Studies in Natural Language Processing

Language and spatial cognition

Studies in Natural Language Processing
Executive Editor: Aravind K. Joshi
Sponsored by the Association for Computational Linguistics

This series publishes monographs, texts, and edited volumes within the interdisciplinary field of computational linguistics. Sponsored by the Association for Computational Linguistics, the series will represent the range of topics of concern to the scholars working in this increasingly important field, whether their background is in formal linguistics, psycholinguistics, cognitive psychology or artificial intelligence.

Also in this series:

Planning English sentences by Douglas E. Appelt
Natural language parsing, edited by David R. Dowty, Lauri Karttunen and Arnold Zwicky
Text generation by Kathleen R. McKeown

Language and spatial cognition

An interdisciplinary study of the prepositions in English

ANNETTE HERSKOVITS

Department of Computer Science, Wellesley College

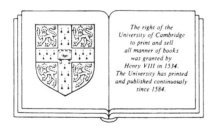

CAMBRIDGE UNIVERSITY PRESS

CAMBRIDGE

LONDON   NEW YORK   NEW ROCHELLE

MELBOURNE   SYDNEY

CAMBRIDGE UNIVERSITY PRESS
Cambridge, New York, Melbourne, Madrid, Cape Town, Singapore, São Paulo, Delhi

Cambridge University Press
The Edinburgh Building, Cambridge CB2 8RU, UK

Published in the United States of America by Cambridge University Press, New York

www.cambridge.org
Information on this title: www.cambridge.org/9780521109185

First published 1986
This digitally printed version 2009

A catalogue record for this publication is available from the British Library

Library of Congress Cataloguing in Publication data
Herskovits, Annette
Language and spatial cognition.
(Studies in natural language processing)
Bibliography
Includes index.
1. English language – Prepositions.   2. English
language – Data processing.   I. Title.   II. Series.
PE1335.H47   1986   425   86-6089

ISBN 978-0-521-26690-1 hardback
ISBN 978-0-521-10918-5 paperback

Table of contents

Preface

Work at the crossroads of two disciplines can be rewarding, but the worker runs the risk of failing to fulfill the expectations of either side. I wrote this book with one eye to linguistics and the other to artificial intelligence, and an uneasy awareness of the discrepancies in outlook between the two. In addition, I had a concern for, though only primitive means to check, psychological reality. A few preliminary remarks should help guide the reader through the resulting analysis.

First, the work has its roots in artificial intelligence. The basic question that shapes all the others is: how can one produce and interpret locative expressions that are appropriate in a given context? This translates into a concern with what have customarily been called "models of comprehension and production" – here renamed "encoding and decoding", because I question the psychological reality of any such models, yet find that looking at the problem in this light raises all the interesting questions about the spatial uses of the prepositions.

But I have also asked questions that generally fall in the province of traditional linguistics, questions about the respective scopes of arbitrariness and motivation, compositionality, and the boundary between semantics and pragmatics. My attempts to set up various categories descriptive of linguistic meaning also resemble the methods of linguistics more than those of artificial intelligence. The result is an unorthodox, nearly theoretical, "descriptive framework". Linguists should not look here for certain familiar categories, such as literal meaning, utterance meaning, presupposition; and distinctions important to traditional linguistic analysis – between truth conditions and appropriateness conditions, and between semantics and pragmatics – though not denied, play a marginal role.

Some will certainly ask, where is the computer program? Well, there is none, and this is deliberate. Writing a program would have required simplifying to such an extent that it would have contributed nothing to a demonstration of the validity of a delicate semantic analysis. Looking at a relatively "simple" domain, it becomes apparent that language use is the result of juggling logic, convention, common sense, vagueness, knowledge of the world and of conversational behavior, implicit assumptions about what "matters", in a manner too devilishly complex for our present programming abilities. Worse yet, it is not even clear what one should want the programs to do.

The introduction presents the main cognitive, linguistic, and computational issues addressed in the book. Chapter 1 states the basic problem, examines the philosophy and method of the work as a whole, and gives a first overall view of the descriptive framework. Six short chapters then lay out the descriptive framework, piece by piece. The problem of decoding and encoding is addressed in Chapter 8. Chapters 9 and 10 are case studies: examinations of the three basic "topological prepositions" (*at, on,* and *in*) , and the "projective prepositions" (*behind, to the right, in front of,* etc.). In the conclusion, I consider the implications of this work.

Most books on semantics start with an apology like "semantics is a notoriously slippery business", "in semantics, a rough road is better than...". This book will not fail to respect the tradition. Semantics is very difficult, and any inroad should be welcome; I hope the reader will forgive gaps and inconsistencies, for the sake of discovering previously concealed aspects of linguistic form and cognitive processes.

This book owes much to many people: to Terry Winograd, who advised, taught and encouraged me at Stanford University, where this work was begun as a doctoral dissertation; to my other advisers at Stanford, Elizabeth Traugott and Ivan Sag, for their attentive and knowledgeable guidance; to the artificial intelligence group at SRI-International, whose interest and support helped me persevere along unconventional tracks, in particular Barbara Grosz, Jerry Hobbs, and Jane Robinson; to Robert Wilensky, principal investigator of the Sloan Foundation Program in Cognitive Science at the University of California at Berkeley, where I completed this work as a post-doctoral fellow, who generously provided space, facilities, and computer time; to the faculty, students, and fellows of the Institute of Cognitive Studies at Berkeley, whose enthusiasm for the mysteries of language and cognition created a stimulating environment, and especially to Paul Kay, Eleanor Rosch, Dan Slobin, and Leonard Talmy, who offered many comments and suggestions on the work; to the administrators at Wellesley College for allowing me time away to complete the book; to Aravind Joshi, who saw the possibility of a book in the dissertation and selected it for publication in this series; to Penny Carter of Cambriige University Press, who combines patience and understanding with a sharp eye; to Rene Yung and Jill Manca for the drawings that grace theses pages; and finally to Peter Solomon, who read the manuscript many more times than I could have tolerated myself, edited many successive versions, listened attentively to frequent ramblings about prepositions – a topic previously of no interest to him – and considerably improved the book's readability.

Introduction

This book presents a fine-grained analysis of the semantics and pragmatics of locative expressions, expressions like *the teapot on the table, the man behind the counter*, and *the circle of light under the lamp*; then examines, in light of that analysis, the possibility of constructing a computational model of comprehension and production in the spatial domain.

This work did not grow out of an interest in space per se, but in the workings of language in general, its relation to cognition, and the plausibility of the computational metaphor. That led me to look for a suitable domain – simple, but neither too simple nor too narrow. Expressions predicating the position of one object relative to another satisfy this requirement. They are simple in several ways: their semantic structure involves a two-place, or at most a three-place predicate (e.g., *between, beyond*); and the position of objects is a concrete, unambiguous, and well-understood physical notion. Yet, the domain defined by these expressions turns out to be surprisingly complex. What one says does not in general correspond in a simple manner to elementary geometric predicates, and, contrary to common belief, a precise geometric definition of the place and shape of the objects in question does not suffice for choosing a preposition appropriately.

But space was compelling because it occupies a privileged place in language and in the cognitive system. Spatial metaphors pervade language, and not solely as a source of colorful expressions; they are necessary to conceptualizing various semantic domains, in particular abstract domains. In addition, much of our reasoning ability relies on visual thinking, on the manipulation of mental images.

In short, the domain of space provides a particularly clear view of most of the fundamental issues pertinent to language and to cognition. I will begin by placing the work in this larger context.

0.1 Spatial cognition and language

Underlying most work in linguistics and artificial intelligence is the belief that the world comes nicely structured along lines defined by universally accepted and objectively definable categories. The physical world seems particularly well-delineated and unambiguously conceptualizable, made up of objects, each with a well-defined shape and position in space. Words and morphemes denote these well-drawn categories, and what people talk about (even if it is not readily apparent because people are not always careful) are these discrete objects and their relations in the world. Such an "objectivist" view of meaning (Lakoff and Johnson 1980) is a little hard to extend to abstract entities, but it seems uncontroversial for the physical world.

In fact, the spatial domain remains incomprehensible when looked at in this way. Careful examination of a range of locative sentences reveals that the spatial objects related often do not actually exist in the world, but are mental constructions – beyond and above that first mental construction produced by perception. Even objecthood is not an unalterable given.

Clearly we cannot know reality objectively, since knowledge is a product of the human organism. Yet there is a "fundamental" or "canonical" view of the physical world, which in everyday life is taken as "the world as it is". But language does not directly reflect that view. Idealizations, approximations, conceptualizations, and selections mediate between the canonical view and language. These are not strictly linguistic: they reflect spatial representational structures that are necessary for action (movement and manipulation), interactional properties (such as the function of a cup, how we hold it), often appearance rather than the actual configuration of the objects, and – most importantly – the concerns and purposes of the speaker.

The objectivist view has given rise to various mistaken hypotheses on the structure of the domain of spatial expressions. In linguistics, it has been assumed commonly that the meaning of locative expressions could be entirely specified as a proposition constructed out of a simple geometric relation applying to the objects. In artificial intelligence, there is a widespread implicit assumption that, given descriptions of the shapes of two objects, given their location (for example, by means of coordinates in some system of reference), and, in some cases, the location of an observer, one can select an appropriate preposition to describe the spatial relation of the objects. The data do not bear out either view, and this book gives abundant proof of their falsity.

Yet, our language obviously maps onto the world as it is. After all, a rose is a rose, and a cup is a cup, and every human being – whatever their individual, linguistic, and cultural differences – sees each as an object with a certain shape, color, substance. I will offer an account of the spatial domain that makes this mapping comprehensible, while avoiding the objectivist fallacy.

0.2 Linguistic issues

Central to the semantic approach taken in this book are the complementary notions of ideal and of deviations from the ideal. Anyone who has looked carefully at a semantic domain knows how elusive comprehensive and accurate semantic descriptions are. Lexical meaning has been remarkably refractory to attempts at formal definition. I will show that one can make sense of many apparent irregularities of semantic data by assuming that word meanings are defined in an ideal world – in the spatial domain, a world of lines, points, surfaces, and of definite relations of inclusion, contact, intersection, and so forth. To describe and communicate facts about the complex and imperfect world that surrounds us, we must bend and stretch these ideal concepts. Obviously, this bending and stretching cannot be done at the speaker's whim; while it may not all be the result of linguistic rules, it is constrained by the need to preserve mutual comprehension, so that our references to objects and facts are, usually, successful. For that reason, ideal concepts must be complemented by a precise account of the way in which such concepts are distorted in a linguistic and situational context.

Thus, I will propose **ideal meanings** for the spatial prepositions, and then describe two types of deviations from the ideal: those based on convention, which basically give rise to polysemy, and those that result from pragmatic processes of allowance, or tolerance. "Polysemy" may not be a fully appropriate term: if we go by the speaker's intuitions, "the meaning" of the preposition is the ideal meaning; but the ideal meaning can be conventionally exploited in various ways, which must be recorded with the preposition in the lexicon. In my description of prepositions, I have therefore devised a series of **use types** to correspond to various classes of uses distinguished by different conventions.

A specification of lexical meaning has little value without an account of how lexical meanings combine to make up the meaning of phrases and sentences – the problem of compositionality – so I will propose meaning representations for complex locative expressions, representations that are built using the semantic information attached to the preposition as well as pragmatic and world knowledge.[1]

A striking feature of the composition process is the degree to which context must be called upon for a full specification of meaning. Spatial expressions in particular present a lot of hidden indexicality – that is, context is frequently necessary to determine what proposition they express. Terms like *to the right, in front of*, and so forth, are known to have indexical uses, where the hearer must determine the relation expressed by considering the location and orientation of an implicit observer. But indexicality extends much beyond these obvious cases (I am of course concerned only with indexicality originating in the use of the preposition not with pronouns or other pro-forms that might occur in the expression). Many contextual factors modify the relation that is being expressed, or the particular spatial objects of which the relation is true, factors implicit in the intentions and concerns of the speaker.

Context also plays a role in allowing pragmatic inferences. We use general and specific world knowledge, and knowledge about communication, to infer facts beyond those entailed by the utterance.

Pragmatic inferences raise the problem of the boundary between pragmatics and semantics. I will firmly distinguish between those aspects of meaning that are the inalienable property of the expression alone, and those elements that depend on the particular context of use – grouping the former into a complex called the **situation type**[2] associated with the expression, or its **interpretation**. Whether this distinction coincides with the semantic/pragmatic distinction is controversial. First, the situation type associated with an expression includes elements of meaning which would normally be considered pragmatic, such as some constraints on the purpose of the expression. Second, linguists do not all agree on a definition of pragmatics: some include the treatment of indexical terms (e.g. Montague 1974); others handle indexical expressions with a standard truth-conditional apparatus and restrict pragmatics to those aspects of meaning that are not truth-conditional, thus excluding indexicality (e.g. Gazdar 1979); still others draw the line between conventional aspects of meaning, and those arrived at by principles of preferred interpretation (e.g. Wilson 1975).

In effect, in the practical context of considering the construction of an artificial intelligence system, I will end up cutting the cake in a way different from any employed in traditional linguistics, using several criteria to sort elements of meaning: determined by the expression versus determined by the context, conventional versus motivated, normal versus "out of the ordinary". The **normal situation type** associated with an expression, more restricted than the situation type in that it assumes conditions to be "normal", will play a central role in the framework proposed. In an informal way, I will call "pragmatic" some principles that guide the evaluation of various indexicals in context, others that restrict the choice of expressions, and also some inferences from world knowledge.

Finally, another essential issue is idiomaticity. Linguistic theories sort idioms from regular expressions. An idiom is often defined as any expression which conventionally conveys elements of meaning other than those obtained by straightforward application of the relevant rules of composition to the meanings of the component morphemes. But we will find many conventional peculiarities of use that cannot be derived from the morphemic meanings (unless they be redefined in rather unintuitive fashion), even with expressions not perceived as idiomatic by native speakers. Idiomaticity seems to be a matter of degree: the meaning of most expressions depends partly on the lexical items combined, and partly on conventions attached to phrase-types; those for which the latter predominates are perceived as more idiomatic. Of course, all conventions must be stated in some part of the lexicon, which motivates the two levels in the lexical information attached to each preposition: the ideal meaning, and the use types – which are phrase types centered on the preposition, each with its own particular semantic and pragmatic features. This division will allow us to account for the mixture of phrasal idiosyncrasy and morphemic motivation that seems so prevalent in language.

0.3 Computer models of language

As researchers in artificial intelligence have discovered over the last ten years, building a faithful model of linguistic activity is quite a difficult task. One need not look at metaphors or abstractions to find this; the concrete and well-defined domain of locatives is as riddled with such difficulties as are more striking feats of linguistic activity, and it yields many clues as to their source.

These difficulties can be traced to three properties of language. The first applies only in the spatial domain – although it may have some equivalent in other domains: the fact, already mentioned, that the spatial objects we relate are mental constructions that I will call **geometric descriptions.** These geometric images are neither contained in, nor directly inferable from, the canonical description.

Another problem is the context-dependence of language. In communicating, we rely on implicit shared beliefs and concerns to a degree which has not been sufficiently recognized in artificial intelligence. Characterizing precisely the context-dependent parameters and how they vary with the context is most difficult.

Vagueness is the third difficulty. Vaguely defined entities and relations occur everywhere, and no satisfactory formal solution has ever been proposed for this problem. Simply allowing degrees of truth (as in Zadeh's "fuzzy logic" (1974)) is no solution; we must understand how we integrate the interplay of many vaguely defined parameters into some definite utterance. It is not clear that this can be solved by making explicit the set of relevant parameters and attaching an appropriate weight to each, because it is not clear that a list of such parameters and weights can be specified once and for all for every expression.

All this does not mean that building computer systems is pointless. One can construct, for specific applications, useful computer systems that simplify in well-defined ways; a good informal description of the meaning and use of locative expressions could allow one to think precisely of the simplifying assumptions needed to meet a particular purpose. More to the point, thinking about computational models of comprehension and production is a very powerful heuristic tool, forcing us to make precise our intuitions about meaning.

1   Meaning and use of locative expressions

Although trying to build computational models of comprehension and production is a good way to start thinking about meaning, there are some legitimate doubts about the soundness of the computational metaphor itself. I will address these, as they have some bearing on my general method and approach, before introducing the central questions guiding this study. One attempt to answer these questions in the domain of locative expressions, widely employed in artificial intelligence and linguistics, uses a "simple relations model", but this, I will show, fails to account for the data in many ways. Examining those deficiencies leads to an outline of the descriptive framework adopted in the book. But to begin, a precise definition of just which expressions are considered will be helpful.

1.1 Locative expressions

A **locative expression** is an expression involving a locative prepositional phrase together with whatever the phrase modifies (noun, clause, etc.).

The simplest type of locative expression is composed of three constituents: the preposition and two noun-phrases as in

> *the spider on the wall*

The spider is the **subject** of the preposition, and *the wall* is the **object**. The subject refers to the **located entity**, the object to the **reference entity**.

A locative expression may be structured around a copulative verb:

> *The spider is on the wall.*

or an existential quantifier:

> *There is a spider on the wall.*

Mostly this book is about locative expressions of these first three simple types. But there are also locative expressions where the subject of the preposition is a clause:

> *Louis is eating snails in the kitchen.*

7

Although most commonly that sentence is assigned the constituent structure:

[[Louis] [[is eating snails] [in the kitchen]]]

I will take the subject of the preposition to be *Louis is eating snails*, as this clause describes the event that is taking place *in the kitchen*.

A spatial prepositional phrase may also fit in the case frame of a verb:

She put the bread in the hutch.

Here the most appropriate constituent structure is:

[[She] [[put] [the bread] [in the hutch]]]

What is being located *in the hutch* is not any object, state, or event, but the "destination" of the action "to put", that is, the end place of the trajectory of the bread, which will be considered the located entity.

Prepositions fall into two categories: some are primarily static (e.g., *at, in, under*); others primarily dynamic (*to, from, via*). But static prepositions can be used in dynamic contexts (*The cat ran under the bed*), and dynamic ones in static contexts (*The lamp is two feet from the wall*). By focusing on locative expressions of the first three simple types, I exclude an in-depth study of dynamic prepositions, or of dynamic contexts for the static ones, but much of what holds true in the simple static cases carries over to dynamic contexts. Usually, some aspect of the action denoted by the verb involves a part of space, which is located with respect to the reference object by means of the preposition exactly as any static physical object would be. Consider for instance

She ran behind the fence to the road.
He writes only on blue paper.

In the first example, a directed line segment – the trajectory of the run – is located *behind the fence*, and its end is on the road. In the second example, the trajectory of the tip of the moving pen is located *on the blue paper*; so is the resulting writing, the trajectory being in fact coincident with the space it occupies. In these and many similar examples, the preposition simply relates the relevant trajectory to the chosen reference object, as it would two ordinary objects; there are, however, examples where this analysis fails, and where special, verb-dependent rules apply.

Basically, this study deals with the use of locative expressions in American English, more specifically West Coast American English. I have generally relied on my own linguistic intuitions, though I have checked with half a dozen people when those intuitions wavered, and note when conflicting opinions appeared.

For detailed study, I have selected two classes of prepositions: the three "basic topological prepositions", which are *at, on,* and *in,* and the projective prepositions, which are fundamentally derived from the experience of viewing, such as *in front of, behind, to the right,* etc. The first group is treated in Chapter 9, the second in Chapter 10.

1.2 The philosophical basis of the computational metaphor

When research in artificial intelligence began, there were forecasts that computers capable of fully intelligent conversational exchanges would soon exist. Even when computer scientists had to give up these unrealistic expectations, they attributed their failure to quantitative complexity; most still held that a computer program could in principle fully perform as a language user, that some well-designed algorithm manipulating physical symbols could fully explain linguistic ability (Winograd 1976; Johnson-Laird 1977; Woods 1978). One dissenting voice was that of Dreyfus, an interpreter of Heidegger, who argued that no algorithmic procedure could account for intelligence or language, and that knowledge could not be exhaustively formalized (1979). By 1980, a number of computer scientists had become more cautious about identifying intelligence with symbol manipulation, and some, such as Winograd (1980), even rejected the idea.

Some of the principal arguments against the computational metaphor involve the notion of "background" (Searle 1979; Dreyfus 1979; Winograd 1980; Winograd and Flores 1985). Very briefly, this holds that what a sentence conveys will vary from context to context, according to the purposes and assumptions of the speaker; these constitute a background that cannot be exhaustively formalized as there is no absolute way of breaking it down. Any one of many possible ways would reflect the biases – the purposes and assumptions – of the analyst.

Another set of arguments centers on the notion of mental representations, and whether they can be said to underlie language use, and to represent the world. Winograd and Flores, for instance, claim that one cannot assume that a language user has mental representations of the regularities observed in language use; that language comprehension and production do not proceed by manipulating representations of such regularities. They argue further that cognition is not based on the manipulation of "mental models" or representations of the world; a sentence is not a description of a state of affairs in the world. Following Maturana (1978), they describe the nervous system as a closed system: "...the system can do only that which is determined by its own structure and activity – its action cannot be understood as a reflection of an external world it perceives". We tend to accept the idea that instinctual behavior is not based on a representation of the world, but on a set of external conditions that cause a certain perturbation to the nervous system.

However, when it comes to cognition, we feel certain that our mind holds a representation of the world. Yet this certainty is unfounded.

Without attempting a full discussion of these ideas, I want to place the analysis proposed in these pages in relation to them, because I find them persuasive.

I will speak of relating a locative expression to a situation type. A situation will be taken to include the current relevant purposes, concerns, and beliefs of the speaker or hearer – though "beliefs" should be interpreted broadly to include the representation of scenes provided by perception. If indefinitely many different complexes of purposes and beliefs may be seen as bearing upon the production or interpretation of a given sentence, it is impossible to give a systematic description of the relation between an utterance and a situation type, or to list necessary and sufficient conditions for the use of an expression. But one can point to some salient and commonly encountered relations between locative expressions and some articulated aspects of experience and purpose. And one can also sometimes discern extensions, processes which stretch the use of expressions beyond those central cases. I will talk of predicting the interpretation of a sentence in a given context, and of predicting the sentence appropriate to a given situation, using as instruments for such predictions the regularities that link locative expressions and situations; but strictly speaking I may only be describing the regularities that link locative expressions and the salient aspects of commonly encountered situations in which they would be used – aspects that present themselves as we imagine some of the ways in which a locative expression would be appropriately used, or on the contrary, ill-formed or misused.

Of course, any semantic description would have the same limitations. Yet, the study of regularities of this kind is worthwhile, even if those regularities remain somewhat intractable. Any student of semantics knows that any attempt to capture the meaning of a word always founders against the encounter of unforeseen uses. But language is not a free-for-all, and even if we do not now see the nature of its rules, there are constraints; without them, there would be no language and no communication. Looking at regularities, attempting to express them formally, and exploring where generalizations fail, is a necessary first step toward building a more adequate theory.

In short, while I share Winograd and Flores' disbelief in the assumption that we can model the use of knowledge by manipulations of symbols, I think such models have been revealing in patches. They also are the only rigorous means we now have of capturing some epistemological phenomena. Exploring further the computational description of language comprehension and production should enable us to more clearly understand its limits, and possibly open the way for an alternate scientific description of language abilities.

Often, for simplicity, I will speak as if the beliefs which make up situations concern real objects and properties in the outside world, even though any description of the world is only something created by the organism in its encounter with it, and not truly "objective". In this study, I will assume that there is an agreed-upon common-sense knowledge of the world (Section 2.4) on which we base our understanding of sentences. Because of the common structure of human organisms, one may assume the common-sense knowledge that relates to spatial properties is well defined.

1.3 Decoding and encoding

The central questions guiding the inquiry in this book involve decoding and encoding.

The decoding question is: given a locative expression used in a particular situation, can one predict what it conveys, how it will be interpreted – that is, provided it has been used appropriately? If not, can one explain the inappropriateness? The encoding question is: given a situation with two spatial objects, can one predict the locative expression that can be used truly and appropriately to describe their spatial relation?

The term "predict" in these formulations naturally implies some rigorously defined procedure. Thus, solutions to the encoding/decoding problems would resemble what are commonly called models of comprehension and production. However, the formulation of decoding and encoding sidesteps some requirements of psychological validity; it makes no reference to psychological processes. Though situations are assumed to be psychological entities (they are made up of beliefs and purposes), decoding and encoding are not assumed to relate such entities to locative expressions by processes that imitate those of comprehension and production. All that is required is that situations and expressions be appropriately paired. Since I do not – nor for the most part do artificial intelligence researchers – use psychological evidence to support the models proposed, other than occasional introspective evidence, such a formulation of the problem and of the proposed solutions seems less misleading. Avoiding the terms "comprehension" and "production" is also meant as a reminder of the doubtfulness of the claim that language ability can be fully described by an algorithmic manipulation of symbols. In any case, an analysis of decoding and encoding paves the way for designing algorithms that would behave like language users, assuming such algorithms possible.

1.4 Simple geometric relations

The first solution to the decoding/encoding problem that comes to mind, and the one semanticists have generally adopted in one form or another, runs as follows. Prepositions are assigned meanings which are simple relations. For instance, the meaning of *in* might be the relation:[1]

$$In(X, Y) \leftrightarrow Located\ (X, Interior(Y))$$

For *on*, one might distinguish two meanings, On_1 for three-dimensional objects (as in *The book is on the desk*), and On_2 if the reference object is a line (as in *The town is on the border*):

$$On_1(X, Y) \leftrightarrow Supports(Y, X)$$
$$\text{and}$$
$$Contiguous\ (Surface(X), Surface(Y))$$
$$On_2(X, Y) \leftrightarrow Contiguous\ (Boundary(X), Y)$$

These relations may be complemented by "preconditions" that must hold for an expression constructed with the preposition to be acceptable; for instance, Cooper (1968) gives for *in* the condition that X must be smaller than Y.

Then, given an expression like *The toy is in the box*, one can apply a simple compositional rule: insert symbols denoting the referents of the noun-phrases as arguments of the relation defining the meaning of *in*. One gets:

$$Located\ (Toy,\ Interior(Box))$$

(This formula involves no analysis of the meanings of *toy* and *box*; for specific purposes, one could substitute for *toy* and *box* more complex formulae involving a componential analysis of those terms.) Such a first order logic formula represents the necessary and sufficient conditions for *The toy is in the box* to be true; it is the "meaning" of the expression.

In general, these prepositional meanings correspond in a straightforward way to clear first intuitions, and yield reasonably good representations for a number of examples. I will refer to them as the "simple geometric relations meanings" of prepositions (save for the intrusion of *Support* in one sense of *on*, such meanings would all be purely geometric relations); such meanings together with the compositional rule constitute the "simple relations model" of the meaning of locative expressions.[2]

But this simple relations model yields wrong or insufficient predictions about the set of situations (intensionally the situation type)[3] described by a locative expression. Meaning representations based on the simple geometric meanings do not provide a solution to the fundamental encoding/decoding problem. This is not surprising – such representations were not meant to predict everything a locative expression conveys or presupposes; part is to be explained by a complementary pragmatic theory. But let us see just what the simple geometric predicates fail to explain[4] before discussing how that should be handled.

• Contrast between converses, and unacceptability of some converses

The proposed simple meanings do not differentiate between *the house behind the church*, and *the church in front of the house*, though the two expressions are clearly not used interchangeably. Nor do the simple predicate meanings explain why one cannot say **the jar in the lid*,[5] but must say instead *the jar with a lid on it*.

• Geometric descriptions

At best, the simple geometric relations apply in fact not to the objects themselves, but to various geometric figures (points, surfaces, or volumes) associated with the objects. For instance, in *the bird in the tree*, the bird is not in the interior of the reference object, as in *the bird in the oven*, but in the interior of the outline of the part of the tree made of branches. In *the key under the mat*, the key is *under* the lower surface of the mat, but in *One could see shiny silver carp under the water*, the carp are *under* the top surface of the water.

Some geometric descriptions arise through clear cases of metonymy, in particular synecdoche, where mention of an object is used to refer to a part of it. For instance, in *the child in the back of the car*, the child is *in the back* of the interior space that holds the passengers.

Other geometric descriptions involve a process of **geometric conceptualization**. For instance, in many uses of prepositions an object is "viewed as" a point, line, or plane, and so forth (Leech (1969) and Fillmore (1971) describe such intuitions). So, in *The village is on the road to London*, the road is seen as a line, the village as a point, and point and line are asserted to be contiguous. The meaning of *on*, On_2, applies here – but to geometric conceptualizations of the objects.

In general, then, the simple geometric meanings of the prepositions apply to geometric descriptions of the objects. In the simplest case, the applicable geometric description is the part of space occupied by the object (the **place**, or **canonical geometric description** of the object); in more complex cases, it can be the outline, a particular surface, a point or line obtained by approximation, the space occupied by a part of the object, etc. The surprisingly large number of possibilities is reviewed in Chapter 5.

• Divergence from the simple relations

The simple geometric relations sometimes do not even hold for the geometric descriptions. For instance, in Figure 1.1(a), one would say *The pear is in the bowl*, although the pear is not in the interior of the bowl, and in 1.1(b), *"Ulysses" is on the desk*, although it is not contiguous with the desk.

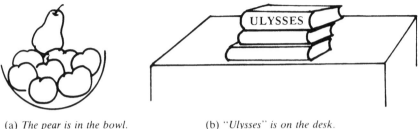

(a) *The pear is in the bowl.*   (b) *"Ulysses" is on the desk.*
Figure 1.1

Take another example. A sensible simple relation meaning for *behind* is:

$$Behind(X, Y) \leftrightarrow Included\ (X, BackSpace(Y))$$

The situation in Figure 1.2(a) conforms strictly to that meaning. But the situation in 1.2(b) does not; yet it might be appropriate to say *X is behind Y*, depending on what kind of objects X and Y are, and on various aspects of the context (purpose of the speaker, presence of other objects nearby, etc.).

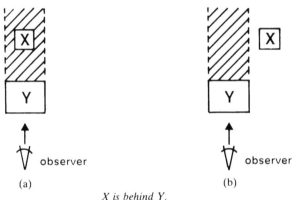

(a)   (b)
X is behind Y.
Figure 1.2

Or, take the simple meaning of *at* to be:

$$At(X, Y) \leftrightarrow Coincides(X, Y)\quad \text{(with X and Y points)}$$

which accounts for

> *The center of the circle is at the intersection of the axes.*

But in

> *Mary is at the gate.*

Mary and the gate are not coincident; they are only very close together.
In all examples given so far, one could say the simple relation is

"almost" true, meaning that a "small" movement of the located object would make it true. But this is not so in

> *the wrinkles on his forehead*

A wrinkle is clearly not an object contiguous with and supported by the forehead.

Thus the simple relation meanings do not strictly apply in a variety of ways.

• Unexpected context dependencies

The "deictic" uses of *behind, to the right,* and the other projective prepositions (for instance *The cat is behind the tree,* where an observer is implied) present well-known cases of context dependency (Fillmore 1971; Clark 1973). There are many less obvious cases. Thus in *The gas station is at the freeway,* the gas station is at the intersection of the freeway with a crossroad, and the speaker is, in reality or imagination, on that crossroad, some distance from the intersection. Because of this implied crosspath, the sentence is indexical.

In Figure 1.3(a), one could say that *A is to the right of X.* But if an object B were introduced as in 1.3(b), then in many contexts, only B is *to the right of X* (in some contexts, one might say *A and B are to the right of X,* but *the building to the right of X* would be identified as B, and *The post-office is to the right of X* would not leave the addressee wondering whether the post-office were A or B). So the appropriate use of *A is to the right of X* depends on the presence in the environment of objects other than A and X.

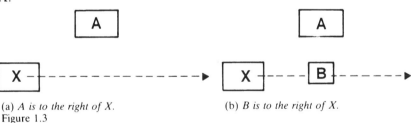

(a) *A is to the right of X.*

(b) *B is to the right of X.*

Figure 1.3

Or take *Lucy is at the supermarket* and *Lucy is in the supermarket.* Although both would often be true according to the simple relations meanings, we do not use them indiscriminately. If both speaker and addressee are in the supermarket, for instance, *at the supermarket* is usually inappropriate.

A sentence like *The train is at the bridge* highlights the route followed by the train, marking the bridge as a landmark on that route, whereas *The train is on the bridge* or *The train is just next to the bridge* do not. The simple meaning of *at,* as contrasted with that of *on* or *just next,* does not account for this highlighting of a background element.

• Unexplained restrictions

There are many cases where the simple meanings indicate that some expression should be acceptable when it is not. For instance, although a football field is an area, with an interior, one does not say *Joe is in the football field*, though one says *Joe is in the field*. Similarly, one will not say *Draw a line in the blackboard*, but rather *Draw a line on the blackboard*.

In describing the situations depicted in Figure 1.4, one will not say *The bulb is under the socket*, or *The potato is in the bowl*, although the situation in 1.4(a) conforms with the simple meaning of *under*, and in 1.4(b), the potato is inside of the bowl.

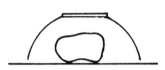

(a) *The bulb is in the socket.*   (b) *The potato is under the bowl.*

Figure 1.4

• Additional constraints

Constraints beyond those implied by the simple relations meanings must be met for a locative expression to be used appropriately. For instance, the use of *above*, *below*, *under*, and so forth, presupposes the existence of a vertical direction, and of gravity, as does the use of *on* with the On_1 sense.

Other constraints not implied by the simple meanings concern the expected behavior of objects. For instance, if told *There is milk in the bowl*, we will generally infer that the bowl has a more or less horizontal underside, and that the milk fills the bowl up to some horizontal plane, as liquids do. We do not assume the bowl is overturned with the milk floating somewhere in its interior.

Some additional constraints occur only with particular uses of particular prepositions. Consider *Maggie is near her desk*. Here we would normally infer that Maggie is not *at her desk*. Assume the following simple relation meaning for *near*:

$$Near(X, Y) \leftrightarrow Distance(X, Y) \leq Threshold$$

(*Threshold* being an implicit variable whose value is contextually determined). The above inference does not follow from the simple meanings of *at* and *near*.

As another example, take *Maggie is at her desk*; it implies that Maggie is very close to her desk, in conformity with the meaning of *at* (albeit with a certain tolerance as explained above), but it also implies that Maggie is using her desk: if she was turning somersaults on top of her desk, she would not be *at her desk*.

1.5 A comprehensive descriptive framework

Using standard linguistic machinery, there are two ways one could try to account for the aspects of locative meaning not predicted by the simple relations model: one is by complementing the model with a pragmatics allowing inferences from world knowledge and conversational principles, and including a way to handle metonymy; the other is by labeling the delinquent uses "idioms", thus placing them outside the model.

It is quite difficult to see how the standard practices of pragmatics could help, except with synecdoche (an appropriate pragmatic account of which remains to be given), and for the "additional constraints" – which, in the examples described, could possibly be construed as pragmatic inferences. But nothing in pragmatics has prepared us to deal with geometric conceptualization, or with the unexpected context dependencies, and the divergences from the simple relation meanings.

Excluding the deviant examples as idioms is undesirable as for the most part native speakers do not perceive them as idiomatic. Even for those that are so perceived, the sense that there is something exceptional is limited; speakers also perceive some motivation, that is, they see these uses as not unrelated to other uses of the same preposition. A model that accounted for such intuitions would be preferable to one that appealed to idiosyncrasy.

One can make sense of the exceptions to the simple relations model by taking each simple relation to be only a geometric ideal, stretched in various ways to adapt to a complex world and a variety of situations. Flexibility in the use of the ideal meaning and adaptability to expressive needs are manifested in several ways. First, in conventionally allowed deviations from the ideal meaning leading to polysemy, which I will call **sense shifts**. Second, in **tolerance** phenomena, that is, in processes by which we allow the ideal relation, or the "sense-shifted" ideal relation, to be "almost true".

Finally, this flexibility is manifested in the variety of transfers to geometric descriptions, reflecting both synecdoche and geometric conceptualization. The ideal relation is defined on pairs or triplets of geometric elements (for instance points (for *at*), lines (for one sense of *on*), regions of space of dimensionality greater than zero (for *in*), etc.). With a particular expression used in a particular context, the arguments of the transformed ideal meaning (transformed by tolerance and sense shifts) will not be the objects referred to, but geometric descriptions of these objects, schematic images matched onto them; naturally these arguments must match the geometric categories specified in the ideal meaning.

So part of the meaning associated with the use of a given locative expression is a proposition asserting that a transformed ideal is true of the geometric descriptions; this proposition is the **geometric meaning** of the expression (note that all indexicals would be resolved in such a proposition). It is only part of the meaning of the expression, because other elements of meaning, preconditions and contextual conditions, come into play.

Clearly, there are stringent constraints on the way the ideal meaning can be bent and adapted, otherwise communication would be impossible. What linguistic and pragmatic rules do speakers abide by? What evidence, what world and pragmatic knowledge do hearers use to interpret utterances? Given a locative expression used in a certain context, how can one predict the transformations of ideal meanings and the geometric descriptions applicable, and make the geometric meaning explicit? How can one explain some of the restrictions on prepositional choice? Are these motivated by pragmatic principles, or are they a matter of convention?

There are pragmatic motivations in some cases, and I will propose a set of pragmatic principles and near-principles which relate to four essential factors: **relevance**, **salience**, **tolerance**, and **typicality**. But many aspects of the interpretation of a locative expression do not follow from world knowledge, from pragmatic principles, or from the ideal meaning and meanings of the subject and object of the expression; they are conventional and must be stated in the lexical entry of the preposition. Each preposition has thus a set of distinct use types, each use type manifesting the ideal meaning in some way. For instance, there is a use type corresponding to a class of uses describable as "person using artifact", an example of which is *Maggie is at her desk.*

In traditional semantics, it is assumed that one level of abstraction is sufficient to define lexical meanings in such a way that they will constitute the material out of which truth-conditions can be built, given rules of composition entirely defined by the syntax (this requires some qualification if the expressions considered are indexical, but that is irrelevant here). Instead, I suggest two levels of abstraction: ideal meaning and use type. The ideal meaning abstraction is not sufficient to build truth-conditions, but is a necessary anchor that organizes the overall set of uses of the preposition. The use type abstraction, with several use types derived from the same ideal meaning, is much richer and provides material that brings us much closer to a definition of truth-conditions; however, it is possible, in out-of-the-ordinary circumstances, to break even use type constraints.

I noted above that for any statement of the meaning of an expression, it always seemed possible to come up with a situation where the expression is true and appropriate, although it does not fit that meaning. That is, meaning appears to depend on speakers' beliefs and goals to an extent that always breaks any limits assigned to it. To cope with this difficulty, I will rely on a notion of normality, considering centrally the relation of an expression to its normal situation type, or normal interpretation. But since an expression can be used in all kinds of non-ordinary situations, I will also consider how one can obtain interpretations that are not normal in the sense prescribed, how one can stretch the normal interpretation.

The normal interpretation of an expression differs from its geometric meaning in two ways; (a) it includes contextual constraints of a pragmatic nature, and (b) it depends only on the associated expression, thus including unresolved indexicals.

This completes a first sketch of the descriptive framework proposed in this book to account for the meaning and use of locative expressions.

A few words about the attitude taken in these pages toward formalization seem in order. I have chosen to be broad and relatively informal, rather than narrow and formal. I have not written any computer program, nor do I offer any precise implementation plan, because the scope and complexity of the phenomena would defeat any attempt to do so, unless one simplified in ways that would make the enterprise useless, since it is precisely this scope and complexity that I want to address. My descriptions are usually discursive, but whenever it appeared useful, I have used first order logic with its ordinary syntax to represent interpretations of locative expressions. I saw no advantage in using such notations as semantic networks, KRL (Bobrow and Winograd 1977), and so forth.

This approach has let me observe the remarkable fluidity allowed in the use of words and syntactic expressions, and to understand some of the principles that regulate that fluidity. Language is not as flat and fixed as simplistic componential systems suggest. Because I wished to give a feeling for the subtlety and complexity of language use, I have avoided the strait-jacket of a precise performance requirement, or a rigid formalism. One can explain certain linguistic choices only by speaking of suggestion, connotation, fuzzy connections and analogies, ways of conceptualizing, of viewing, contextual highlighting, and so forth, all of which are impossible now to represent formally. I have preferred to give some discursive account, however imprecise, of any regularities perceived in the data, rather than push them under a rug. Formalization can come later, if it proves appropriate to the topic.

2   Normal situation types

This chapter and the five which follow offer detailed descriptions of the various components of the descriptive framework, starting with normal situation types. These represent the first abstraction from raw empirical data: statements of the normal conditions under which speakers use a certain locative expression, they make explicit the interpretation of locative expressions spontaneously offered by speakers. This is where we must start to look for motivation for the other constructs of the framework. A concluding section offers a sketch of the common sense knowledge of the physical world, the backdrop to normal situation types.

I assume that we can associate with each locative expression a set of characteristic constraints – constraints that must hold for the expression to be used truly and appropriately under normal conditions. These constraints do not constitute a set of necessary and sufficient conditions for the true and appropriate use of the expression – since I doubt such a set exists – but are simply characteristic, or canonical, constraints. This set of constraints defines the normal situation type associated with the locative expression, or its normal interpretation; extensionally,[1] a normal situation type is a set of particular situations, each conforming to the constraints, or conditions, defining the type.

2.1 Defining normality

"Normal" can be defined with some precision. First, a normal situation conforms to the laws of physics – the common sense physics of ordinary solid objects, liquids and gaseous substances. Thus *The woman walked through the wall* would imply that there was a gap in the wall, not that the woman dematerialized. Second, objects are where they belong – most of them near the earth, within the field of gravity. Travellers in outer space may manage to use *above*, *below*, *on*, and so forth, in some consistent manner, but one should consider the use of those words under conditions involving gravity before making predictions about extensions. Finally, the objects are "normal", interact according to their normal function, and people interact with them in normal fashion. Thus, given *The teapot is on the table*, the table stands with its top horizontal and its legs below, and the teapot sits on it. The table is not made out of gingerbread, hanging upside down from the ceiling, with the teapot glued to it. And a person sitting *in an armchair* is not encased in its backrest.

The most problematic part of this definition is the one concerning the normality of the objects and of their interactions. A table with a broken leg is not so exceptional; shall we consider abnormal a situation where a teapot is on the inclined top of a damaged table? Obviously, such decisions will sometimes be arbitrary, but since I will propose ways to interpret a sentence where the normal conditions do not hold, this will not be a crucial problem.

Normal is distinct from prototypical. A prototype corresponds to a "best example", so a prototypical scene with a teapot on a table might be something like this: the ceramic teapot is directly on top of a four-legged, medium-sized wood table, not too far from the center of the table top. Such a scene is much more specific than the normal scene, which would only specify that the teapot be made of any appropriate material, that the table have a horizontal top at usual height supporting the teapot in the ordinary way, with or without thin objects (a cloth, hotpad, etc.) between the table and the teapot.

2.2 Normal situation types and semantics

Every linguistic description and natural language system needs to deal with the problem of normality. As Searle notes in "Literal Meaning" (1979), *The cat is on the mat* would be literally true if the mat had been stiffened so it could hold at an angle when stuck in the floor and the cat had been drugged into a stupor and balanced on the upper edge of the mat. Yet, this is not what comes to the mind of ordinary speakers. Clearly, a linguistic theory must account for the way language users associate normal interpretations with expressions.

In linguistics, this problem is traditionally handled in the pragmatics. It is assumed that expressions have a literal meaning strictly based on the meanings of the morphemes and their mode of combination. For non-indexical sentences, the literal meaning is identical to the truth-conditions of the sentence. But the truth-conditions of an indexical sentence (e.g., *I am hungry*) vary systematically with the context of utterance (e.g., with *I am hungry*, they vary with the speaker and time of utterance). The literal meaning then involves indexical variable(s); these will take particular values in particular contexts, yielding a set of truth-conditions for the sentence-context pair. The truth-conditions of a sentence ordinarily define an interpretation much less constrained than what the speaker intends to communicate; additional constraints must be pragmatically inferred to account for the interpretation intended by the speaker (which the addressee can be expected to recover, if the speaker has been skillful).

This approach depends crucially on being able to define, on the basis of the sentence alone, a literal meaning related in very specific fashion to the truth of the sentence in every context. Leaving out indexical sentences to simplify this argument, it should be possible to specify a set of necessary and sufficient conditions for the truth of the sentence; and the contribution of each lexical item to the truth-conditions should be invariable (assuming the sentence unambiguous). There are difficulties with these requirements.

Searle (1978) and Winograd (1980) claim, and support with examples, that one cannot devise truth-conditions for a sentence that will account for all its possible uses. One can always fabricate an odd context in which the sentence will be false, although the proposed truth-conditions fit. Winograd, for instance, considers the question *Is there water in the refrigerator?* The answer depends on the purposes of the questioner. Water in the eggplants, the orange juice, or as ice, would not normally count as water, but tap water, though it contains a variety of chemicals, normally does. Strictly speaking, the truth-conditions of *There is water in the refrigerator* should reflect these facts; unfortunately, there is no end to the number of possible inclusions and exceptions.

Then, if the classical theory is to be consistent with linguistic intuitions, a speaker should be able to judge whether a sentence is true or not in every context. But it is often difficult to predict what people would say in typical circumstances – how then can we evaluate the meaning of an expression by considering its truth in every possible world? We know what to say in typical situations. Beyond those, our processes of extension often give uncertain results, and results that frequently diverge from speaker to speaker (Kameyama 1980; Coleman and Kay 1981). Would one say *the shop on Polk Street* in a world where shops float in mid-air above the center of the street? Which way is *up the wall* in a gravity-free world?

In short, it is not possible to assign truth-conditions to an expression distilled from all its possible uses; neither can one define a constant contribution of a lexical item to the truth-conditions of the sentences in which it occurs. The simple meanings typically proposed as meanings of the prepositions do not satisfy those requirements, as shown in Section 1.4, and I doubt that lexical meanings that do could be found. So the use types I will propose do not function like senses in the classical theory, as I will explain below.

In fact, normal interpretations play a much more central role than the traditional model assumes. Normal situation types are so firmly associated with expressions that speakers may use them as points of reference to judge the appropriateness of a term, rather than rely on predetermined lexical meanings valid for every possible use of the term. So if someone referred to the scene in Figure 2.1 as *The bread is in the bowl*, the addressee might reply *The bread is not in the bowl, it is under the bowl*, stressing *not*, thus implying that *The bread is in the bowl* is false.

The bread is not in the bowl.
Figure 2.1

The classical theory would claim that the bread is in fact in the bowl in Figure 2.1, but that the statement is pragmatically misleading, because it suggests the normal interpretation. But one does not negate a pragmatic implication in this way.[2] There are thus problems with the neat separation of pragmatics and semantics assumed by the traditional theory.

The approach proposed in this book attempts to deal with some of these objections to the classical theory. Roughly, the fixed points in our descriptive framework are not lexical meanings, but the pairing of a phrase type with an interpretation that will most commonly consist of a set of central cases falling clearly within the use type, together with processes of extension from those central cases (processes that may occasionally give inconclusive answers). But, importantly, there may even be uses that fall clearly outside the use type, but are yet derived from it through the normal situation type: given a sentence, interpretations can be obtained on the basis of their resemblance to its normal interpretation; this comparison process does not require that any particular use type constraint remain satisfied. In other words, the structure I have aimed for is: a set of cases unambiguously associated with the use type, together with ways to extend the use of the phrase type to other cases on the basis of resemblance to the central set of cases – some specified in the use type, others the results of much less well-specified processes involving normal situation types. Although I find this structure revealing about the nature of language, extension processes are very difficult to capture rigorously – they involve world knowledge and context in complex ways – and this work barely begins to explore them, as its main focus remains the description of the central cases.

Certainly, this makes use types very different from senses in the standard understanding of the term, particularly as a use type is not required to bring a constant contribution to the truth-conditions of expressions derived from it. In addition, use types may be much more elaborate than senses; use type interpretations are, in fact, as classes of normal situation types, say "hyper" situation types themselves: there is no simplicity requirement on use type definitions (as there seems to be, though tacitly, for linguists when they define lexical meanings – for instance, disjunctions are frowned upon); they may include both semantic and (what would usually be considered) pragmatic constraints, and particularities of use of any sort (e.g., conventional tolerance conditions).

In the description of decoding (Chapter 8), obtaining a normal interpretation will proceed first by instantiating a use type (i.e., by applying the constraints of the relevant use type to the particular object kinds denoted in the expression), then by drawing pragmatic inferences arising from an assumption of normality, as instantiating the use type leaves out some normality conditions. Normal situation types thus come to play a more central role (in both use type definitions and extension processes). This approach also reflects the fact that sentence meanings cannot be the result of strict compositional processes. It makes room for the variability of lexical meaning, and it eschews the impossible requirement of defining context-free literal meanings related to truth in the fashion prescribed in traditional theory.

2.3 Structure of normal situation types

So far, I have argued as if a locative expression had always only one normal interpretation, but it can have several. For instance, in *the painting to the right of the couch*, "the right" may be defined intrinsically to the couch (by reference to someone sitting on it in the normal way), or by an observer away from the couch. This yields two distinct normal interpretations for the phrase. For simplicity, I will use the singular in all arguments where the possible multiplicity of normal interpretations has no bearing.

Since normal situation types are meant as pre-theoretical points of departure, they are unprejudiced by theory about how to separate semantics from pragmatics. So normal situation types will be quite comprehensive, including conditions for truth as well as conditions for appropriateness, with no line drawn between the two (though the distinction between truth and appropriateness, inasmuch as it can be made precise, is not incompatible with the notion of situation type). In some cases, one can clearly see that a sentence may be true, though inappropriate (e.g., *The pencil is south of the inkwell*). But often deciding which conditions contribute to the truth of the sentence, and which to its appropriateness, is theory-bound and controversial, and will be sidestepped (witness the polemics concerning whether the existence and uniqueness of the king of France should be among the truth-conditions of *The king of France is bald* (Russell 1905; Strawson 1950)),[3] as this is not a crucial issue in the context of building of decoding and encoding procedures.

Before going on to describe different parts of normal situation types, three aspects of their nature must be considered: (a) the description of normal interpretations as prototypically structured categories; (b) index-icality; and (c) the distinction between meaning conveyed and meaning presupposed.

(a) It is possible for the canonical conditions that characterize normal situation types to take the form of a prototype[4] together with a specification of the permissible deviations from it. This will generally introduce a grey zone where some language users cannot definitely answer the question "is this particular situation in this category?" (in other words, "can this expression be used in that situation?"). Such fuzziness will generally be compatible with everything I will say about situation types, and I will go on speaking of canonical conditions, even though some of these may, occasionally, be neither clearly true nor false.

(b) Since normal interpretations of locative expressions are abstracted from particular contexts of use, they may contain indexical variables with no values assigned. But the expression and general world knowledge do provide general constraints on the values of indexicals, so a normal interpretation will include a specification of the functions of context which allow one to assign values to such indexical variables. Consider for instance *The cat is behind the tree*: it involves an observer in the context as a "free variable"; the referents of *the cat* and *the tree* are also undefined. In a particular context, all these will be assigned particular values. General constraints that are part of the normal interpretation include: the referent of *the cat* must be a cat, it must be uniquely recoverable from context as indicated by the determiner *the*, there is an implied observer who is located away from the tree, looking toward the tree, and so forth.

(c) Among the canonical conditions of use of a locative expression, that is as part of its normal interpretation, are some conditions one would not think of as conveyed by the expression, but rather as "preconditions" for its appropriateness. For instance, a condition for the appropriateness of the phrase "A is near B" is that A be typically more mobile than B, as the oddity of *The house is near the bicycle* shows.[5] Clearly, *The bicycle is near the house* does not "convey" that the bicycle is more mobile than the house, but one might say that it presupposes it. Indeed, both the sentence and its negation require the same relative mobility condition, which is reminiscent of the logical definition of presupposition (a proposition P presupposes a proposition Q if both P and *Not* P entail Q). Yet, since the conditions I consider are canonical rather than necessary and sufficient, I cannot speak of actual logical entailment; "entails" would have to be qualified, perhaps by "characteristically". Thus, although my use of "presuppose" does not fit in a formal logic framework, it is not intuitively unmotivated. So I will divide the canonical conditions defining the normal situation type into those that are conveyed by the expression and those that are presupposed, or are preconditions of every use of the expression, assuming normality.

To conclude this section, let us survey different aspects of normal situation types, different types of canonical conditions. First, there is the purpose to which locative expressions are normally put. Since normal situation types include conditions for truth and appropriateness, and since the notion of appropriateness is subordinate to that of purpose, a definition of purpose should be part of the normal interpretation of an expression.

Another aspect of normal situation types is the arrangement of the objects, or the scene. The scene can be described at a level of canonical description and at a level of geometric conceptualization. The former is part of the "fundamental description of the world" – a general naive description of all existing objects, their physical properties, interactions and place in the world – a notion explored in the next section. But the motivation for the use of a preposition cannot always be found at this canonical level; instead it must be sought at a level of geometric conceptualization. So *Maggie is at her desk*, at the canonical level, describes a person sitting at a desk, in a position to use it: desk and person are three-dimensional objects, with normal shapes; the desk is made of solid and hard material, has a horizontal top at standard height, and so forth (details such as the exact material of the desk, its precise shape, Maggie's height, etc., are of course left unspecified, as they go beyond what is entailed by normality). At the level of geometric conceptualization, Maggie and her desk are seen as points (the geometric descriptions), and the two points are coincident; this description corresponds to the geometric meaning. The introduction of ideal meanings and geometric descriptions is motivated by the conceptualization level.

Finally, canonical conditions may include constraints on context that are unrelated to the purpose of the expression. For instance, *Lucy is at the supermarket* is inappropriate if both speaker and addressee are themselves in the supermarket – unless the speaker somehow takes the point of view of someone away from the supermarket (e.g., saying *John thinks Jerry is at the supermarket*). Further analysis will show that *at the supermarket* implies a "remote" point of view, while *in the supermarket* would imply a "close-up" one. Thus, if both speaker and addressee are in the supermarket, *at the supermarket* is ordinarily inappropriate, because a remote viewpoint on the supermarket is then inapplicable.

Clearly, many aspects of the normal interpretation of an expression cannot be deduced from the ideal meanings together with canonical descriptions of the objects. This will require us to introduce various pragmatic near-principles and, finally, use types.

2.4 A fundamental description of the physical world

The common-sense view of the physical world underlies our perception of it and every linguistic description of its physical aspect. There is much evidence of its primacy and of the faith most people have in its universality: workers in artificial intelligence, for instance, refer to that view with few misgivings whenever they talk about "representing knowledge of the physical world". This is a "naive" view, in the sense that it appeals only to a common-sense conception of space and objects. It may also be called "objective", and "viewpoint-free" (it is not a view of how things might appear to someone standing in a certain place, but how they would appear to an "ubiquitous" eye), but such judgments are of course valid only within the context of a human, thus ultimately subjective, experience. Even within a single human being's mind, several "theories" of the world can coexist, and one appears objective only relative to another. Thus, there is no contradiction here between naive and objective: the fundamental view is naive with respect to more scientific theories; it is objective with respect to visual illusions, deformations of perspective, and so forth. In other words, this view is the ideal toward which the reconstructive work of our perceptual processes tends – adopting a traditional view of perception.

In this view, space is three-dimensional, isotropic, and Euclidean. The earth is immobile; its surface – the ground – extends to infinity in all directions and keeps overall, despite bumps and hollows, within an horizontal plane. Above the ground is empty space; underneath, earth and rocks to unknown depth. In places, solid ground gives way to seas, lakes, and rivers, with more or less horizontal top surfaces except, for example, where rivers fall.

The ground supports solid objects, which are connected,[6] discrete wholes. At a given instant, these objects have a well-defined surface, which separates their inner substance from the outside world. Each has a shape, and a location in space. The surface of an object may appear totally plane and smooth, but it may also have an apparent texture, that is, some more or less periodic three-dimensional superficial patterns.

Liquids may be still, or agitated, or flowing. When still, they are contained, and have an horizontal top surface. Liquid in motion may maintain the same overall shape, and thus constitute an "object", although none of its parts are the same from one moment to the next. Some "objects" have even less definite shapes: air, clouds, fog, and so forth. Light, darkness, shadows are immaterial, but may have a more or less definite shape.

Gravity pervades space. Every object, unless it is in motion, or lighter than air, must be supported, either by the ground, or by another object which is itself supported. Water will support some objects and not others.

One could in principle give an almost complete account of this naive view at a given time, by specifying the shape of the ground, the place and shape of each object, and the support relations between objects; almost complete, because fluids and gases may have no definite shape (but one might for these find a somewhat more refined mode of description, e.g., indicating how the gas density varies through space).

We can also follow the evolution of the world through time, and consider a continuous succession of such instantaneous fundamental views. Objects will move through space, break, or be made from parts, behaving at least sometimes in predictable ways. All this constitutes the canonical description of the world.

However fundamental, this description does not provide the knowledge needed to explain the use of spatial terms, since what we say does not always reveal fact, but rather appearance and various geometric conceptualizations. Some conceptualizations come from "mental maps", which are made of lines and points approximating the canonical view of the world. The origin of others is more puzzling, as with *the crack in the surface*, where the surface is conceived as a thin lamina without any physical counterpart. Also, language allows us to refer to geometrical objects (*walk in a straight line between the trees*), objects or parts of objects with vague boundaries (*in the valley, in the neighborhood, the carvings on the stone*), or "entities" with undefined boundaries (*She walked through the water*). None of these has an exact physical correlate. There are abundant examples of divergence between this fundamental description of the world and the conceptualizations revealed by language.

Yet, the canonical view of the world is important; it is always in the background of appearances and conceptualizations, and, in contrast with these, is assumed to be "reality". Reference to the canonical view explains many assumptions we make when hearing a given sentence, although they are not warranted by the sentence itself. For instance, when told *The chair is behind the desk*, we will generally assume that both are supported by the ground, or some floor, as we know things usually are in that fundamental view.

One cannot assume that the canonical view is everywhere unambiguously defined, or that it is uniform for all speakers of a given language – much less for all human beings. There are domains of knowledge where several inconsistent views may mix, with no one view having a decisive claim to being fundamental; for instance, counterintuitive scientific views (such as the rotundity of the earth) have become partially integrated with our intuitive views, and it is not always clear which should be seen as canonical. What is the canonical view of the sun? of sugar dissolved in coffee? or of the eye? There are also objects invisible to the naked eye: cells, bacteria, microscopic irregularities in the surface of a polished piece of metal, molecules and atoms. What is the naive view of these? It might be necessary in such cases to admit locally several canonical views.

Often, one can assume that the canonical view of a phenomenon exists, but is not fully known, while what matter linguistically are well-defined non-canonical views. For instance, in most locative sentences about the sun, we need not know the canonical view of the sun; it is enough to know how it appears in the sky, since this appearance is what enters into the spatial relation. Presumably, the appearance is related in some fashion to the unknown canonical view. Note also that in areas where the canonical view is not clearly and uniquely defined, there are often such divergences between different members of the community that any assumption of universality will be most strained.

"Naive physics" as conceived by Hayes (1979) is closely related to the canonical view of the world (and presents some of the same difficulties). Hayes proposes "the formalization of a sizable portion of common-sense knowledge about the everyday physical world: about objects; shape; space; movement; substances (solids and liquids); time, etc.". A formalization of the canonical view of the world would be part of naive physics, but Hayes would probably include as well a formalization of other views, for instance the map view, or any others that are reflected in language. One difficulty of his proposal is the assumption that all naive views can be integrated into one consistent theory. A person holds several distinct naive theories of objects, shapes, etc. I have singled out one of these as fundamental, closest to "reality". I doubt that the other naive views, except for the map view, could be given a consistent and coherent theory, and certainly they need not be consistent with each other; human beings seem almost to play with how they view, or imagine, things in ways that are not systematic enough to be expressed in the form of some physical theory, even a naive one.

3   Purpose

Now that normal situation types have been introduced, I want to begin to disassemble them, to consider several types of normal conditions of use associated with locative expressions. Some of the linguistic choices manifested in a locative expression are correlated with elements of meaning that are best described as part of the purpose of the speaker,[1] and this is the first aspect of normal situation types I will consider. This leads to an examination of the notion of place, and of some constraints on the choice of subject and object that arise in connection with the prototypical purpose of locative expressions: the specification of place.

3.1 Prototypical purpose

Anyone asked the purpose of phrases like *at the store* or *on the table* will very likely give an explanation along the following lines: a sentence like *The teapot is on the kitchen table* most commonly answers the question *Where is the teapot?*, and its purpose is to give a spatial constraint on the place of the teapot sufficient for the hearer to easily find it, but not so precise as to be needlessly cumbersome. Of course, what "easily" implies varies with the particular physical situation, and the knowledge and/or perceptual abilities of the addressee.

The spatial constraint takes the form of a relation linking the object looked for and a reference object. One can conceive of a procedure designed to select an appropriate reference object.[2] Its place should be either known to the addressee, or easy to discover (for instance because the object is perceptually salient – relatively big, or bright, or odd, etc.). It should also be spatially related to the located object so simply and directly that one single locative phrase, or perhaps two, can express the relation (as a consequence, all objects closely associated with the located object normally have priority over more distant ones). The selection procedure thus requires a representation of the particular physical situation, and of the addressee's relevant knowledge of the world and particular environment, focus of attention, and perceptual abilities. Such a representation would often follow from expecting the addressee to have typical human abilities, spatial understanding, and judgments; thus one can often speak of the relative salience of objects independently of any particular perceiver. Note that to find an object that conforms to all the desired conditions, the selection procedure must have access to the lexicon, since whether a reference object leads to unwieldy expressions depends on which spatial relations are simply expressed in the particular language considered.

3.2 Non-prototypical purposes

Locative phrases may serve other, non-prototypical purposes, instead of, or in addition to, providing a constraint on the location. Most often, the latter remains a goal, but it is subordinate to another goal (as it is even in the prototypical case, where the high level goal is to allow the addressee to find an object). One can test whether constraining the location of object X is relevant by seeing whether the prepositional phrase could answer the question *where is X?*.

- Identification

In *The store at the corner sells cigarettes*, the purpose of the locative phrase is to allow the addressee to identify the store the speaker has in mind; it should apply uniquely to that store. Presumably, the speaker generates a subgoal "try the location as a sufficient characteristic", so that, at a lower level, the purpose of *at the corner* is to constrain appropriately the place of the particular store. The prepositional phrase itself could answer the question *Where is that store you wish to talk about?*. Choosing an appropriate constraint in this case could be done by a procedure essentially similar to the one that selected *on the kitchen table* in answer to *Where is the teapot?*, but with the additional condition that the resulting spatial constraint should apply to one store only.

- Suggesting inferences

If I say *I bought this present in a store on Fifth Avenue*, I may not wish to help the addressee find the store; instead, I may want to draw attention to some of the consequences of the specified location (the present is of good quality, it was expensive, etc.). An upper level goal was to describe some characteristics of the present; this led to a subgoal specifiable as "to give a constraint on the place of the store where it was bought". The locative phrase *on Fifth Avenue* could also answer the question *Where is the store?*, but the choice of *Fifth Avenue* as a reference object was not motivated solely by its salience as a physical place.

- Highlighting a relation

In

He had bright blue eyes in a long thin face.

the purpose of the locative phrase is not to inform the addressee of the location of the eyes, but rather to introduce the description of the face. Note that the speaker could have said:

> *He had bright blue eyes and a long thin face.*

The use of *in* rather than *and* highlights the relation of the eyes to the face, suggesting that there is something worth notice in the meeting of the face and the eyes.

- Describing the located object, location irrelevant

In all cases so far described, one purpose of the locative phrase is to give an appropriate constraint on the place of an object, where appropriateness varies with the context. But with *a man in a red hat, in a red hat* is not an answer to *Where was the man?* except as a joke (a standard joke of French children is to answer *Où est Jean?* by *dans sa chemise*). *In a red hat* may be relevant to identifying a certain type of man, but there is no subgoal "to give a constraint on the place of the man". As we will see, the usual Figure/Ground relationship is inverted here. *In the red hat* does not constrain the place of the man, because normally one cannot work one's way from the place of the hat to that of the man, and the hat is moved onto the person, and not the person into the hat. Only *with*, which is not basically locative, allows the same inversion (*the church with a steeple*).

3.3 Further specifications of purpose

So with one exception the purpose of a locative expression is partially specified as "to give an appropriate constraint on the place of an object". Additional specifications of purpose will often be necessary to explain how, given the same reference and located objects, a speaker selects one of several plausible prepositions, and how the addressee can infer the values of some indexical variables and draw various pragmatic inferences. Here, purpose becomes entangled with relevance and tolerance. For instance, take chess pieces on a board, and specify the purpose as "to give a place description for someone concerned with distinguishing game positions". Clearly, the speaker must use a preposition indicating direction (such as *behind, on the left of*, etc.), rather than the imprecise *near*, though both *The queen is near/behind the bishop* might be true. Such a definition of the purpose also permits us to constrain the values of two indexical variables: the direction of the back axis which defines *behind* should be parallel to the chessboard axis joining two players in standard position; and the tolerable deviation from being exactly located on the back axis is defined by the grid size of the board. Relevance and tolerance are considered in detail in Chapter 6.

As this discussion shows, purpose is not as clearly definable an entity as the place and time of an utterance. Purpose is not observable like time or place; there exists no universally agreed-upon procedure for determining it. Purposes are normally multiple and imbedded, a given expression may fulfill a multiplicity of purposes, and any formulation of the purpose(s) will involve implicit references to indefinite amounts of complex world knowledge. Yet one can work backward from linguistic choices to a partial specification of the corresponding purpose that is useful.

Since in its most general specification purpose involves the notion of place, it will be useful to have a clear understanding of what "place" is.

3.4 The notion of place

Aristotle, in the Physics, describes the place of an object as that part of space it occupies. In this naive common-sense view, space constitutes a fixed frame in which objects move, and of which they occupy parts at given times. "The existence of place is held obvious from the fact of mutual replacement. Where water now is, then in turn, when the water has gone out as from a vessel, air is present. When therefore another body occupies this same place, the place is thought to be different from all the bodies which come to be in it and replace one another. What now contains air formerly contained water, so that clearly the place of space into which and out of which they passed was something different from both." (McKeon 1941).

A place can thus be thought of as any piece of empty space, as in

> *Under the bed is a good place to hide.*
> *No two objects can occupy the same place at the same time.*

or – relationally – precisely as that part of space occupied by an object (note the description of purpose as "giving an appropriate constraint on the place of an object"). Normally, we conceive of the earth itself – Galileo notwithstanding – as immobile within space so that it serves as the absolute frame of reference.

Since the only way to describe the place of an object is by using other objects as reference, place is linguistically specified by means of a locative expression; this expression provides a constraint on the place, by indicating a certain spatial relation between it and the place of the reference object. This should, by the same token, constrain the place of the reference object, but there is actually a basic asymmetry between the two objects: the place of the reference object is assumed known, and the expression thus in principle gives information on the place of the first object.

Since the truth of a spatial relation is always time-dependent, one must think of spatial relations either as 3-place predicates, for instance:

> *In (A, X,t)*

(with A the located object, X the reference object, and t the time), or as 2-place predicates relating the places of objects rather than the objects themselves:

In (Place (A,t), Place (X,t))

Since *in* and other spatial predicates are usually thought of as purely spatial, and since *Place* is certainly time-dependent, the second formulation seems preferable. However, in my occasional use of predicate calculus, I will for brevity simply write

In (Place(A), Place(X))

In this formula, we can assume *Place* to be implicitly indexed by the time t.

There are looser spatial uses of the word *place* (which might in fact be considered other, closely related, senses). Objects, such as a school, a city, a garden, a terrace, can be described as *places* contrary to, say, a teapot, a painting, a coat:

This garden is a beautiful place.

Such objects are mostly thought of as offering a surface for support, or an interior for inclusion; they are attached to the earth and "immobile" like it; in locative expressions, they are most often used as reference objects. There is here a kind of conceptual confusion[3] between the reference object itself and the space it offers for support and inclusion, as these examples reveal:

The bedroom is a pleasant place to work.
The worst place for a store is this street corner.
The bed is the best place to put the blanket.

In these an underlying *in, at,* or *on* has been deleted (their meaning being respectively something like *In the bedroom is a pleasant place to work*, and *at this street corner...* and *on the bed...*). In this process, the distinctions between *at, on,* and *in* are neutralized; yet, inasmuch as the reference object is identified with a privileged space (the space enclosed, or above and adjacent, etc.), no misunderstanding will arise. The same deletions would not be acceptable with other prepositions; the two sentences below are not synonymous:

The best place to hide this letter is the cabinet.
The best place to hide this letter is under the cabinet.

In the same way, there is a double use of the term *where*. "Where" relative clauses may refer to the exact "place" of an object, as in

The house is near where the bicycle is.

but in sentences like

The room where the double bed is has no bathroom.

where stands for *in which*.

From here on, I will use "place" in the strict Aristotelian sense.

3.5 The Figure/Ground relationship

At least at first sight, several prepositions appear to express symmetrical relations, for instance, *near*, *against*, *along*, and *at* in certain uses, glossed sometimes as "indicating close proximity". Thus:

$$Near\ (A, X) \leftrightarrow Near\ (X, A)$$

Other prepositions have converses:

$$Above\ (A, X) \leftrightarrow Below\ (X, A)$$

Finally, although some prepositions such as *on* and *in* do not have converses across the board, in some contexts converse prepositional expressions do exist to draw attention to a different aspect of the interaction of complex-shaped objects. For instance,

The shoes are on my feet.
My feet are in the shoes.

Note that *in* does not "mean" the converse of *on*.

What conditions the choice between converse expressions? In the prototypical case where the purpose of the locative expression is to inform the addressee of an object's location, this choice is determined by which of the two objects' location is at issue. That entity is referred to in the subject position of the expression; the entity whose location is taken for granted is referred to in the object position. Compare

The house is near the church.
The church is near the house.

This rule is clearly related to the fact that, in the "unmarked" case, the topic is also the logical subject of a sentence in English. The object whose location is at stake will tend to be the topic, and the logical subject of the expression.

Following Talmy (1978a), I will sometimes call the first object the "Figure", and the second the "Ground". Here are Talmy's definitions of these semantic roles:

...the terms 'Figure' and 'Ground' – taken from Gestalt psychology – can be given the following characterization in the area of semantics:
The Figure object is a moving or *conceptually movable* point

whose path or site is conceived as a variable the particular value of which is the salient issue.

The Ground object is a reference-point, having a stationary setting within a reference-frame, with respect to which the Figure's path or sites receives characterization. (emphasis in the original)[4]

Suppose the speaker wishes to describe the location of an object A to a given addressee. Assume A is in the field of view and there is an object B, near A, that the speaker believes visible to the addressee; or, alternately, assume the speaker believes that the addressee knows the location of an object B near A, but cannot see it. Even so, the speaker may not be able to use a locative expression with A as Figure and B as Ground, though the relation expressed appears true. For instance, the sentences

> *Mary's house is near the bicycle.*[5]
> *The gate is at Mary.*

are not acceptable, even if the addressee knows where the bicycle is; or if Mary is quite visible against a very long fence in the distance, while the gate does not stand out. In such contexts, one may use periphrases

> Mary's house is near where the bicycle is.
> The gate is where Mary is standing.

To explain this, we must look at the typical properties of pairs of objects, such that one is used as a reference for locating the other. As noted, a reference object should either be easy to see, or its location known to the addressee. In the former case, the Figure would normally be less discernible than the Ground – otherwise the addressee could discover the Figure's location without locative information. In the latter case, the Ground object will often have a permanent location, since such objects are more likely to have their location known than objects which move freely.

In short, there is a tendency to use relatively large fixed objects as references, and pairs of objects which greatly violate these conditions are unacceptable, even if the choice of reference object is perfectly rational in the particular context. The need for a fixed Ground-object is fulfilled by substituting *where the bicycle is* for *the bicycle*, or *where Mary stands* for *Mary* – by having a place, that is, a fixed point of the earth's surface, as reference object instead of a typically very mobile object.

Consider now the case where the main purpose of the locative expression is not to inform the addressee of an object's location, but to identify an object, as in

> Give me the book next to the pencil!

The particular book the speaker has in mind can be inferred from its location. Where identification is the main purpose, the reference object apparently need not be more salient than the located object; since the speaker wants the addressee to pick one out of several objects, the selected object need only be the only one to bear the relation expressed to the chosen Ground object. Yet, often the sort of Figure/Ground relationship that would be unacceptable with the prototypical use remains unacceptable here as well. So, as expected

> *The bottle is under the cap.*

sounds absurd; the addressee would be unlikely to see the cap but not the bottle. But

> *The cognac bottle is the one under the cap.*

sounds no better, although such an expression should make sense if there were several similar bottles, and only the cognac bottle had a cap. Then one would say instead:

> *The cognac bottle is the one with the cap on it.*

(*with* is not basically locative, and does not demand a fixed and/or salient reference object). In the same way,

> *I painted the wall against the chair.*

is unacceptable. Our linguistic ear demands the same relative fixity and salience of Figure and Ground in the identification case as in the prototypical locative case.

It is difficult to state exactly the conditions that make a locative expression unacceptable because the typical relative salience and fixity of Figure and Ground are inappropriate. The unacceptability depends on the preposition, and also seems to vary idiosyncratically with particular contexts. Thus *at* and *against* strictly require a Ground that is fixed in relation to the Figure; *next to*, *by* and *behind* are less strict, as exemplified by

> *The gate is just next to Mary.*
> *I painted the wall by/behind the chair.*

Such variable restrictions should probably be considered as conventional properties of particular prepositions. When one tries to infer these restrictions from connotations of the preposition, the resulting explanations are very elusive. For instance, *against* suggests a movement of the Figure toward the Ground; in the static case, this might exclude situations with a moveable Ground and a fixed Figure. Such connections may underlie speakers' intuitions, but that would be difficult to prove.

Restrictions on Figure/Ground choices depend on more than the relative fixity and salience of the objects, and vary somewhat idiosyncratically with the context as the following examples show:

> *The mountain under the plane just now is Mount Shasta.*
> ** The cognac bottle is the one under the cap.*

It seems that connotations of the preposition, the accumulation of experiences with the objects and with similar linguistic expressions, combine to make certain Figure/Ground assignments unacceptable in ways that are difficult to make explicit. In some cases, explanations suggest themselves – for example, human beings, though quite movable and often relatively inconspicuous, can be used as Grounds for much bigger, fixed objects, presumably because of the human tendency to picture oneself as the center of the universe:

> *The Empire State building is near us.*
> ** The Empire State building is near the bicycle.*

In summary, there are typical patterns of conceptual movability; that is, for some pairs of object kinds, A and B, one will typically locate object of type A with respect to object of type B, and expressions that relate them in converse order are often unacceptable, however rational they might be in terms of the speaker's purposes. The acceptability of a certain Figure/ Ground choice also varies with the preposition. Finally, with a given preposition, the unacceptability of a given locative expression cannot always be traced to a few properties of the objects involved; it varies in somewhat idiosyncratic fashion with the types of objects.

4   Ideal meanings

There have traditionally been two ways to conceive of the meaning(s) of a lexical item:

(a) The meaning of a word – assuming it has only one – consists in a list of conditions corresponding to its contribution to the truth-conditions of the sentences in which it occurs. This is sometimes called the "checklist" theory of meaning (Fillmore 1975). Of course, a given word may have several meanings; one will often distinguish several types of contribution to the truth-conditions of the sentences in which it occurs.

(b) Another way to view lexical meaning involves the notion of prototype. Rosch (1977) looked at prototypes for natural kinds from a psychological perspective. A prototypical bird, for instance, is the "best instance" of a bird. Most North Americans have a remarkably similar description of the prototypical bird: in size, color, habits, and so forth, it is somewhat like a robin. Other members of the bird category are then described in terms of their resemblance to the prototype, and may vary in their "degree of membership" in the category. (Strictly speaking, there may be no prototype object, but only degrees of prototypicality; speaking of a prototype is only a shortcut.) Resemblance being a matter of degree, we can see why natural kind categories would be fuzzy, and why some questions about membership in the category (e.g., "Is a whale a fish?") would occasionally elicit the answer "yes and no". Also, speakers may accept a given label in a given context, and reject it in another (speaking to a small child, one may call a whale a fish; in a zoology paper, that would be unacceptable).

The meanings I propose for the prepositions, the ideal meanings, share properties with prototypes, but are better suited to the domain of spatial relations. The ideal meaning of a preposition is a geometrical idea, from which all uses of that preposition derive by means of various adaptations and shifts. An ideal meaning is generally a relation between two or three ideal geometric objects (e.g., points, lines, surfaces, volumes, vectors) – in fact, ideal meanings are usually those simple relations that most linguists and workers in artificial intelligence have proposed as meanings of the prepositions. These relations play indeed an important role, but as something akin to prototypes, not as truth-conditional meanings.

In a particular use of a preposition, the ideal meaning may have been "transferred" to another relation, one that is in some way closely related; this new relation may in turn be only approximately true. Moreover, the objects related are mapped onto geometric objects (matching the categories specified for the arguments of the ideal meaning) by processes of geometric imagination, idealization and selection. These mappings onto geometric descriptions, corresponding to various geometric conceptualizations and metonymies, are accomplished by a variety of functions (Chapter 5).

The geometric meaning of a locative expression is thus a proposition involving a relation applying to geometric descriptions of the objects, and that relation may be the result of two transformations applying in succession to the ideal meaning, which I call sense shifts and tolerance shifts:

• Sense shifts

These are discontinuous shifts to another, conceptually close relation. So, for instance, the ideal meaning of *on* is not true of the situation described by *the wrinkles on his forehead*, but that situation "resembles" one of contiguity and support, and this resemblance motivates the use of *on*. Thus one would not say

> *the ruts on the road

because the depth of the surface accident prevents one from seeing a resemblance with a situation of contiguity and support. Where the surface accident is deep, *in* is required, expressing the relation of a gap to the "interrupted" object:

> *the deep wrinkles in his forehead*
> *the ruts in the road*

Or consider

> *the apple on the branch*
> *the medal on a chain*

The relation centrally expressed here is one of attachment. But, most often, attachment co-occurs with contiguity and support: the apple is contiguous with the branch through its stem, and ordinarily supported by the branch, though from above; and the same can be said of the medal and the chain. That attachment is implied, however, is shown by the fact that the first example would be appropriate if the branch were on the ground and the apple supported by the ground instead of the branch, or if the chain and medal were in a box. Although the meaning expressed is not the ideal meaning of *on*, it is closely connected to that meaning.

● Tolerance shifts

The ideal meaning or transformed ideal meaning may be only approx-imately true, as in *The book is on the table* when there is a table-cloth between the book and the table, or in the use of *behind* in Figure 1.2. Tolerance shifts involve gradual deviations measurable as an angle or distance.

The term ideal meaning is used rather than prototype, first, because there is little agreement about the nature and role of prototypes, and second, because a prototype, being a best example, is rather concrete. But in the case of prepositions, a very abstract geometric relation functions as a central model to shape the category, while the best example of use, more concrete, plays no such role. For instance, informants usually say the best instance of use of *in* is something like "containment in a medium-size box". We clearly do not want to describe the whole category of uses of *in* in terms of such a concept, but rather in terms of the topological relation of inclusion, whatever the dimensionality, size, or kind of the reference object.

Since the ideal meaning is the irreducible ideal associated with a preposition, it should allow one to understand novel use types. From it, from knowledge of the objects involved and of the context, one might be able to guess at the likely interpretation of an unfamiliar locative express-ion. So, for instance, if a non-native speaker were to speak of **the characters in the screen*, we would have no trouble interpreting the expression, using the ideal meaning of *in* and our knowledge of screens, although the correct expression is *the characters on the screen*.

I believe that such ideal meanings are best suited to describing linguistic intuitions about the spatial uses of the prepositions. I consider them both a psychological and a linguistic hypothesis and assume such a unitary geometric meaning exists in people's minds as a kind of "model", as the concept from which all uses of the preposition radiate. Psychological experiments might help confirm this claim. But the linguistic data them-selves give clues – if not definitive evidence – to the validity of the concept. Using the preposition *in*, I will attempt to show that all instances of use gravitate around such an ideal meaning.

4.1 An example: the preposition "in"

Consider

1. *the water in the vase*
2. *the crack in the vase*
3. *the crack in the surface*
4. *the bird in the tree*
5. *the chair in the corner*

6. *the nail in the box*
7. *the muscles in his leg*
8. *the pear in the bowl*
9. *the block in the box*
10. *the block in the rectangular area*
11. *the gap in the border*
12. *the bird in the field*

What is the contribution of *in* to the normal situation type associated with each locative expression? Without question, *in* conveys an idea of inclusion or surrounding in all these examples. But in each case, this idea applies to geometric objects related to the real objects in different ways – in some cases, strictly speaking, it may not apply at all. Geometric conceptualization, sense shifts, tolerance, and metonymies, allow one and the same lexical item, *in*, to serve in a wide variety of ways.

The first five examples illustrate the use of geometric imagination, and the mapping of geometric conceptualizations onto the real objects. Consider first the reference objects. In each example, the function mapping that object onto the relevant geometric description is different. The water is within the volume of containment defined by the concavity of the vase – a volume limited by the inner side of the vase and by a plane through its rim (Figure 4.1(a)) (if the rim does not fit in a plane, take a plane through the lowest point of the rim, when the vase sits on a horizontal surface). The crack is within what I call the "normal" volume of the vase – that is, within the part of space the vase would occupy if it had no crack; the crack is then seen as a "negative part" (Figure 4.1(b)). In example 3, the surface is imagined as some very thin lamina in which the crack is included. In example 4, the bird is in a volume bounded by the outline of the tree's branches (Figure 4.1(c)). In example 5, the including volume is a cylinder[1] delimited on two sides by implied walls (presumably of a room), above and below by two horizontal planes (one at the top of the walls, the other at the bottom), and, completing the closure, by an imaginary surface whose location, vaguely defined, depends on context (on the overall size of the room, on the size of the located object, on the presence of other objects in the corner area). Possibly, in some contexts, the projection of that surface on the horizontal floor would be something like the dotted line in Figure 4.1(d).

In each example, the located object is mapped onto the same geometric description: the place of the object (as defined in Section 3.4).

Example 6 (*the nail in the box*) shows how a phrase can be ambiguous when two different geometric descriptions of the reference object are equally plausible (lacking further specification by context). The nail could

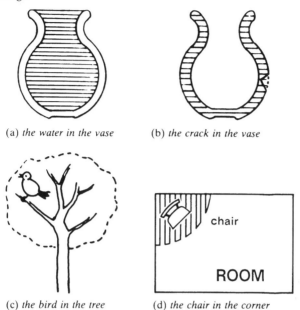

(a) *the water in the vase*   (b) *the crack in the vase*

(c) *the bird in the tree*   (d) *the chair in the corner*
Figure 4.1

be embedded, nailed into the walls of the box, or it could be contained within the box. Two distinct normal situation types correspond to this expression.

One can see how the expression "geometric imagination" applies: geometric figures are imaginatively projected onto the real objects. Piaget and Inhelder (1967) note that the child's idea of space, while developing under the influence of motor and perceptual mechanisms, builds upon sensorimotor constructs "at the level of thought and imagination". Not surprisingly, mental constructs which do not merely reflect perceptual representations arise also in connection with language (though these may originate in linguistic convention rather than the direct interpretation of spatial experience). This is easily granted in the context of geographical knowledge and mental maps, but it is also true in the context of scenes that can be perceived at a glance.

What constitutes an appropriate geometric description for various kinds of objects in various contexts is often arbitrary; it may appear very natural, given our subjective experience and interaction with the objects, but often it cannot be deduced from the canonical description of the object, and from the properties of the other objects referred to in the expression. Thus the fundamental description of a tree, or of a surface, does not allow one to conclude that "the outline" and "a very thin lamina" are appropriate geometric conceptualizations, justifying respectively *the bird in the tree* and *the crack in the surface*.

There are also cases where a geometric description appears justifiable but is unacceptable. Thus, though a dish and a tray may be essentially identical in shape, one would say

   the potato in the dish

but not

   *the potato in the tray

This reflects a functional difference: a dish contains, but a tray is for support. Functional salience often conditions the appropriateness of geometric descriptions.

Example 7 – *the muscles in his leg* – illustrates sense shifts. The actual relation between muscles and leg is not one of containment, but the relation "part of". *In* can be used in such cases only if the part is surrounded by the rest of the object;

   *the knee in his leg

is odd: "part of" relations that may be expressed by *in* are distinctly related to the idea of spatial inclusion.

Example 8 (Figure 4.2) allows us to illustrate tolerance.

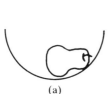 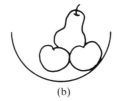 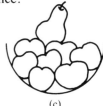

   (a)   (b)   (c)
the pear in the bowl
Figure 4.2

In 4.2(a), the pear is entirely within the associated volume contained by the bowl. In 4.2(b), it is partially contained in that volume. But in 4.2(c), the pear is not at all in that volume. Somehow, if an object is part of a group of objects supported by the bowl, some of which are strictly *in the bowl*, it is commonly said to be *in the bowl*. The distinctions between situation (a), (b), and (c) – as regards the location of the pear – are generally overlooked. *In* is the best choice, given the range of lexical possibilities.

Yet it will not do to say that an object is in a container if it is supported by it; the chopstick in 4.3(a) is *on the bowl*. If, however, it is one of a bunch of chopsticks, as in 4.3(b), then one might say *The chopstick is in the bowl*.

Examples 9, 10, and 11:

   9. *the block in the box*
   10. *the block in the rectangular area*
   11. *the gap in the border*

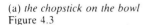
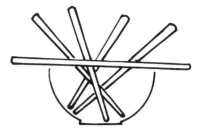

(a) *the chopstick on the bowl*   (b) *the chopstick in the bowl*

Figure 4.3

show how inclusion is generalized across dimensions. Examples 10 and 11 illustrate respectively inclusion in a two- and one-dimensional object. There is a difference, however, between these two uses of *in*. The block in the two-dimensional rectangular area is, strictly speaking, on top of it – in the third dimension; whereas in the case of a one-dimensional object, the gap is a part of the associated geometric description – namely the border – were it not interrupted. In the two-dimensional case, there is synecdoche; only the base of the block is strictly speaking in the area; this is an instance of a larger class of synecdoche motivated by salience, which I will consider in Section 6.1.

Inclusion in a one-dimensional object is not a widely useful conceptualization, and all examples are exactly patterned on 11:

    a notch in the edge / an opening in the boundary / ...

Examples where the reference object is not absolutely thin (a road, a string, a queue, etc.) tend to be doubtful, since the object is then not necessarily conceptualized as a line without thickness, but possibly as a cylinder, or a strip. For instance, in

    a person in the (waiting) line
    a truck in the road

there is no reason to think of the line or the road as linear objects without thickness (as one must with the road in *a city on the road to London*, since the city may extend on both sides of the road). The road is seen rather as a strip within which area the truck sits, and the line as some sort of irregular string of which one person is a piece.

It is instructive to note the prepositions used in English with actual geometrical objects. One will say:

    a point on a line

and although in Euclidean geometry, line and point having no extension, the point is actually part of the line, the conceptualization here is one of a point distinct from the line, having so to speak alighted on it. But one could say:

> *There are points in the line which do not correspond to any rational*
> *number.*

where the conceptualization is one of inclusion. Whereas the latter conceptualization accurately reflects geometric reality, the former, although not inconsistent with the Euclidean model, has no place in it: distinguishing a point in the line from a point having alighted on it is outside Euclidean geometry with its extensionless lines and points. However, to discard this use of *on* as some exception, or as an idiom, is to ignore the very natural conceptualization underlying it. There are discrepancies between Euclidean geometry and the conceptualizations involved in describing it in natural language, just as there are with the fundamental description of the physical world.

The last example, *the bird in the field*, illustrates the fact that there may be several ways to conceptualize a given situation. It would be appropriate if the bird were at some altitude above the field (note that this use of *above* points to a conceptualization of a field as a layer of soil bounded by the ground surface, or maybe as the ground surface itself). There are two possible interpretations for this example. In the first, the field is conceptualized as a three-dimensional layer including some soil under and some air above (an alternate to the conceptualization involved in the use of *above*). In the second, the field is conceptualized as an area, but there is a certain tolerance; the located object may be somewhat above or below the area. It is not clear what evidence we could use to choose between these alternatives; introspectively, both seem plausible. We will encounter more examples of alternate conceptualizations of the same real situation: it seems that the language user need not choose between the two interpretations, since, as far as the canonical level is concerned, they do not conflict. It is as if they worked together in corroborating the canonical description.

There are constraints on what can be conceptualized as an area. It is not sufficient that an object be geometrically two-dimensional; it must also be part of a surface divided into cells, so one can contrast inclusion in one cell with inclusion in another. One does not say:

> **Draw a line in the blackboard!*

but

> *Draw a line in the margin!*

is acceptable, because the margin is a subdivision of a page. Geographical areas are sections of a divided surface, namely the ground, whence the expressions *in (England/the county/the province/...)*

One will say:

the child in the (window/door)

although windows and doors are not properly subdivisions of a surface; but they are "holes", framed empty spaces, and *in* does not then conflict with *on*.

There may be constraints on the use of a given prepositional expression that have nothing to do with the ideal meaning, nor with any of the standard mechanisms that allow us to extend the use of the ideal meaning. For instance, *the truck in the road*, as opposed to *on the road*, implies that the truck is an obstacle. *Joan is in the hospital*, as contrasted with *at the hospital*, implies that Joan is hospitalized, rather than visiting or working there.

Some constraints depend on context. Let us consider *the chair in the corner* again. In Figure 4.4, if the speaker is close enough to that corner, the phrase is not appropriate unless the armchair is removed. If the

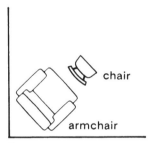

Figure 4.4

speaker is far from that corner, then the difference between chair and armchair in relation to the corner may be ignored, and the above phrase is appropriate. This difference is also ignored in

The chair and the armchair are in the corner.

It is built into the concept of a "corner" that *in the corner* becomes less appropriate as one gets further from the vertex itself, but the effect of this gradation depends on the distance from the corner to the vantage point adopted, which changes the resolution, allotting distinct or identical locations to the chair and armchair with respect to the corner.

It is surprising to find so many idiosyncratic conditions in uses that are not perceived as idiomatic. Even if one were to argue that these express-ions are idiomatic, this would not deny that the ideal meaning of *in* is yet expressed in them. In other words, although there may be an arbitrary

element in the normal interpretation of these expressions, there is also a
strong element of motivation. They are, in Fillmore's words (1979),
"motivated", but not "compositional".

Finally, before settling on an ideal meaning for *in*, what about the
contrast between partial and complete inclusion? Mostly, partial inclusion
suffices for the use of *in*, but it is possible to mean only complete inclusion:

> *I cannot put my foot in that shoe.*[2]
> *Put this rice in the bag!*

Whether strict or partial inclusion is meant depends on implicit assumptions as to what matters. Since the essential idea associated with *in* is that
of inclusion, and since the partial/complete distinction is a matter of
contextualization, I will take simply as the ideal meaning of *in*:

> *in*: inclusion of a geometric construct in a one-, two-, or
> three-dimensional geometric construct.

4.2 Other prepositions

Clearly, there is no general procedure for deciding whether an ideal
meaning exists, and, when it exists, what that ideal meaning is. Rather, the
ideal meaning reflects the intuition of a central idea, and of adaptations
making the preposition suitable for a broad variety of contexts. Deciding
on an ideal meaning is a matter of carefully considering for each preposition its range of uses, so as to perceive the complex inherent regularities. A
preposition may have several ideal meanings, as do the projective prepositions, and the applicable adaptation processes vary from preposition to
preposition. While only a thorough review of all types of use of a given
preposition can give a clear idea of the validity of an ideal meaning, I want
to provide here some sense of the basis for choice, and of the various shifts
and adaptations I have allowed to apply to ideal meanings in particular
uses.

Chapter 9 deals with "the three basic topological prepositions": *at*, *on*,
and *in*. Of these, the definition of an ideal meaning is least clear-cut for *on*.
The idea most consistently associated with *on* is contiguity – with a surface,
or with a line:

1. *the carpet on the floor*
2. *the village on the road*
3. *the house on the lake*

(this last example should be interpreted as meaning that the house is on
land contiguous with the edge of the lake). *On* can be used also with

geometrical objects or shadows as located objects – contiguity being a matter of appearance in the latter case:

    4. *a point on a plane*
    5. *the shadow on the wall*

With three-dimensional physical objects, *on* implies support, with a few exceptions: the reference object supports the located object. Thus one does not say of a chair against a door:

    **the chair on the door*

Occasionally, support will be indirect, as with a book said to be *on the desk* when on top of a pile of books on the desk. One can then say that the related objects are "almost" contiguous, because the intermediary objects must be thin, or, more generally, without salience. Exceptions to the support requirement are exemplified by

    6. *On the left wall is a couch.*
    7. *the lock on his forehead*

Example 6 is quite idiomatic, since without a qualifier like *left* or *opposite*, it is not acceptable:

    *?*A chest of drawers is on the wall.*

Example 7 is one of a restricted class where the located object is a body part. One can say here that support is irrelevant, as it is not a property one would pay attention to when concerned with contact between body parts. Similarly, in examples 4 and 5, support is irrelevant. Thus, in all examples so far, except one very idiomatic one, support is required if it is relevant.

In some cases, contiguity and support are either absent, or are not the central idea expressed:

    8. *the carving on the stone*
    9. *a table on three legs*
  10. *the cafeteria on the campus*
  11. *the man on the bus*

These eleven examples represent the range of uses of *on*. What should the ideal meaning(s) be? Should there be one ideal meaning implying only contiguity, or one implying contiguity and support, or two – one with contiguity and one with support – or even more than two ideal meanings? I believe the best solution is to adopt a single ideal meaning as follows:

    on: for a geometric construct X to be contiguous with a line or
        surface Y; if Y is the surface of an object O_Y, and X is the space
        occupied by another object O_X, for O_Y to support O_X.

(The predicate *Contiguous* is defined so that, if line or surface are oriented – that is, if they have an outer and inner side – the geometric construct *X* must be entirely situated in the region of space bounded by the outer side of *Y*. The outer side of the line or surface will naturally be defined by the actual object which they bound (the table in *the book on the table* and the lake in *the house on the lake*). Note that line or surface are not necessarily so oriented; in *The village is on the border*, the border has no orientation, and the village could be on either side of it.)

Such a relation sits at the center of all uses of *on*, and seems to satisfactorily represent the central meaning intuition associated with *on*. In examples 1 to 4, this ideal meaning either applies exactly, or is "approximately true" (in cases of indirect support). In examples 6 and 7, which correspond to very restricted classes of use, the support condition is released, while contiguity is required. Note that although there is no support, there is still some resemblance to a situation of support: the reference object must be larger than the located object, and act as a background to it. Those expressions are not reversible:

> *the forehead on his lock*
> *the wall on the chest of drawers*

In example 8, the located object is part of the reference object, and in example 9, the reverse is true, but in both cases, the situation resembles one of contiguity and support: the carving is conceptualized as separate, and it must be superficial (otherwise *in* would be preferred to *on*); and the table is conceptualized as supported by its legs. In 10, the idea expressed is one of general location in an area; but in the great majority of cases, such general location implies also contiguity and support (not always since the cafeteria *on campus* might be on top of a highrise). In other words, support and contiguity are highly correlated with general location in an area; we have here a process by which a typical, but not necessary, occurrence has brought about a certain use of the preposition. As for example 11, there is support and contiguity, but with the floor instead of the top surface of the bus.

The above ideal meaning lies thus at the center of all uses of *on* as a sort of model; approximation, resemblance, a process involving typicality, and the selection of a variety of geometric descriptions, all link this model to the various situations in which *on* is used appropriately.

For *at*, I will content myself with a few arguments in favor of the ideal meaning proposed:

> *at*:   for a point to coincide with another.

Reference and located objects need not actually be points, but their extension and internal properties are ignored; they are "viewed" as points and mapped onto punctual geometric descriptions. Thus, in

> *The train is at Victoria Station.*

the station is conceived as a point on a travel trajectory. Time expressions also support the proposed ideal meaning: time is conceptualized as a real line, and in

> *We met at six o'clock.*

the punctual time of the event coincides with a reference point in time.

Coincidence need be true only given a certain tolerance. Mary, in

> *Mary is at the window.*

is only very close to the window. *At* will imply the closest relationship between two objects, "closest" being defined relative to the range of relevant possible interactions between the objects and the significant distinctions within that range; so, for instance, *at* will imply coincidence where possible and where the contrast between coincidence and separation is significant. Thus, coincidence is implied in the case of geometrical objects:

> *The center of the circle is at the intersection of the axes.*

since the difference between exact coincidence and very close proximity is of great matter in geometry. But exact coincidence cannot be inferred in

> *The car is at the corner of 6th and Broadway.*

which is true if the car is a good many feet from the corner, since that difference is not ordinarily significant for cars and street corners. We see here how an ideal meaning can, so to speak, pick out different contrasts in different domains.

The range of uses of *at* indicates that *at* is a **graded concept**, that its applicability, in some sense, is a monotonic decreasing function of a distance or angle (some projective prepositions are also graded concepts). Evidence that *at* "tends" toward coincidence is also provided by the role of modifiers such as *exactly, precisely*, etc. The phrase *exactly at* reduces the allowed deviation from coincidence; it is as if *at* were more or less true, and truer if the objects are closer.

There are cases where located and reference object are one- or two-dimensional:[3]

> *The temperature is highest at the equator.*
> *There is a film of oil at the surface of the water.*

These sentences imply respectively that the locus of the highest temperature points is coincident with the equator, and that the location of the film of oil, seen as infinitely thin, is coincident with the surface of the water. But such uses are clearly not prototypical; it seems reasonable to describe them as generalizations to higher dimensions of an ideal meaning with punctual (zero-dimensional) arguments.

For the projective prepositions, deciding about an ideal meaning is straightforward. Each of *in front of, behind, to the right of*, and *to the left of* has two ideal meanings, corresponding to the distinction between *The cat is in front of the tree from where I stand* and *The cat is in front of me* (sometimes referred to as egocentric versus intrinsic (Fillmore 1971; Clark 1973), though I will show in Chapter 10 that these terms are too simple). Take *to the right*, for instance: one ideal meaning takes three arguments, two points and a point of observation; the other takes two arguments, one point and a point of observation. A "point of observation" consists of two vectors attached to the same point: one vertical, the other horizontal, and corresponds to a "canonical observer" (Clark 1973) who stands upright on an horizontal plane, and looks straight ahead; the horizontal vector is along the line of sight. In the case of each ideal meaning, one can define four half-axes centered on the point corresponding to the reference object; the sequence front, right, back, left, is in counter-clockwise order in the first ideal meaning, and in clockwise-order in the second (see Chapter 10 for details). For *to the right*, the point corresponding to the located object must be on the right axis.

Among the adaptations of the ideal meaning for these prepositions, one finds rotation, to account for the fact that

> *to the right of the painting*

is acceptable when the painting is tilted; and curving of the axes, to account for the fact that

> *John is behind me.*

is acceptable if John is behind me on a curved road. In addition, there is the usual mapping of geometric descriptions on the objects related; in

> *the man to the right of the car*

the located object is assimilated to a point, and a point of observation is matched onto the car (by analogy with a human being). And there are also processes of relational approximation, since

> *The Knight is directly to the right of the Queen.*

is true given a certain tolerance.

At least at first sight, it is easy to define ideal meanings for the other prepositions. Take for instance *under*. The following ideal meaning seems appropriate:

> *under*: partial inclusion of a geometrical construct in the lower space defined by some surface, line, or point.

Any surface in a space with a vertical direction defines several infinite subspaces, one of which is *under* the surface. One can similarly define an infinite surface under a line, and an infinite vertical line extending downward under a point.

When the reference object is three-dimensional, its associated geometric description is usually the lower surface of the object. The lower surface is not necessarily a plane through the lowest points of the object, but it is the locus of where vertical lines moving upward impinge on the object. See

> *The boat is under the bridge.*

which is acceptable if the boat is in the cross-hatched space in Figure 4.5 below.

Figure 4.5

However in

> *One could see shiny silver carp under the water.*

the geometric description is "the upper free surface of the water". A whole category of objects allows this metonymic transfer: snow, lake, ocean, sand, and so forth. Thus,

> *The Eskimo buried the seal under the snow.*
> *Ants dig burrows under the sand.*

These all present an extensive surface at ground level. The appropriateness of the metonymy depends on context; most people do not accept

> *The fish is under the water.*

because in such an expression the surface of the water is not salient. Interestingly, with *underneath*, the geometric description is restricted to the lower surface since

> *underneath the lake*

is usually interpreted as "below the bottom of the lake".

4.3 Elementary spatial concepts and ideal meanings

Looking at two domains, color and physical objects, Rosch and Mervis (1975; Rosch 1977) state that a prototype – or clearest case of category membership – is determined by different criteria in each domain. For color, the basis of prototypes is physiological: some colors are perceptually salient and act as focal points for each category. But for concrete objects, prototypicality is linked with the distribution of attributes: the more prototypical a member is rated, the more attributes it has in common with other members of the category, and the fewer attributes in common with members of contrasting categories.

The domain of spatial relations has some similarity with color, in that ideal meanings are constructed out of perceptually salient spatial objects and relations. The definition of a relation in general, and of an ideal meaning in particular, involves two components: the domain of the relation – the set of pairs, or triples, etc., on which it is defined; and the relation proper (extensionally, this would correspond to the subset of pairs of which the relation is true). Ideal meanings are defined for geometric objects which are generally salient (e.g., points, planes, the vertical direction), although sometimes unspecified (e.g., "any geometric construct"), and correspond generally to perceptually salient relations (e.g., parallelism of lines, enclosure, contiguity). These are objects and relations that are easily, quickly and accurately perceivable (this includes both visual or coenesthetic perception, since perception of the vertical, for instance, involves coenesthetic perception). Psychological experiments might help support this claim, but it is in part quite obvious. Child development also provides evidence. Piaget and Inhelder (1967) showed that children's first representation of space is based on "topological relations" – among which they include proximity, separation, order (or spatial succession), enclosure or surrounding.[4] These basic relations are involved in the ideal meanings of a number of prepositions: proximity in *by*, *next to*, etc., separation and its opposite, contiguity, in *on*, *against*, order in *between*, *beyond*, *behind*, etc., and enclosure and surrounding in *in*, *inside*.

Of all the possible perceptually salient relations, whether elementary or complex, only a few are lexicalized in English (or for that matter in any language). The need for simplicity and practical usefulness limits the relations effectively coded in language to a subset. The requirements for perceptual salience, simplicity, and usefulness make it unlikely that a language would have a term meaning "for two punctual objects to be separated by seven feet", or "for two punctual objects to make an equilateral triangle with the observer", or "for three people to look along parallel lines". Also, there exist words referring to three-place relations (the projective prepositions, *beyond*, *between*, etc.), but not to four.

Table 4.1 lists elementary spatial concepts that occur in the ideal meanings of prepositions. I have distinguished five classes of concepts: (1) topological, (2) geometric, (3) physical, (4) projective, (5) metric. Each

Table 4.1. *Elementary spatial concepts in ideal meanings*

(1) topological:

    attributes/properties
        dimensionality (*at, on, ...*)
        boundedness (*across, through*)[†]

    objects
        inner side (*inside*)

    relations
        enclosure (*in, inside, around*)
        contiguity with line or surface(*on, against*)
        order of three points on a line (*between, beyond*)
        order of two points on an oriented line (*above, under, ...*)
        coincidence of two points (*at*)
        line in/on a plane (*across*)

(2) geometrical:

    objects
        straight line (*along, behind, ...*)
        plane (horizontal plane with *behind, in front of, ...*)
        cross axis of a two dimensional strip (*across*)

    relations
        alignment of points (*between, behind, ...*)
        parallelism of lines (*along*)
        alignment with direction (e.g. vertical) (*over, under, ...*)
        orthogonality of lines (*to the right/left ...*)

(3) physical:

    objects
        vertical direction (*above, below, ...*)

    relations
        support (*on*)

(4) projective:

    objects
        point of observation

    relations
        on line of sight (*behind, in front of ...*)
        on orthogonal to line of sight (*to the right*)

(5) metric:

    attributes
        distance (*near, close to, ...*)

[†] (*Across* and *through* contrast along the dimension of boundedness (Talmy 1978b). Compare *She walked through the water* with *She walked across the water*; with *across*, there is a bounded body of water and "she" walked from one end to another; but with *through*, *the water* is not conceived as bounded.)

attribute, property, object, or relation, is followed by prepositions in whose ideal meaning it plays a role (this is only a guess in the case of the prepositions that I have not closely studied).

*   *   *

In summary, ideal meanings are an attempt to represent intuitions of a geometric ideal together with transformations that adapt and extend this ideal to a range of contexts of use. These transformations take a variety of forms: transfers to geometric descriptions, conventional sense shifts, relaxation of some constraints through approximation. This characterization of ideal meanings does not entail a precise procedure for defining them (in fact the usual characterization of truth-conditions and compositionality does not entail a precise procedure for defining truth-conditions or morphemic meaning either). But a careful examination of the set of uses of all closely studied prepositions reveals regularities fitting this characterization.

5 Geometric descriptions

To understand the use of locative prepositions, one must assume that geometric descriptions are mapped onto the objects by a process of geometric imagination, a mapping accomplished by **geometric description functions**. Objects other than those explicitly referred to in the locative expression may also be relevant to its interpretation – most frequently, but not uniquely, an observer – and those, too, are mapped onto geometric descriptions.

Geometric description functions are meant to represent: (a) how we view a particular object as some geometric entity (e.g., a tree as a point, a surface as a very thin lamina, a person as a frame of reference); (b) indirect references to a part of an object, or an adjacent region of space (e.g., an interior), or a projection, etc. (Section 5.2), by means of a noun-phrase that refers to the object. These may in general be called "metonymies" – though this is often stretching the intuitive idea of metonymy, since a speaker may not be as aware of an indirect reference as he or she would be if told *The ham sandwich is waiting for his check*.[1] The various geometric descriptions are systematically related to the object as it is located in space at the time the utterance applies. In the simplest case, we see the object as it is in the fundamental description of the world. Then, the geometric description applicable is simply the region of space occupied by the object (taking a "naive" view), that is, the "place" of the object. Given any object at a given time *t*, we can assign to it a place; we thus have a geometric description function which I will call *Place*.

Since it is not the objects themselves that we relate by means of a spatial expression, but regions of space associated with the objects at a given time, an element of the domain of a geometric description function is a pair consisting of an object and a time. I use the term "object" broadly, to include not only physical objects, but anything that might be referred to in a locative expression (or might be relevant to its interpretation). To avoid confusion, I sometimes use the more general term "spatial entity". Spatial entities will include geometric objects (e.g., circles, planes), object parts (the handle of a cup, the leg of a table; also an object's surface, edges, front, top, back, sides), parts of space ("the space between the seats", "a place to build a house", "here"), holes, groups of objects (the mountains,

the trees, a building complex), environments (a neighborhood, the sub-
urbs). As for the range of a geometric description function, it is contained
in the set of all possible regions of space.

To make things more precise, let us assume the ideal meaning of a
preposition is a two-place relation I, and consider first locative expressions
such that the ideal meaning applies exactly. This means that for any such
locative expression, the corresponding normal situation type is partially
defined by a scene constrained thus: given that the expression refers to a
located object O_1 and a reference object O_2, there exist two functions,
GD_1 and GD_2, such that the following relation holds:

$$I\,(GD_1\,(O_1,t),\,GD_2\,(O_2,t))$$

With a three-place relation, we would have:

$$I(GD_1(O_1,t),\,GD_2(O_2,t),\,GD_3(O_3,t))$$

The GD_i functions are the geometric description functions applicable in
the case of this situation type. I will introduce new functions, G_1, G_2, and
G_3; each G_i is implicitly indexed by t, and such that for every pair $<O,t>$,
$GD_i(O,t)$ and $G_i(O)$ have the same value. The relations above can then be
shortened to:

$$I(G_1(O_1),\,G_2(O_2))$$
$$I(G_1(O_1),\,G_2(O_2),\,G_3(O_3))$$

But the ideal meaning may have been transferred by a sense shift that
yields a new relation, which we will denote by S_I to stress its relatedness to
the ideal meaning I. Moreover, this new relation may be only approximately true; the resulting approximate relation will be denoted by $A(S_I)$.

$$[A(S_I)](G_1(O_1),\,G_2(O_2))$$
$$[A(S_I)](G_1(O_1),\,G_2(O_2),\,G_3(O_3))$$

In some cases, A is simply the identity. If we also allow the identity as a
sense shift, then we need only the two formulae above; these are general
schemata for the geometric meaning of locative expressions (they are only
indicative; in some cases, the relation expressed may not fit such a schema,
as, for instance, with uses of *on* implying support, as we will see below).

The ideal meaning or transferred ideal meaning may also involve
selection restrictions; that is, the pairs or triples which constitute the
arguments of the relation I or S_I will be subject to conditions. For instance,
for *in*, the second argument must refer to a region of dimensionality
greater than zero (there is no inclusion in a point), thus the range of G_2 for
in is restricted to regions of dimensionality greater than zero.

The functions G_1, G_2, and G_3 are often decomposable. For instance,
with *The bird is in the bush*, one can assume:

Included (Part(Place(Bird)),
Interior(Outline(VisiblePart(Place (Bush)))))

where the geometric description applicable to the bush is the product of the **elementary geometric description functions** *Interior, Outline, VisiblePart,* and *Place* (*VisiblePart* maps a region onto the part of it that is above ground). The function *Place* is implicitly indexed by *t*; given a time *t*, it maps spatial entities onto regions of space of any dimensionality. All other elementary geometric description functions map regions onto other regions.

In the first order logic representations of the geometric meaning of locative expressions I will propose, I will either simply use the preposition itself (*Under, ToTheRight*, etc.) as the ideal meaning, or the ideal meaning expressions established in Chapter 4. Variables corresponding to the subject and object of the preposition, though they have transparent names for readability (*TopOfCabinet, VictoriaStation*, etc.), are not analyzed; as far as the internal structure of the formulae is concerned, I could just as well have used *X* or *Y*. In any system designed to do "reasoning " or "comprehension" tasks however, these entities would have to be further described, and the content of the various elementary functions (*Outline, LineApprox, Interior*, etc.) would have to be made explicit, for instance, by axiomatizing the notions involved, or as algorithms computing the corresponding functions.

I will first describe the *Place* function for different types of spatial entities, then consider the other elementary geometric description functions.

5.1 Place

I consider here the problems involved in defining the place of various types of spatial entity. A taxonomy of spatial entities is in Table 5.1. Certain

Table 5.1. *A taxonomy of spatial entities*

ordinary solid objects	parts
loose solid substances	geometric objects
groups of solid objects	parts of space
liquid or gaseous "objects"	holes
geographical objects	unbounded "entities"

"places" will have boundaries which are vague (parts, environments, etc.), or even undefined (as in *He walked through the water*). I will not propose any mode of representation for vagueness and unboundedness, but simply indicate where they occur, and assume that the value of the function *Place* represents in some way what is vague (to what extent, with what constraints, etc.), or unbounded, and that associated formal deductive processes handle such representations in a way matching human reasoning.

• ordinary solid objects

An object such as a book, cup, shirt, is entirely bounded by a closed surface, on the inside of which is matter; the region bounded by this surface is the object's place. In the naive view, the surface is well-defined.

Let us make clear how *Place* relates to the shape of an object. At a certain time *t*, given the shape of an object, and the location of three of its points within a fixed frame of reference, its place is determined. For many solid objects (tables, cups, etc.), the shape remains essentially constant through time, except in the case of violent irreversible changes (cutting, breaking); but there are also flexible solid objects (clothes, strings, etc.), whose shape does not remain constant when they are moved, though there are certain constraints on the range of shapes they may assume.

• loose solid substances

In the expressions

> *There is a crab in the heap of sand.*
> *the dust on the table*
> *the rice in the bag*
> *the animals in the straw*

the heap of sand, the dust, the rice, and *the straw* are made up of disjoint parts. Their place is the sum of the places of their various parts; the place of each part is unproblematic, as each is an ordinary solid object. In contrast, substances such as flour and ash are conceived of as continuous; their place would be whatever regions of space are occupied by the amount the speaker has in mind, though it could consist of several disjoint amounts, as in *the ash in the ashtrays*.

• groups of solid objects

These spatial entities can be distinguished from those like sand and flour, because they cannot be conceptualized as solid masses. The place of a group of solid objects is the set of disconnected individual object places. If these objects are contiguous, that place will be identical to the space enclosed in the outline of the group (*She walked across the tiles*). The following example,

> *There are worms in the strawberries.*

illustrates the possibility of ambiguity between two geometric descriptions: the worms could be inside the berries, or among and around them in their container. In the first case the geometric description applying to the reference object is simply the place of the group of berries, in the second, it is the outline of this group, a function considered in Section 5.2.

• liquid or gaseous "objects"

Some bodies of liquid have well defined boundaries at a given time just as solid objects do, for example, the body of coffee of *There is sugar in that cup of coffee*. Others have vaguely defined boundaries, as most "gaseous objects" do:

> *the dew on the grass*
> *the air above the city*
> *the fog in San Francisco*

Many large "liquid objects" fall into the category described next.

• geographical objects

A geographical object is or includes a part of the earth's crust. There are fields, gardens, islands, peninsulas, plains, meadows, mountains, valleys, coasts, continents, pathways, and so forth – complex three-dimensional objects including a piece of ground with more or less precise boundaries. A similar description applies to cities, villages, streets, buildings, neighborhoods. There are accidents of the ground such as cliffs, slopes, crevices, ravines, summits, ridges, etc. There are three-dimensional bodies of water: lakes, oceans, rivers, waterfalls, pools, bays, inlets, and so forth, most with a nearly horizontal top surface, practically all vaguely bounded.

The canonical description of any such geographical object is as it would appear if every part of it were viewed at some short distance with the naked eye. In most contexts however, the view adopted only approximates that description: a field is seen as a relatively flat surface, a city as an area, a path as a flat strip, a river as a line, and so forth. Also, there is a basic indeterminacy involved in deciding what some of these objects include. Is a meadow a ground area? Is it a layer of earth – and if so how deep? Does it include the trees and grass? the air above? Language users seem undisturbed by this indeterminacy, and adopt one or the other definition as convenient. For instance, in saying *the grass and the trees on the meadow*, one takes the point of view that the meadow does not include the grass and trees; a meadow would then be an area of ground covered with grass, but the grass itself would not be part of it. The fact that the meadow remains the same meadow if trees and grass are cut argues in favor of that view. On the other hand, one can walk *through the meadow* which, since *through* implies movement in a volume, makes the meadow into a layer including part of the space above ground. Also, both *billions of creatures live in/under this meadow* are acceptable; in the first the meadow includes a layer of ground; in the second, it either is simply a surface or consists of the surface with space above.

To deal with this indeterminacy, one could consider *meadow* ambiguous, but this is clearly unsatisfactory as language users see no ambiguity. A better solution is to make *meadow* maximally inclusive, with the surface and a layer of ground and one of air, and allow for two geometric conceptualizations, the canonical one, and one as a ground area. Particular examples then either imply one or the other conceptualization, or they allow both, and there is no reason why that indeterminacy needs to be resolved, as we saw with *the bird in the field* (Section 4.1).

Other geographical objects like the sky and the horizon are appearances rather than actual objects: the sky is infinite space, but defined as what "appears" empty above the earth, and is bounded by the horizon. As for the sun, stars, and moon, in the naive view they are known essentially by their appearance in the sky.

• parts

Some words refer to objects which are normally parts of other complete objects: body parts, handles, the cover of a book, a door knob, and so forth. The limits of a part are sometimes vague where it joins other parts of the object. It is difficult to say where a person's wrist begins and ends, yet one can assume that a wrist occupies a place, with two boundaries fuzzily defined.

With the exception of geometrical entities, all two-dimensional entities, such as the margin of a page, the sides of a solid object, or geographical areas, are parts of other objects. For instance, the global surface of an object is a part of a sort: it is an oriented surface (one side of it is the outside). Such a surface is the reference object in *There is paint on the surface of the table*. Faces, edges, and corners are also parts of objects. Faces are parts of the object's surface, delimited more or less precisely as the bounding edges are more or less precisely locatable. The places of an edge and a corner may be respectively a line and a point, but they may also be vaguely bounded, oriented surfaces for objects with rounded edges. The places of edges and corners may be vague: where is the edge of a river?

Parts referred to by the words *side, front, top*, and so forth (considered in detail in 10.2.1) can be faces, edges, or "chunks" of two- or three-dimensional objects. They are also often vaguely bounded: see *the front of the theater* in *the seats at the front of the theater*. Context often determines the mean position of the vague boundary.

As another way to define parts, consider *The ceiling above the lamp is stained*. One would not be speaking here of the entire ceiling (as one might speak of one entire wall in *The wall in back of the chair is dirty* where *the* acts to select one of several walls), but only of a part of it – that is, the area directly above the lamp on the ceiling (although the utterance will often be appropriate if the stained part only intersects that area).

Finally, geometric accidents such as bends, turns, curves, folds, bumps, hollows, angles, define more or less vaguely bounded object parts. For example, *the bump in the road* defines a piece of the road surface with imprecise boundaries. How such places should be defined is often ambiguous: is a fold in a carpet a piece of the carpet, or a piece of its surface, or is it some immaterial shape? It is not clear that any linguistic example offers a reason to choose between these conceptualizations.

● geometric objects

Euclidean points without extension, infinitely thin lines, figures, surfaces, volumes, and so forth, often occur in non-technical (non-mathematical) language, for instance in *The children were standing in a circle,* and *The well is on a straight line from here to the village.* In more technical text (e.g., mathematical discourse), the semantics of the language may become so specialized as to require a distinct specification, placing it outside the scope of the present study.

● parts of space

These are, in general, vaguely bounded:

> *People grow vegetables in the intervals between the houses.*
> *I put the painting above where the table was.*
> *There are nice flowers in this place.*

There are also parts of "apparent" space, as in

> *the planes crossing the blue sky between the two buildings*

● holes

Not every concavity is a hole. A hole is defined only in relation to another object in which it occurs:

> *There is a hole in my shirt.*

A hole may be entirely bounded by its associated object, or part of its boundary may be virtual, defined by extrapolating the object's surfaces past the hole. Thus the hole in a shirt is bounded by planes defined by extending the two sides of the fabric over the hole, and by the edges of the fabric around the hole.

● unbounded "entities"

This refers to a part of a whole entity defined only by the fact that it alone is being paid attention to, the rest being out of view or of no concern, as in

> *He walked through the water.*
> *The fog around me was very thick.*
> *A silhouette appeared from the darkness.*

There would be little sense in trying to specify, in some directions, even a vague boundary for the unbounded object in all of these examples (though some boundaries may be well-defined – for instance *the fog* in the second example extends precisely to *me*); that is, to define a limited range in which the boundary is to be found, or beyond which no part of the object could be found.

5.2 Other elementary geometric description functions

The list of elementary geometric description functions other than *Place* in Table 5.2 is not complete, but it covers all the more common occurrences.

Table 5.2. *Elementary geometric description functions.*

(1) **parts**:	(3) **good forms**:
– three-dimensional part	– outline
– edge	– completed enclosure
– base	– normalized region
– oriented total outer surface	(4) **adjacent volumes**:
– oriented free top surface	– interior
– underside	– volume/area associated with vertex
– overside	– lamina associated with surface
	(5) **axes**:
(2) **idealizations**:	– main axis
– approximation to a point	– associated point of observation
– approximation to a line	(6) **projections**:
– approximation to a surface	– projection on plane at infinity
– approximation to a horizontal plane	– projection on ground
– approximation to a strip	

Remember that all elementary functions, except *Place*, map regions of space onto regions of space. *Place*, however, has for its domain the product of the set of all spatial entities by the set of time instants, and for its range the set of regions of space. It applies first to the located and reference objects, and to any other spatial entity bearing on the interpretation of the expression (e.g., an observer); then the product of some other elementary functions may apply to the value of *Place*. Defining elementary geometric description functions in this way avoids type inconsistencies; every elementary function always gets the right type of argument, and the global geometric description function maps a spatial entity taken at time *t* onto a part of space.[2]

Given a predicate *P*, the predicate *A(P)* designates a predicate which is true whenever *P* is "almost" true; since what counts as almost true depends on context, this notation hides complexities which cannot yet be made fully explicit (Section 6.3 on tolerance is a first inquiry into this problem). For each elementary function, I will give some linguistic examples that illustrate its role in building up meaning.

Elementary geometric description functions fall into six categories:

5.2.1 Functions that map a region of space onto a part of it
• three-dimensional part

This mapping occurs generally when indirect reference is made to a salient part of an object (Section 6.1).

Examples:

> *the tree on the meadow*
> *Contiguous(VisiblePart(Place(Tree)),*
> *GroundSurface(Place(Meadow)))*

Only the region occupied by the visible part of the tree (obtained from the region occupied by the tree by the function *VisiblePart*) can be said to be *on* the meadow. We assume that a geographical entity like a meadow includes a layer of earth together with the grass and a layer of air above; *GroundSurface* maps such entities onto their oriented ground area. There is no support here, only contiguity, since the ground does not directly act as a support for the visible part of the tree, as it would support a stone (although the situation does look as if it did).

> *She is under the tree.*

(she is actually under the branch part of the tree):

> *Under(Place(She),*
> *UnderSide(Outline(BranchPart(Place(Tree)))))*

Outline is a function that maps a geometric construct onto a smoothed out version of it.

> *The child must sit at the back of the chair.*

(the seat is then the relevant part):

> *AtTheBack(Place(Child),SeatPart(Place(Chair)))*

> *the waiting line at the counter*

(the head of the line, and the front of the counter, are the relevant parts):

> *[A(Coincide)](PtApprox(Head(Place(Line))),*
> *PtApprox(Front(Place(Counter))))*

• edge

> *the path along the ocean*

Assume the ideal meaning of *along* to be: for two lines to be parallel and "very" close to each other or coincident. Note that the path could vary in height as it follows the edge of a cliff, so the phrase indicates that the projection onto an horizontal plane at sea level of a line approximating the path is parallel and close to a line approximating the edge of the ocean:

[A(Along)](HProj(LineApprox(Place(Path))),
LineApprox(Edge (Place(Ocean)))))

HProj is the function projecting onto sea level.

• base

This is the surface composed of the set of points of a region which are in the lowest horizontal plane. It will be identical to the underside, if that underside is plane and horizontal. Example (Figure 5.1):

> *The house is above the apartment building.*
> *Above(Base(VisiblePart(Place(House))),*
> *Base(VisiblePart(Place (Building)))))*

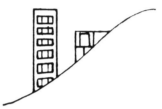

The house is above the apartment building.
Figure 5.1

• oriented total outer surface

> *the fly on the table*
> *Contiguous(Place(Fly),OrientedSurface(Place(Table)))*
> and
> *Support(Table,Fly)*

• oriented free top surface

This is the oriented surface composed of the set of points of a three-dimensional region which are in the highest horizontal plane. Its orientation is defined so it faces the outside of the region.

> *the chopstick on the bowl*
> *Contiguous(Place(Chopstick),*
> *OrientedTopSurface(Place(Bowl)))*
> and
> *Support(Bowl,Chopstick)*

• underside

Consider the smallest vertical cylinder enclosing a three-dimensional connected region of space; it divides the boundary of the region into two parts, one above, the other below; the one below is the underside, the one above I will dub the "overside". *Underside* is involved in:

> *the boat under the bridge*
> *Under(Place(Boat),Underside(Place(Bridge)))*

- overside

Overside is involved in:

> *One could see shiny silver carp under the water.*
> *Under(Place(Carp), Overside(Place(BodyOfWater)))*

5.2.2 Functions that map a region onto some idealization of it

- approximation to a point

The function *PtApprox* is involved in the following examples:

> *the train at Victoria Station*
> *Coincide(PtApprox(Place(Train)),*
> *PtApprox(Place(VictoriaStation)))*

> *The box is three feet from the wall.*
> *Distance(PtApprox(Place(Box)), Surface(Place(Wall)))*
> *= 3 feet*

> *The target is at ten feet.*
> *Distance(PtApprox(Place(Observer)),*
> *PtApprox(Place(Target)))*
> *= 10 feet*

- approximation to a line

> *the city on the road to London*
> *Contiguous(PtApprox(Place(City)),*
> *LineApprox(Place(Road)))*

- approximation to a surface

> *the cat on the grass*

There are two ways to conceptualize this example. In one the layer of grass is viewed as a surface:

> *Contiguous(Place(Cat), SurfApprox(Place(Grass)))*
> and
> *Support(Grass, Cat)*

In the other, the cat would be contiguous with the overside of the outline of the layer of grass:

> *Contiguous(Place(Cat), Overside(Outline(Place(Grass))))*
> and
> *Support(Grass, Cat)*

- approximation to an horizontal plane

  The function *HorPlnApprox* is involved in:

> *The top of the cloud cover is at 3000 feet.*
> Distance(HorPlnApprox(Place(SeaSurface)),
>   HorPlnApprox(Place(TopCloudCover)))
> = 3000 feet

- approximation to a strip

  the house across the street

Assuming the house across the street from the speaker, we get:

> Across(PtApprox(Place(House)),
>   StripApprox(Place(Street)),
>   PtApprox(Place(Speaker)))

5.2.3 Functions that map a region onto some associated "good form"
Good forms are obtained by filling out the irregularities or gaps in a region: such functions implement the Gestalt principle of "closure" or "good form" (Koffka 1935).
- outline
  The outline is not identical to the convex closure of a region (Figure 5.2); it takes into account the global shape of a region, ignoring negligible interruptions and irregularities.

> *The bird is in the bush*
> Included(Part(Place(Bird)),
>   Interior(Outline(VisiblePart(Place(Bush)))))
> *cars along the waterfront*
> [A(Along)](Outline(Place(GroupOfCars)),
>   LineApprox(Place(WaterFront)))
> *man under the ladder*
> Under(Place(Man),Underside(Outline(Place(Ladder))))

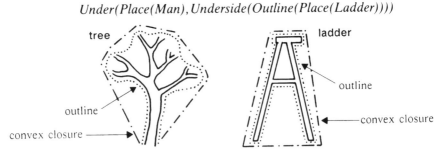

Outline and convex closure

Figure 5.2

- completed enclosure
  In uses of *around*, the surrounding spatial entity may consist of a few

disconnected regions; an imaginary complete enclosure is then mapped onto it.

> *the three houses around the lake*
> *Around(CompletedEnclosure(Place(ThreeHouses)),*
> *Overside(Place(Lake)))*

(The *Overside* function yields the top "face" of the lake.)

> *the clouds around the earth*
> *Around(CompletedEnclosure(Place(Clouds)), Place(Earth))*

● normalized region

As speaking of a hole implies a reference to a complete, "normal" shape, the geometric description applicable to the reference objects in the following examples is the region of space occupied by that complete normal shape:

> *the hole in the wall*
> *the crack in the cup*

Here is a representation of the first example:

> *Included(Place(Hole), NormalRegion(Place(Wall)))*

5.2.4 Functions that map a region onto an adjacent volume
● interior

The interior is not the difference between the convex closure of a body and the space occupied by the body itself, since the outer boundary of an object may have concavities which are part of the closure but not of the interior. The interior should be defined topologically. Often one has to overlook certain interruptions of the boundary (e.g., doors and windows in a building, or the space between bars in a cage). For containers, the interior is generally bounded by a plane through the rim. The representation for *the milk in the bowl* would be:

> *Included(Place(Milk), Interior(Place(Bowl)))*

The interior may consist of several disjoint parts, and a locative expression may refer to one of them; e.g. *your seat is at the front of the theater*:

> *AtTheFrontOf(Place(Seat),*
> *AudiencePart(ShowInterior(Place(Theater))))*

where the relevant portion of the interior is where the show takes place, the portion occupied by the audience.

- volume/area associated with vertex

> *chair in the corner*
> *Included(Place(Chair),VertexVolume(Place(Corner)))*

The function *VertexVolume* takes as argument a vertex in a parallel-epipedic empty space bounded by solid matter; its value is some cylinder as described in Section 4.1; this cylinder actually depends on other contextual parameters, not made explicit in the formula above.

- lamina associated with surface
  With:

> *crack in the surface*

an imaginary very thin lamina is matched onto the surface.

> *Included(Place(Crack),Lamina(Place(Surface)))*

5.2.5 Functions that map a region onto axes

- main axis

Objects whose shape is more or less that of a ribbon or a parallelepiped have one main (longest) axis.

> *The car moved along the road.*
> *Along(Place(Path),MainAxis(Place(Road)))*

(This represents only the location of the path of the car's movement.)

> *She rewound the vine along an horizontal lath.*

The location of the vine after it has been rewound is such that the axis of its spiral shape is coincident with the main axis of the lath:

> *[A(Along)](MainAxis(Outline(Place(Vine)))),*
> *MainAxis(Place(Lath)))*

- associated point of observation

The two orthogonal vectors that constitute a point of observation can be mapped either onto a person, or onto an inanimate object. In the following examples of use of the projective prepositions, each three-argument ideal meaning carries a "3" subscript; each two-argument a "2".

In the first example, there is an implied observer; a point of observation is associated with that observer by the function *PtofObs* in the obvious way:

> *the cat to the right of the tree*
> *[A(ToTheRight$_3$)](PtApprox(Place(Cat)),*
> *PtApprox(Place(Tree)),*
> *PtofObs(Place(Observer)))*

In the next two examples, a point of observation is associated with the reference object itself. In the first case, that reference object is a person, and the association of the point of observation is straightforward. In the second case, the object is a chair; points of observation are associated with inanimate objects by taking into consideration their symmetry properties, or the position of their typical user, or other properties considered in detail in Chapter 10.

> *The church is in front of you.*
> *[A(InFrontOf$_2$)](PtApprox(Place(Church)),*
> *PtofObs(Place(You)))*
> *Jessie is behind the car.*
> *[A(Behind$_2$)](PtApprox(Place(Jessie)),PtofObs(Place(Car)))*

5.2.6 Functions that map a region onto a projection

- projection on plane at infinity

> *The North Star is to the left of the mountain peak.*

In this use of *to the left*, a point of observation is mapped onto an implicit observer (*Observer* in the geometric meaning). *To the left* could not be true of the mountain peak and the North Star themselves; one must instead consider the apparent relative position of star and peak in the plane of view, in other words, the relative positions of their projections on the plane at infinity. More precisely, from the observer's point of view, the projection on the horizon of the image of the star is to the left of a point approximating the image of the mountain peak (the horizon being a line in the plane of view).

> *[A(ToTheLeft$_3$)](HorizonProj(InfinProj(Place(NorthStar))),*
> *PtApprox(InfinProj(Place(Peak))),*
> *PtofObs(Place(Observer)))*

- projection on the ground

> *The painting is to the right of the chair.*

The painting is to the right of the chair.
Figure 5.3

Since this sentence would be true in Figure 5.3, the geometric meaning is:

$[A(ToTheRight_3)](PtApprox(GroundProj(Painting)),$
$\qquad PtApprox(Place(Chair)),$
$\qquad PtofObs(Place(Observer))))$

5.3 Geometric descriptions and mental imagery

The spatial uses of the prepositions cannot be understood unless an intermediary level of geometric conceptualization is postulated. Although I have postulated this intermediary level purely on the basis of an examination of the data, it leads naturally to a psycholinguistic hypothesis, namely that a level of mental imagery (Shepard 1978; Kosslyn 1981) mediates between perceptual representations and language. This imagery level naturally shares points of anchorage with the canonical level.

Similar intuitions are expressed by Lakoff and Johnson in "Metaphors we live by" (1980): "...understanding a situation where we see the fog as being in front of the mountain requires us to view the fog and the mountain as entities. It also requires us to project a front-back orientation upon the mountain." For Lakoff and Johnson, the processes involved are essentially metaphorical – the sentence *The fog is in front of the mountain* manifests a comprehension of a situation in terms of three conventional metaphors: *the fog* and *the mountain* are seen as entities, and *the mountain* is seen as having a front. But using the term metaphor tends to hide one important property: these interpretations are spatial, too, and can be mapped in precise, systematic fashion on the perceptual representation. The mountain is seen as a finite closed volume matching the upper surface of its terrain down to the base, which is vaguely defined, though one can specify a zone in which it must be. A mental image could correspond to such a metaphor – or geometric description, in my terminology. There could in fact be several successive layers of imagery, with mappings between the layers. For instance, there would be a level at which the mountain is viewed as an entity as described above, and another level at which it is seen as having an orientation.

It is because such mental images are anchored on the canonical description – systematically related to it – and because the canonical description has some fit with the world, that we can count on utterances such as *The fog is in front of the mountain* to be functional, to provide information on which others can act. If our perceptual representations did not intersect the outside world in the right places, we would walk into walls, and if the mental images evoked by words did not map to a degree the perceptual representation, we would direct others to walk into walls.

6   Pragmatic factors

Are there principles that can be used to predict the applicable geometric descriptions and the acceptable shifts from the ideal meaning, or are these purely a matter of convention? One can ask similar questions about the other apparent irregularities described, such as unexplained context dependencies and restrictions and additional constraints. Can all or any of these phenomena be explained by inferences from world knowledge, conversational principles, or other pragmatic principles yet to be formulated?

I believe that systematic behavior and rules are most likely to be found by looking at some fundamental properties – primarily salience, relevance, typicality, and tolerance – and I have formulated some sort of pragmatic principles relating to these properties. But although one can discern some systematicity, it is actually very difficult to formulate rigorous principles and find rigorous inferential paths from them; I will thus speak of "near principles". These are not predictive; they embody necessary but not sufficient conditions for the appropriateness of a certain use, and are formulated in terms of factors for which we lack a formal account. Similar problems arise when one tries to apply Grice's cooperative principle and maxims (Grice 1974), which appeal to "quantity," "quality," "relevance," etc., and provide no clue on how those should be evaluated. Yet these maxims, like the near principles described here, reveal some of the forces that shape language use.

6.1 Salience

Salience explains the direction of metonymic shifts. It may arise in several ways: visually, or in the context of a concern for a given use of the objects, or for some action performed with, or in close association with, the objects.

Here is a first near principle that motivates certain synecdoches:

> One can use a noun which basically denotes a whole object to refer to the region occupied by a part of it that is typically salient.

To illustrate, in *a waiting line at the counter*, a functionally salient part of the line, its head, should be substituted for the line itself; the phrase is appropriate only if the head of the line, not any other part, is very close to the counter. A salient interior is substituted for the whole reference object in *the child in the back of the car*. In *the cat under the table*, the cat is probably not under the legs of the table; *table* here stands for the table top, a functionally salient part of the table.

The word "typically" in the formulation of this principle is important. There must be an experience shared by all speakers in which the relevant part is salient. One cannot use a noun-phrase denoting a whole object to refer to a part simply because that part is in focus in the particular context. For instance, one cannot say

*He held the cup by putting two fingers through it.

using *cup* to refer to its handle, since the most important part of a cup is typically the containing part, not the handle.

This near principle has a corollary:

One can use a noun-phrase which basically denotes a whole object to refer to the region occupied by a part of it that is typically visible.

So, in

There is a rabbit under the bush.

the rabbit is not under the whole bush, which would be under the roots. And in

the house on top of the hill

only the visible part of the house, not the cellar or the foundations, is *on top of the hill*.

A second corollary is:

The geometric description applicable may be the base of the object (i.e., its area of contact with the ground plane).

This would account for

the house above the apartment building

in Figure 5.1.

Also, whenever we describe an object as being *in an area*, only the base of the object is in the area. For instance, one would describe Figure 6.1 by *The block is in the circle*, although, in fact, only the lowest surface of the block is within the area of the circle. This has come to be so natural to us that it is hard to think it involves any special process such as metonymy. Yet, if we consider the analogous situation in two dimensions, a similar

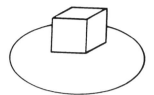

The block is in the circle.
Figure 6.1

metonymy does not pertain. One could not say, in Figure 6.2: *The rectangle is in the line.*

One cannot say:

> *Mary was standing in the edge of the cliff.*
> *The town is in the border.*

although one can express inclusion in a line, as in

> *a notch in the edge*
> *an opening in the boundary*

Typically, knowing where an object is located involves knowing on which part of the earth's surface that object sits; the location of the base is what matters.

The rectangle is in the line
Figure 6.2

Two other near principles authorize metonymies on the basis of salience. First:

> The geometric description applicable may be the projection of the object on the plane at infinity.

In other words, one can locate according to appearance rather than fact. Thus, in

> *The Morning Star is to the left of the church.*

to the left could be strictly true only of the appearances of the Morning Star and the church in the plane of view. This near principle relates to salience, since appearance is a salient aspect of one's experience of objects.

Second:

> The geometric description applicable may be the projection of the object on the ground plane.

In the example of Figure 5.3, one may say *The painting is to the right of the chair*, although the painting is actually higher than the chair; *to the right* is in fact true of point approximations of the chair and of the projection of the painting on the ground.

Horizontal coordinates stand out in our experience of objects, because we are normally bound to the ground, and move on it to approach objects, so we often ignore altitude when using prepositions like *to the right*, *in front of*, etc.

6. 2 Relevance

Relevance bears on prepositional choice in ways that are not immediately obvious; among the necessary near principles, I thus propose to include some offshoot of Grice's maxim, "Be relevant." I distinguish relevance from salience thus: salience refers to the kind of foregrounding of objects or object parts that arises in our interactions with and perception of our environment, while relevance has to do with communicative goals, with what the speaker wishes to express or imply in the present context.

the milk in the bowl
Figure 6.3

Take for instance something in a container, like milk in a bowl (Figure 6.3). The body of milk is contiguous with and supported by the bowl, yet one cannot say

    the milk on the bowl

One must use *in* to describe its relation to the bowl. To account for this restriction, one could posit a hierarchy among prepositions, such that when both *in* and *on* apply, the expression of containment – therefore *in* – has priority. This would reflect the perceptual salience of containment. But in Figure 6.4, *on* can be appropriate, although there is containment.

Relevance helps explain these examples. One uses *in* or *on* according to whether containment or contact is most relevant. If one is most concerned with contact and its consequences – such as whether the surface of the pan

(a) *the dust in/on the bowl*
Figure 6.4

(b) *the oil in/on the pan*

is oiled, or the surface of the bowl is soiled – then one will use *on*. If one is most concerned with containment and its consequences – such as, the milk can be carried around – then one will use *in*. Usually, with milk in a bowl, there is no reason to focus on contact, which is why the use of *on* sounds very odd.

Another example of the role of relevance is provided by the bulb and socket depicted in Figure 1.4(a). Both *in* and *under* are strictly speaking true, but generally one is concerned with the objects' function, whether the bulb will work, and this can be inferred from *in*, but not from *under*, as *in* is associated with the bulb functioning. Therefore, *under* sounds odd, though not impossible – precisely in contexts where function is not the topic, for instance: *Place bulb and socket assembly in such a way that the bulb is under the socket.*

Similarly, the potato in Figure 1.4(b) is *under*, not *in* the bowl, because *in* is typically associated with the bowl functioning as a container. If it is important for the addressee to know that the bowl is not in a position to function as a container (i.e., if function is most relevant), then one must not use a preposition that will suggest that it does. Note that two facts condition the choice of *under*: first, function is important to the addressee; second, *in* is closely associated with the bowl's normal function, where the bowl faces upwards.

The bulb is in the socket.
Figure 6.5

It is difficult to ascertain why a particular preposition is associated with a given functional interaction. *The bulb is in the socket* does not necessarily entail the situation pictured in Figure 1.4(a); strictly speaking, the sentence could be said to be true in Figure 6.5. In a traditional approach to meaning, restricting the interpretation to the desired situation would require a pragmatic inference. But this only displaces the problem, since it leaves unexplained why *in* and not *under* allows the pragmatic inference leading to the appropriate situation. The explanation seems to lie in the fact that surrounding, though not sufficient, is necessary to bulb function; this is not true of "being under" – the bulb and socket assembly might be in horizontal position or even with the bulb above, and still be functional. In the case of objects in a container, surrounding (rather than being supported, or being above) is the most salient property associated with the functional aspects of containment (such as restriction of movement). The forces that regulate the assignment of lexical items to specific functional situations are not appropriately accounted for by the notion of entailment or pragmatic inference.

A few more examples of the role of relevance follow. Consider the space under a desk; it is frequently four-sided, and constitutes as good an enclosure as, say, a gutter. Yet, one says

>   *the water in the gutter*

but not

>   **I stretched my legs in the desk.*

Instead one will say *under the desk*. This surrounding is irrelevant, because it has no functional significance; an alternative to *in*, namely *under*, is preferred.

Finally, consider Figure 6.6.

the finger in/on the glass
Figure 6.6

Whether the finger is *in* or *on* the glass depends on whether one is most concerned with the consequences of contact or containment. Two legends could be used to illustrate this picture:

>   *If you put your finger on the glass, the sound will stop.*
>   *Never put your finger in the jelly glass!*

Besides motivating in several cases the choice between two prepositions, relevance is involved when a situation does not fit clearly into the normal situation type associated with an expression. For instance, if only the front paws of the cat are *on the mat*, is the cat on the mat or not? A speaker concerned with keeping cat fur off the mat might say, *Move the cat off the mat*, thus implying the cat is on the mat. But a speaker concerned with keeping cat fur off the floor around the mat might say *Move the cat onto the mat*, thus implying the cat is not on the mat. So what is most relevant to the speaker affects the truth of a sentence, given the same objective situation. This is another troublesome example of the way meaning depends on the speaker's implicit concerns.

6.3 Tolerance and idealizations

How can we characterize the relational tolerance, that is, the permitted deviation from the ideal meaning (or from the sense shifted ideal meaning)? How does such tolerance relate to idealizations of objects (approximations to points, lines, surfaces, etc.)? How can we describe the contexts that make certain idealizations appropriate? Since these questions are in effect related, they will be considered together.

Let us first examine some prepositional uses involving relational tolerance. In uses of *at* such as

> *Mary is at the gate.*

I have argued that both Mary and the gate are seen as points, and those points as coincident. In the following examples:

> *The runners are at the starting line.*
> *Jim sat at the edge of the cliff.*

the reference object is conceptualized as a line, and the located object as a point on the line.

These examples suggest several questions. How far can Mary be from the gate – the runners from the starting line, or Jim from the edge of the cliff – for these sentences to be true? How does this distance vary with the objects related and the context? Is there a general, uniform, way to transform the Euclidean space into a space where the images of Mary and the gate will be coincident points? Should tolerance be characterized in general pragmatic terms, or is it idiosyncratic and must it be specified in the use types?

Similar questions arise with the other prepositions. Take *on*. Tolerance is involved in both the three- and two-dimensional cases:

> *The book is on the desk.*
> *The woman was standing on the edge of the diving board.*
> *The house is on the edge of the park.*

The book may be separated from the desk by non-salient objects. Boggess (1979) carefully describes the conditions under which these intermediary objects can be ignored, conditions that depend on search strategies used to reach objects and on groupings that these strategies induce (Section 9.2); such conditions are quite specific, so it seems sensible to include them in the use type "physical object supported by another".

Similarly, there must not be any salient object nor a great distance between the woman and the edge of the board, or between the house and the edge of the park. The threshold distances are different in the two examples. Search strategies do not seem helpful here – they are irrelevant in the second example, and it is not clear how they could relate to the tolerance in the third. To see whether any general pragmatic principles can be invoked to predict the tolerance, a thorough empirical study would be needed; one that considers a large number of examples in this use type of *on*, varying the size of the objects and the context.

Note that in the examples with *on*, the distance between the objects must be considered negligible, but their internal dimensions need not be seen as negligible, or even relatively small, as is the case for *at*.

Consider now the use type of *in* that will be labeled "spatial entity in container"; if the container is an ordinary container opening upward, under certain specific conditions (Section 4.1), one can say that an object is *in* another even if it is outside its volume of containment; these idiosyncratic conditions should be made part of the use type.

Finally, consider *to the right*. How close to the right axis must an object be, for

> *A is directly to the right of X.*

to be true? How does the required accuracy vary with different kinds of objects, say houses on a block, chess pieces on a board, or silverware on the table? Again, there are no obvious general predictive principles and a thorough empirical study is needed. But these examples suggest some general statements about the way tolerance depends on the objects related and the context. Two phenomena define lower bounds on tolerance. First, there is a basic indeterminacy stemming from the nature of the objects. Consider

> *Put the napkin to the right of the plate!*

How precisely can one define the right axis of a plate? That axis would normally be parallel to the edge of the table, and that edge can not be defined with more than a certain accuracy, given the surface texture of any physical object (there always are surface irregularities, which can be made apparent by magnification).

Another source of indeterminacy is perception, and the degree to which two positions can be distinguished. For instance, the truth of

> *The white horse is at the finish line.*

depends on the means available to determine the position of horses, which changed once high-speed cameras became available.

But primarily, tolerance depends on what the speaker deems to matter, on relevance. So, for instance, with chess-pieces on a board, if the game is what matters, then the grid of the board defines the relevant precision. If I say:

> *The Knight is directly to the right of the Queen.*

the allowed distance from the right axis that preserves truth is defined by the size of the squares. Or, if I say of a horse running away from me *The horse is already at the fence*, the tolerance will be different from that in *The horse is at the finish line* in a race.

So tolerance depends on the nature of the objects, on perception, and on what is relevant.

Two pragmatic near principles can be stated that reflect the link between tolerance and relevance: the "shifting contrast" principle, and the "background grid" principle.

- Shifting contrast

> If two objects, A and B, are placed in relation to a reference object in such a way that the ideal meaning of a preposition (or the sense-shifted ideal meaning) is truer of A than of B, then one can use that preposition to discriminate A from B – so that the locative phrase will be assumed true of A but not of B.

Two examples of this shifting contrast near principle (so named because the contrast expressed by the preposition "shifts") follow.

Consider again the use of *to the right* in Figures 1.3(a) and 1.3(b), reproduced in 6.7. One would say that A is *to the right* of X in 6.7(a), but if B is placed as in 6.7(b), then the ideal meaning applies better to B than to A, and, in many contexts, only B is *to the right* of X; *to the right* can be used to discriminate A from B.

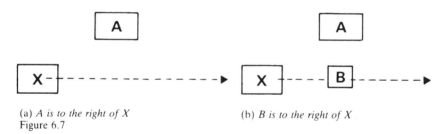

(a) *A is to the right of X*   (b) *B is to the right of X*
Figure 6.7

Consider also the pear and bowl of Figure 1.1(a). Although one would ordinarily describe it as *The pear is in the bowl*, a photographer might say

> *Move the pear so that it is in the bowl!*

The ideal meaning of *in* applies better to the apples than to the pear; one can use *in* to contrast their location, although most often that contrast will be ignored.

Finally, a child racing with another might say:

> *I was at the door before you.*

implying that the second child was not *at the door* when she herself reached it, even though the second child might have been only one foot from the door and could have been described as *at the door* in another context.

● Background grid

> If there is in the context a grid-like pattern and if that grid-like
> pattern is relevant to the speaker's point, then that grid-like
> pattern will define the tolerance in the use of the projective
> prepositions.

The grid-like pattern may be that of a network of streets and yard divisions, of a chess-board, or of a set of rooms in a building.

Let us now turn to the question of object idealizations, the processes that let us see an object with extension in three dimensions as zero-dimensional, a long thin object as one-dimensional, an irregular surface as a plane, an area with an irregular boundary as a ribbon, and so forth. With these phenomena, as with relational tolerance, certain distances are considered negligible. This suggests that a uniform treatment of both might be possible, a question considered below. Under what conditions are such idealizations appropriate? Let us reconsider some examples involving idealizations:

> *John is at the store.*
> *the city on the road to London*
> *the house across the street*
> *The box is 6 feet from the wall.*
> *The cloud cover is at 3000 feet.*

(The box example concerns the interpretation where the box is seen as a point, not where 6 feet is the shortest distance between some point of the box and the wall.) Note that the last two examples involve approximations which could be characterized mathematically in metric terms – the ratio of the maximum dimension of the box to 6 feet, and the ratio of the maximum vertical distance between the highest and lowest point of the cover to 3000 feet. Approximation to a point (or a plane) will be good enough for certain purposes, if the relevant ratio is smaller than a certain context-dependent threshold (dependent on those particular purposes).

No such precise characterizations are available in the three first examples; the approximations are imposed by symbolic linguistic schemata, and their appropriateness does not depend on specific ratios of the objects' size to some reference distance. The use of *at* implies a remote viewpoint; this shows in certain appropriateness conditions, such as that speaker and addressee must not be both in the store, but that condition is not expressible in terms of thresholds on distance ratios. The appropriateness of such idealizations will be conventionally determined in the use type; rather than asking what dimension ratios make it appropriate to see these objects as points, lines, and so forth, one should ask with what types of objects, in what standard situations is it appropriate to use *at*, or *on*, or *across*, with these senses? So the last two examples suggest an entirely pragmatic treatment, relating precise measures of approximation to specific tasks; but the appropriateness of idealizations in the first three examples should be specified in the use types.

The examples and observations in this section suggest two essential research questions: First, how precisely does the relational tolerance vary with the objects related and the context? A systematic answer to this question will require extensive empirical studies. Possibly general principles would emerge from such a study; if not, idiosyncratic tolerance conditions must be specified in the use types. The search for a general theory leads to the second question: is there a mathematical model involving a simple uniform transformation of the real space, such that the ideal meanings, or sense-shifted ideal meanings, will be true of the images of the objects in the transformed space, and these images will be the appropriate geometric descriptions (considering only geometric descriptions arising from idealizations)?

One possibly useful notion in that regard is that of a "tolerance space"[1] (Zeeman 1962; Roberts 1973). A tolerance space is a metric space with a reflexive and symmetric relation between points, such that any two points less than a certain distance apart are not distinguished; this distance is called the "resolution" of the space. This concept appears to provide a valid representation of some of the processes by which we "see" an object as a point, a road as a line, and so forth, but it is rather difficult to define the resolution when considering linguistic usage. The resolution would not be homogeneous. Essentially, it should be defined so as to result in only a few distinguishable descriptions of objects (e.g., description as a point, and the canonical description). But this is quite different from how resolution must be defined, in visual perception, to represent the change in appearance as one moves further and further away from the objects looked at. Even if tolerance spaces were a useful notion, the resolution would have to be made a function of the objects' position in space, of properties of the objects, such as the particular ways one interacts with them, and of various contextual factors, importantly of "what matters in the context"; how this could be done is difficult to imagine. In short, it is not clear how tolerance spaces could be used to explain linguistic examples.

Another approach is that of "fuzzy logic" (Zadeh 1971, 1974). I have talked about meanings being "almost true", an expression reminiscent of Zadeh's fuzzy sets and asymptotic truth function. But by themselves, these concepts are of limited usefulness in describing the role of fuzziness in the use of locative expressions: they must be complemented by a theory of relevance. Thus, one could represent the truth of *The stool is to the right of the desk* as a monotonic decreasing function of the angle *A* in Figure 6.8

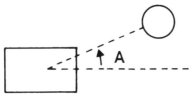

Figure 6.8

(the figure is a view from above). But such a function does not allow us to specify the circumstances in which we accept the sentence, and those in which we do not. These depend on our purpose, on what we deem useful to communicate, on what we know, on what we judge "important" in the given context, on the presence in context of contrasting situations, and so forth – factors I am attempting to make explicit in this book.

Because relational tolerance and idealizations reflect an accumulation of practices, of interactions with the objects, making predictions out of general principles will be at best difficult. In our constant intercourse with the objects in our world, we have integrated into our knowledge strategies that allow us to count or discount some fact according to context; the exact nature of those strategies is still very much a mystery. Yet tolerance is one direction in which the search for systematicity should proceed.

6.4 Typicality

It is difficult to enunciate even near principles involving typicality, but it is easy to see its pervasive influence on language use. Its role in motivating pragmatic inferences has been widely studied in artificial intelligence, but it has rarely been observed that typicality also motivates metonymies and certain linguistic choices.

As an example of a pragmatic inference, consider the following. If I say

The fountain is behind the city hall.

you will assume that the fountain is close to the city hall, in fact that it is *next to* the city hall, meaning that no other salient architectural object is between the two objects. This "nextness condition" is not part of the meaning of *behind*, because in

The treasure is buried 600 feet in a straight line behind you.

there is no proximity. Still, we find it most useful to relate objects by means of *behind* when they are close together for several reasons: the direction defined by *behind* is otherwise difficult to evaluate, and as it is generally more rational to choose a reference object close to the object one wishes to locate, most typically objects will be close together. As a consequence, "nextness" is the unmarked case, the default, the inference one should draw, lacking evidence to the contrary.

As for metonymies, the first salience near principle made an explicit reference to typicality: metonymies are allowed on the basis of typically salient properties of the objects. If one simply referred to any part of an object that is in focus in the particular context by means of a phrase denoting the whole object, one would often fail to communicate. The corollary stating that one can use a term referring to a whole object while strictly speaking locating its base also depends on typicality, as in our world objects typically sit somewhere on the ground, and we generally focus on the location of that base.

We have also seen how typicality restricts the assignments of the roles of Figure and Ground: when two kinds of objects get typically involved in a locative relation with a certain Figure/Ground assignment, it is sometimes impossible to use a converse assignment, even when it would be rational to do so in the particular current situation. So, one does not say

*the bottle under the cap

because, typically, caps are conceptually moveable with respect to bottles.

Note that typical characteristics we need to consider are not only physical characteristics: the typical use of, or intercourse with, an object is just as important, and one must even consider typical characteristics of the communication act of locating – the fact that reference objects are usually close to the located object, that the location of the base of an object is generally what matters, and that certain kinds of objects are not normally used as references for other kinds.

7   Use types

The pragmatic near principles provide constraints on the interpretation of a locative expression, but still leave many phenomena unaccounted for, and although further study might reveal additional pragmatic principles, it is clear that some facts of use will remain a matter of convention. For instance, there is no way to predict that one cannot say

> *the cat in the lawn

or that *in* can be used with the following kinds of geometric descriptions: the volume of containment, the normal volume, and the outline. There is no explanation for the fact that *at* can be used indexically, as in *The gas station is at the freeway*. After all, in French, where *à* takes on many of the functions of *at*, one cannot say

> *La station-service est à la route.

And convention is also involved in the type of use exemplified by

> Jim is at his desk.

The implication that Jim is using his desk might seem obtainable as a pragmatic inference: if Jim is *at* his desk, he is very close to his desk, therefore he is very probably using it. But since

> Jim is by his desk.
> Jim is just next to his desk.

do not give rise to the same implication, there is an element of conventionality involved in this use of *at*.

Similarly, the use of *on* to refer to attachment (*the pear on the tree*) and other kinds of divergence from the ideal meaning that I have called sense shifts are not deducible from the ideal meaning and pragmatic information about the objects.

So all such conventional facts of use – facts that are neither determined by the ideal meaning of the preposition and the meanings of the subject and object of the expression, nor pragmatically inferable – will have to be somehow specified in the lexicon, as characteristics of additional senses of the preposition or of idiomatic forms. The kind of lexical representation I suggest, the use type, preserves the relation of the various uses of the preposition to the ideal meaning(s). It is also a uniform representation that does not distinguish between senses and idioms – one reason why I chose the coinage "use type" rather than the word "sense"; the other being that a use type will include more aspects of meaning than linguists would normally put in a sense. A collection of use types will be attached to each ideal meaning of each preposition.

7.1 Distinguishing use types

Suppose we can discern two classes of use of a given preposition; how do we decide whether these correspond to two use types, or to a single more general one? Just as there are no fully satisfying procedures for deciding whether a word has one or two senses where polysemy rather than homonymy is involved, or whether one should have two grammatical cases rather than one more general one, there are no strict theoretical criteria for distinguishing use types, but there are some heuristic guidelines.

Two use types are distinguished by means of one or several "significant" distinctions: while this might seem subjective, there is a good degree of agreement as to what is significant. For instance, a locative expression will correspond to two different use types if some distinction is generally important to a language user, if an addressee who wishes to act upon the description offered by the speaker will almost certainly need a clarification. Thus,

> *the nails in the box*

corresponds to two use types, one that implies containment, the other embedding. Each involves a different geometric description of the reference object: the interior in the first case, the normal volume in the second. One could have a single use type with a disjunctive condition in its representation; something like "the located object must be included in the interior or in the normal volume of the reference object". But first, language users would agree that the distinction between containment and embedding is significant, and, second, conjunctions such as:[1]

> **There is plutonium and a crack in the vat.*

are unacceptable. Such a conjunction represents the application of a classic "identity test" for detecting ambiguity (Lakoff 1970; Zwicky and Saddock 1975); that is, *Joe and Lucy ate pudding* is assumed to be the result of deleting the first [ate pudding] from *Joe ate pudding and Lucy ate pudding* under identity of meaning in the two conjoined clauses. That it is impossible to delete the first [in the vat] from *There is plutonium in the vat and there is a crack in the vat* suggests that that phrase has different meanings in the two clauses; this in turn suggests that two distinct use types correspond to the expressions underlying the conjunction. The use type categorization fits well the sorting that this identity test would induce; it seems that "significant" distinctions forbid such conjunctions.

It is tempting to account for the distinction between use types in terms of the following "principle": situation types within the same use type should have many properties in common, while two situation types across use types would share many fewer common properties.[2] But clearly, it is not simply a matter of the number of common properties, but of their relevance. There is potentially an infinity of possible differences between situation types (corresponding to the potential infinity of locative expressions), and some differences are taken to matter, while others are not.

It is possible for an expression to allow interpretation by two use types, with no difference in the actual situation at the canonical level. The same referent situation may give rise to two interpretations that differ only in geometric conceptualization. So, for instance, *the motel on the road* can be interpreted with the motel seen as a point and the road as a line (instantiating the use type "physical/geometrical object contiguous with a line"), or it can be interpreted with the motel touching the edge of the area defined by the road (instantiating "physical object contiguous with edge of area"). These two interpretations specify identical real world situations.

7.2 Idiomaticity

In the present framework, idioms are put on the same footing as regular uses. I will argue that the difference between the two is only a matter of generality and does not justify two distinct kinds of lexical entities. Compare:

> *the book on the desk*
> *the man on the bus*

Speakers have an intuition that the first is regular – i.e., generated by the core grammar together with perfectly straightforward rules of semantic interpretation – but the second is idiomatic. Let us compare the two phrases.

(1) Both phrases imply support and contiguity (with the floor of the bus in the second example), but the second expression carries an additional implication that the man is traveling on the bus, since

> **?The family is living on a converted bus.*

is odd to most speakers. Note that in both cases, contiguity can be relaxed; the book may be on top of a pile of books, and the man sitting on a suitcase.

(2) The oddity with *the man on the bus* is that when an object is in another, one would more typically use *in*, unless support was especially relevant; since that is not the case, this use of *on* suggests an element of conventionality. In other words, the geometric description applicable to the reference object is not the most typical one, namely its top surface.

(3) Each phrase corresponds to a productive pattern – that is, one can substitute a number of noun- phrases for *book*, *man*, *desk*, and *bus*, while preserving the relation between Figure and Ground – but the selection restrictions for the second pattern are tighter than for the first. In the first, almost any physical object could take the place of *desk*, but in the second, the reference object must be some "large" vehicle.

To summarize: in the idiomatic pattern, the meaning of *on* is further from the ideal meaning, the selection restrictions are tighter, and the geometric description applying to the Ground is not the one expected. But these do not amount to differences of nature; idiomaticity is a matter of degree determined by factors such as the distance from the ideal meaning, the scope of the selection restrictions, and the deviation from the geometric descriptions normally expected. I will suggest a uniform representation for both patterns, assuming that each phrase is generated by a use type.

This provides, for the locative expressions considered, an account of idiomaticity congruent with linguistic intuitions. An idiom is then just a pattern less general than patterns underlying regular expressions (but this account is not satisfactory for all idioms; so for instance, with *to take the wind out of one's sails*, one needs to explain the metaphorical relation of the phrasal meaning to the compositional meaning).

The idea that one's linguistic competence consists of a repertory of syntactic patterns, each associated with its own partially idiosyncratic semantic interpretation and pragmatic information, with "regular" cases just patterns among others, runs counter to traditional linguistic theory. Naturally, this would not be limited to locative expressions, but should pertain throughout language. Recent work by Fillmore, Kay, and O'Connor (1985) on "minor" grammatical constructions (e.g., expressions involving *let alone*, as in *He never made first lieutenant, let alone general*) supports this view. They find that a large part of a speaker' s competence consists of such "peripheral" constructions; given that the machinery required to handle these would be powerful enough to handle the regular structures, they suggest a uniform treatment for both.

7.3 Representation of use types

A use type is made of two parts: a phrase pattern centered around a preposition, and the interpretation associated with the pattern, that is, a

set of conditions defining the appropriate, characteristic conditions of use
of such a pattern.

Most often, the phrase pattern is simply a preposition with selection
restrictions for the subject and object of the preposition, So there will be a
use type pattern:

"Person *at* Artifact"

with the interpretation that the person is using the artifact. From this use
type one can generate examples such as:

Jim is at his desk.
the man at the stove

But some use types involve a specific word as object of the preposition:

"Spatial Entity *at sea*"

where the very word *sea* must occur as object of the preposition, and this
will yield examples such as:

The Titanic will never be at sea again.
We had a ball at sea.

Here is another example of a use type:

"Object viewed as Point *at* Object viewed as Line"

with the interpretation that the first object is at the intersection of the
second with a crosspath, for phrases like

The gas station is at the freeway.
The turn in the road is at the river.

In speaking of conditions of use, I do not mean to imply that there is
some checklist; conditions of use might be expressed as a set of prototypical conditions, together with a procedure for deciding which deviations from
these conditions are tolerable. Occasionally, such a procedure might give
inconclusive answers. For instance, a use type labelled "physical object
transported by a large vehicle" accounts for examples like: *the man on the
bus, the crew on the boat*. Not only must the reference object be a large
vehicle, but it must also be referred to in the context of travel. Yet, "a
large vehicle", and "in the context of travel", are not conditions that can
be evaluated in a clear-cut way. In the prototypical case, one would
demand that the vehicle be (if wheeled) as big as a bus, and that it be in the
course of traveling (though possibly at a stopping place). These conditions
may not obtain and *on* may still be appropriate for some speakers,
unacceptable to others. Thus, with "jitneys" (a public transport vehicle
little bigger than some taxis), some speakers accept, sometimes hesitantly,

Jody is on the jitney. (One cannot say "public transport" is a necessary condition – see *Rockefeller is on his yacht*; but if the vehicle is used for public transport of large groups of people,. that factor weighs in favor of using *on*.) More accept *I came on the jitney.* This variation and hesitancy are typical of fuzzy semantic categories; such fuzziness is normally best represented by means of a prototype and of deviations from the prototype.

The representation of use types poses the same difficulties as any other representation of meaning, because of this context-dependent fuzziness, which carries over to normal situation types.

7.4 Knowledge in use types

I see use types as complex entities. One might specify in a use type a whole range of elements of meaning, anything that holds true for any phrase generated by the use type pattern. It will be useful to separate the constraints in use types between those that bear directly on the scene, and those that concern exclusively the context, though the constraints on the scene may in fact involve the context indirectly, in particular the aim of the communication.

Table 7.1. *A taxonomy of constraints in use types.*

constraints on the scene	constraints on context
selection restrictions	constraint on purpose
allowed spatial relation between the objects	highlighting of a background element
constraints on indexicals	particular conditions on context
constraints on geometric description functions	

7.4.1 Constraints on the scene
● selection restrictions
The categories of the subject and object noun-phrases of expressions in the use type must satisfy certain constraints. The phrase pattern itself gives a first specification of the selection restrictions, in the form of the main categories to which subject and object must belong (unless of course it specifies words, as with "spatial entity 'at sea'"). More detailed specifications of restrictions, when needed, are in the interpretation part – because, as the example with jitneys demonstrates, the selection restrictions cannot always be expressed in clear-cut fashion.

Here are other examples of selection restrictions: In the use type "physical object contiguous with edge of geographical area", the located objects must be fixed and relatively large; one says *The house is on the lake* but not **The car is on the lake.* "Spatial entity in container" permits as reference objects seats that surround somewhat the sitter's body as in *the man in the chair*, but excludes **the man in the stool*.

Selection restrictions concern the categories denoted by the linguistic labels rather than the objects themselves. Indeed, if the football field was referred to as *the rectangular area*, one could use *in*; see *the players in the rectangular area*.

• allowed spatial relation between the objects

Spatial constraints on the geometric descriptions of the objects related consist of: (a) one central constraint, either the ideal meaning, or derived from the ideal meaning by a sense shift; and (b) the allowed deviation from that central constraint, when it cannot be inferred from general considerations involving tolerance.

So with the use type "physical object contiguous with a wall", for examples like

> *On the left wall, there is a chest of drawers.*

the ideal meaning of *on* (implying contiguity and support) is sense shifted; the support condition is dropped. Also, if there were a tapestry between the wall and the chest, the chest would still be *on the left wall*; so there is a tolerance shift, constrained in the use type by the condition that the intermediary object not be salient.

• constraints on indexicals

This concerns indexicals corresponding to an added argument to the relation binding located and reference object, not the determination of the geometric descriptions and of the tolerance, which also involves context dependency, thus indexicality of a sort.

Use types will include a representation of how to compute the values of indexicals, that is, they will specify the functions of context that yield the appropriate referents. For instance, some of the use types of the projective prepositions include detailed characterizations of the way to compute the location and viewing direction of an implicit observer (as in *The cat is to the right of the tree*). For the preposition *near*, Denofsky (1976) describes how an implicit (fuzzy) distance threshold must be computed. Finally, with *the door opposite the window*, a room must be recovered from the context to interpret this expression. The corresponding use type will specify that there must be an implied space, with two approximately parallel boundaries, and with the reference object on one of these boundaries.

• constraints on geometric description functions

A use type may constrain the geometric descriptions involved. For instance, with *in*, one use type specifies that the geometric description function applying to the reference object must be *NormalRegion*, the other that it must be *Outline*. The use type "spatial entity at location" specifies that the range of the two geometric description functions must be the set of points.

7.4.2 Constraints on the context

• constraint on purpose

Every use type, except two (corresponding respectively to expressions like *the man in a red hat*, and those like *the man with a long nose*), specifies that the purpose of the expression must be to constrain the location of the object referred to in subject position. In the two exceptions, the purpose is to provide a description of the located object.

• highlighting of some background element

The choice between expressions is often a matter of bringing attention to some background element rather than signalling differences of fact. Such effects are often conventional properties of the types of expression. Thus *to the right*, as contrasted with *on the right*, tends to highlight the distance between the two objects, and to evoke travel away from the reference object; the contrast cannot always be described in terms of objective differences in the situations (it sometimes is: thus if a third object of the same kind is between the two considered, only *to the right* is appropriate). Consider also

> *Bogota is at/on the equator.*

at will be preferred if one wishes to signal the presence in the background of some transverse line (e.g., a travel trajectory). In

> *The temperature is highest at(*?on) the equator.*

at is more appropriate than *on*, because reference to the highest temperature points implies an infinity of transverse lines corresponding to the domains of the temperature curves considered, and *at* highlights such transverse lines.

• other particular constraints on the context.

Some use types will include a description of the context of use at a rather specific level. Thus, the use type "spatial entity at location", which underlies the expression *Suzy is at the supermarket*, includes complex conditions specifying the allowed contexts of utterance.

7.5 Sense shifts

No general principle regulates sense shifts, but I will survey the range of possibilities, to support the claim that every use type manifests the ideal meaning; in other words, the occurrence of the preposition in the expressions generated by the use type is motivated – a motivation that stems from a link to a basic core of meaning inherent in the preposition.

Remember that two distinct use types may differ by more than a sense-shifted relation, or they may involve the same relation but differ in another characteristic, such as the geometric description function applicable. So sense shifts constitute only part of an account of polysemy for prepositions.

Here are some of the processes by which the relation in a use type is derived from the ideal meaning:

(1) When the ideal meaning is a conjunction of conditions, the transformed meaning may be derived by dropping one of the defining conditions. For instance, in three dimensions the ideal meaning of *on* involves contiguity and support, but there is a set of cases where only contiguity is required, as with *The chest of drawers is on the left wall.*

(2) The transformed ideal meaning may involve an added condition as exemplified by *the man at the desk.*

(3) The transformed ideal meaning may be related to the ideal meaning by a process involving resemblance, as in *the wrinkles on his forehead.*

(4) The conditions of the ideal meaning may hold in the majority of situations where the transformed meaning is true – in other words the two relations generally co-occur in the everyday world. Thus *on* is used to mean attachment, but attachment most often co-occurs with contiguity and support.

(5) The ideal meaning of *at* has been defined as the coincidence of two points. Uses with one- or two-dimensional objects (Section 4.2) are generalizations of that ideal meaning to higher dimensions.

(6) The ideal meaning may be, so to speak, "embedded" in the relation of the use type. So in *The target is at 10 feet*, the ideal meaning of *at* holds between a punctual approximation of the target and a point 10 feet from an implied observer.

Literature on prototypes for object categories (e.g., Rosch and Mervis 1975) and one study of a verb (the study of *lie* by Coleman and Kay (1981)) generally account for "family" resemblance by means of attributes or features: the prototype of a category – which may or may not match an actual member of the category – shares some features with any member in the category, but there is no criterial set of features for category membership. In the case of the prototypical structure of prepositional categories, resemblance to the prototype (the ideal meaning) involves more complex processes than the sharing of features (only the transformations in 1 and 2 above are covered by that description).

7.6 Conclusion

The chapters in this first part of the book have introduced a descriptive framework intended to capture the regularities of the domain of locative prepositions. Numerous examples have demonstrated that these regularities are more complex than previous semantic models allowed. The examples have exposed the malleability and fuzziness of meaning, its hidden dependence on context – on the speaker's unexpressed concerns, on shared perceptual descriptions and spatial conceptualizations. The descriptive framework is an attempt to marshal some of these properties into a systematic description.

8   Decoding and encoding

Having presented a framework in which to describe the meaning and use of locative expressions, I will now explore the possibility of using this framework as a basis for constructing encoding and decoding procedures.

Remember that the decoding/encoding problem was couched in terms of prediction: can one predict all that is conveyed by a locative expression uttered in a given situation? can one predict which locative expressions are unacceptable, and which inappropriate to which contexts? can one predict the locative expression to be used truly and appropriately in a given context? Since I assume such predictions should proceed by means of rigorously defined algorithms, the result would be much like what workers in artificial intelligence call models of comprehension and production, though with less claim to psychological reality.

Yet terms like "contexts" and "situations" refer to states of belief of the language user, so the question of psychological reality is still there to stalk us. Claims about the form and nature of these beliefs are usually based in part on introspective evidence, in part on the success of attempts at imitating human linguistic behavior: a program that behaves like a human being must work like the human mind. Both justifications present problems – introspection for obvious reasons, but behavior is not clearly an appropriate yardstick either. First, outside artificially constrained domains, there is no obvious way to circumscribe appropriate linguistic behavior; second, no program has so far succeeded in simulating naturalistic discourse. Still, the attempt to devise knowledge representations and processes is a worthwhile endeavor.

The reader should now be well aware of the inherent complexity of spatial knowledge and its linguistic expression. There is no way, given our present understanding of knowledge and language, to offer full solutions to the decoding/encoding problem (even if we leave aside qualms about the nature and form of underlying beliefs), but neither is there definite evidence that the task is impossible. This chapter should throw some light on the range of problems that confront any effort to develop such solutions, and in the process move us one step further toward understanding the adequacy of the computational metaphor.

I will not be concerned with details of implementation, with adopting a particular knowledge representation scheme (frames, semantic nets, formal logic, etc.), or with designing precise algorithms, but will focus instead on the tasks that an encoding/decoding system must accomplish. To use Marr's distinction (1981), I will be concerned with the "computational theory" of encoding and decoding, that is, with determining what information is to be represented, and what is to be computed and why; not with how to carry out the computations, or with the form of the representations. Even this is a very difficult task, and these pages will offer only a first characterization of the underlying representations needed, of the results to be obtained, of which knowledge is needed for which task, and of the fundamental abilities the whole process presupposes. I will often do no more than illustrate the problems involved with an example. In discussing what must be computed, I will occasionally assume some operations performed in some sequence, where it seems helpful to introduce some order in an otherwise unwieldy complexity, but this is not to be taken as an actual plan for computation.

For all that it ends up everywhere in unresolved questions, I find this tour of the problem instructive. Cognitive scientists frequently complain that everything in cognition is tied to everything else, and therefore work hard at cutting out a piece of the problem, trying to make reliable statements in spite of doubts about how they would survive the breaking of the somewhat artificial boundaries. This chapter is meant to be a bird's-eye view of the scope of the problem, pursuing all the connections that appear: with perception, planning, action, meaning, imagination, etc. My aim has not been a preliminary to a practical system, but a first assessment of what it would take to make computer models in the spatial domain that would bring together all that we know, or assume with some confidence, concerning cognition.

8.1 Decoding and encoding: a first look

What can we say about the term "situations" in the definitions of decoding and encoding? A situation would consist of the beliefs, concerns, and purposes of the speaker (in the case of encoding), or addressee (for decoding). "Beliefs" should be interpreted broadly, since some beliefs concern a scene (as above, I use this term to refer to any configuration of objects, whether perceivable instantaneously or involving vast regions, and also whether it is real, remembered, or imaginary); so I assume that a situation includes representations of spatial environments, and will address the question of how these – and, more generally, how spatial knowledge – could be represented.

The descriptive framework outlined in the preceding chapters relied on the notion of a normal situation type, a set of conditions for the true and appropriate use of an expression under normal circumstances (there will be several such sets if the expression is ambiguous). This notion will play an important role in decoding. Indeed, a first step of the decoding process will consist in generating the normal situation type(s) associated with the expression. In a second step, one uses the normal situation type(s) and the particular context of utterance to specify the particular interpretation suggested by the context.

To construct the normal situation type(s) – the normal interpretation(s) – of an expression, one can try all use types of the preposition, assuming the particular objects[1] specified in the expression. One or several "matching" use types should be selected – those which, when instantiated with these objects, do not lead to inconsistencies with general world knowledge. In testing for a matching use type, one must take into account possible metonymies and tolerance, as suggested by the pragmatic principles. All the constraints of a matching use type can be assumed true of the objects referred to in the expression, given appropriate geometric descriptions and tolerance. This yields part of the definition of the normal interpretation; the remainder consists of constraints originating in the assumption that these objects behave normally. For instance, the use type "physical object supported by another" does not prescribe that the supporting object surface must be horizontal, or which surfaces of the objects are involved; in *the teapot on the table*, under normal conditions, the teapot is upright on the horizontal table top – this must be inferred from general knowledge about tables, teapots, and their use.

Using the normal interpretation(s) obtained in the first step of decoding, a second step exploits the particular context of utterance to accomplish three tasks:

(a) Fully disambiguate the expression, that is, select one normal interpretation, if the initial step of decoding yielded more than one – as with *the nails in the box*, where the nails could be contained in the box, or holding the box together, each situation corresponding to a different use type. Usually, knowledge of what is at stake in the particular context would allow us to select one.

(b) Instantiate the normal situation type selected, assigning values to its variables as suggested by the current context. (Remember that a situation type involves a number of unassigned variables, including those representing the referents of the subject and object of the preposition, since the situation type is strictly a function of the locative expression, independent of the particular context of use.)

(c) Draw inferences allowed by the current context in conjunction with the instantiated normal situation type.

The discussion so far considers only normal contexts. Unless the addressee has evidence to the contrary, he or she will assume that conditions are normal, and will use an instantiation of the normal situation type as the default interpretation of the expression. An interpretation can differ from the normal in two ways: either it conforms to the use type selected in building the normal interpretation, but some of the pragmatic inferences based on an assumption of normality cannot be drawn; or it actually breaks the constraints of all use types, though one provides a "close" match.

Decoding must accomplish two additional goals. Since an addressee can detect when an expression is in some way defective, decoding must involve checking for acceptability and appropriateness; this falls out of the matching processes: if no use type matches (i.e., if some inconsistency pops up for every use type tried) and if no out of the ordinary interpretation can be obtained, then the expression is unacceptable. Depending on what the addressee knows about the situation the speaker is attempting to describe, he or she may also be able to detect inappropriateness to the particular context of utterance by checking the relevance of the expression to that context.

Finally, any proposition derived by the decoding process and relating to the spatial arrangement of objects must be integrated into the spatial representation scheme, that is, the end result of comprehension should be to create the representation of an imaginary scene, or modify that of a remembered scene. This last task depends on one's assumptions about the form of such spatial representations.

In encoding, conversely, one starts from a representation of a scene, possibly some propositions representing relevant non-spatial external facts, and some speaker's goals and concerns. These combine to give rise to an utterance. The speaker's goals define which objects to relate and which of these is to be the located object (constraints on appropriate Figure/ Ground assignment may force one to reject the resulting reference object and aim at some periphrase). After a reference object has been chosen, and referring noun-phrases have been constructed, one must then:

(a) Find a use type of some preposition, geometric descriptions, and a tolerance, such that the geometric meaning constructed from these elements is true of the particular situation described, and the use type constraints other than those contributing to the geometric meaning are satisfied in that situation.

(b) Ensure that the resulting expression is relevant to the communicative purposes of the speaker, appropriate to his or her discourse plans.

Before considering encoding and decoding in more detail, I will turn to the question of the representation of spatial knowledge.

8.2 Representation of scenes

This section discusses representations of visual scenes and large-scale environments, focusing on the location and orientation of objects. Neither psychology nor artificial intelligence offer any firm knowledge on this topic, so much of what follows should be taken as speculative. Yet even a rough map of the problems involved is useful, as it lets us see the use of spatial expressions in their natural context of perception and of spatial knowledge.

There are *a priori* several kinds of spatial representations. First, there is the output of visual perception. Second, there is knowledge of large environments – of the arrangement of rooms in a house, or the configuration of a city – and this knowledge "touches ground" only in places with direct perception, with the knowledge of a scene gathered at one glance. Third, we have memories of scenes perceived. Finally, we imagine scenes. These last two are particularly important in relation to language, since usually when a scene is described we construct a mental image of it, blending remembered with imagined details (there is in fact no reason to assume that mental images differ according to whether they are the product of imagination or memory).

There are in fact other possible spatial representations involved in moving about, manipulating objects, and reasoning. Presumably, no single representation can support all these activities. Language itself seems to create its own conceptualizations. In any case, if several representations must be devised, correspondences between them should be clear.

I will consider perceptual representations, briefly discuss imagery, and speculate about representations adequate for some reasoning tasks and for action; finally, I will talk about mental maps (their function is clearly restricted to action – travel – and to the reasoning that supports action).

8.2.1 Visual scenes

The question of representing visual scenes is central to that branch of artificial intelligence concerned with modeling visual perception (Brady 1981; Marr 1982). That research, however, has focused on the representation of shape; almost nothing is said about location. Marr (1982) devotes a short paragraph to the question. He suggests that the visual system should incorporate three types of description: one that is viewer-centered, involving angles (say, altitude and lateral deviation) and distances of objects from the retina; one that records configurations of objects relative to the viewer (e.g., the notion that viewer and two objects happen to create an equilateral triangle); and finally, one that records the relative positions of a number of external objects independent of the viewer (e.g., the fact that three trees are in a straight line, or four buildings make a square). Marr notes that the problems here involve choosing an appropriate coordinate frame within which to make explicit the spatial relations of the configurations – problems very similar to those involved in shape description.

Another problem is how to decide just what groups of objects make up configurations recorded in perception (this question does not arise when describing shape as a configuration of parts, since what constitutes an object is a given). Marr's examples all point to the extraction of good shapes – lines, squares, equilateral triangles – but this is clearly not enough. Proximity seems one important key. Several facts point to its importance in spatial representations for location. We can apprehend the relative position of two objects near each other in a fairly precise and immediate way, but that is not the case with objects that are far apart in the visual scene and/or separated by other salient objects. Then, too, proximity is the first relation to organize the child's conception of space (Piaget and Inhelder 1967). But most importantly, one basic principle of perceptual organization, the Gestalt principle of proximity, states that elements which are close together tend to organize into units.

So part of the problem of extracting configurations involves defining proximity precisely (i.e., perceptually significant proximity, not the concept underlying the word *near*), and understanding how it induces groupings of objects. Contiguity and direct support should be considered at the same time, since contiguity is a limit case of proximity, and direct support implies contiguity. These relations should provide a structural description analogous to the hierarchy of parts often seen as underlying the representation of shape (Palmer 1975; Marr 1982) – though it might not be a simple hierarchy. Given a configuration, it should be possible to define a frame of reference attached to it based on some of its global properties: the locations of the objects in each configuration would then be defined with respect to that frame of reference. For instance, the objects on a table would make up a configuration, and their location and orientation would be specified with respect to its main axes, (and/or the edges of the table, since there is no reason to exclude redundancies from the representation).

To specify orientation, one needs a description of the object's shape. If that description, as Marr (1982) proposes, includes a main axis (generally defined on the basis of symmetry and elongation) for every part of the part hierarchy (including the whole object at the top of the hierarchy), orientation could be specified by the angles of the global main axis with the axes of reference of the configuration; more refined descriptions would include the angles of the main axes of parts.

If the objects on the table sort themselves into several subconfigurations, for instance, several piles of books, each could provide a local reference frame in which its objects' location and orientation would be specified. In fact, one could assume that any two proximate objects make up a configuration, and specify the angles and distances between them.

But proximity is not the only relation to organize perceptual representations; some spatial relations are undoubtedly givens of perception, and those provide other locational information – for instance surrounding, or the alignment of three objects (I have referred to this as a good form, but one can think of objects in such an arrangement as fulfilling a certain spatial relation).

In conclusion, extending Marr's work to include the description of objects' location would seem to involve specifying a structural description (in which proximity and other spatial relations would play an important role), defining local frames of reference for various configurations of objects, and specifying the location and orientation of objects with respect to the local axes by appropriate analogical (metric) information (measures of angles and distances).

8.2.2 Mental images

There is abundant psychological evidence that the representations and processes of perception are of the same kind as those of mental imagery (Shepard and Podgorny 1978; Finke 1980; Block 1981, 1983). But mental images are more vague and blurred than visual percepts. For instance, one may imagine a striped tiger without a determinate number of stripes (Dennett 1981), or one may recall that a painting is in a room without recalling its exact location. The representation of this vagueness remains a basic puzzle (Anderson 1978; Block 1981). If mental images blend abstract elements with more specific pictorial elements, we must ask what sort of abstract elements are involved beyond the relations we posited as parts of perceptual representations. Do we imagine scenes with the same definiteness as percepts, but tag some elements as "uncertain"? This might work for the painting example, but is implausible with the tiger.

8.2.3 Spatial representations for action and reasoning

Representations appropriate for action and for spatial reasoning and problem solving are studied in robotics (Paul 1981; Brady et al. 1983) (for instance, in attempts to get a robot to find a path through a cluttered environment) and spatial problem solving (e.g., Forbus 1983; McDermott and Davis 1984). I will discuss only some elements of representation which are necessary for spatial reasoning and are particularly important to language. These are schematizations of perceptual representations occurring in several "grains": either each object is seen as a point, or groups of nearby objects are seen as points, and nearby groups of such groups, and so forth. Such idealizations serve a clear function. If one wants to reach a distant object, it is normally of no use to consider its dimensions; a more appropriate representation is to mark the object as a point on various possible paths (this is most obvious in the case of large-scale environments – to reach a distant place, a picture of the world in all its naive detail would be very inconvenient – but it should also apply to visual scenes). The same idealization may be applied to groups of objects.

Other idealizations of objects are probably useful in spatial reasoning as well, specifically the stick figures, corresponding to the main axes of objects and of their parts, which play a role in the specification of perceptual representations for shape; for instance, a long and narrow object might be approximated by its main axis.

All such idealizations are obviously relevant to language. Naturally enough, some of the idealizations operative in language spring from the spatial representations we use in action and reasoning.

8.2.4 Large scale environments

By moving about and by integrating successive visual scenes, a human being can construct mental maps of his or her environment. Real maps (pictures) and general geographical principles (e.g., a city street will not usually be spiral-shaped, it will not rise at an 80 degree angle) also contribute to this. There have been psychological and artificial intelligence studies of mental maps (Lynch 1960; Siegel and White 1975; Kuipers 1976). Kuipers proposes the following basic elements for mental maps of cities: "places", which correspond to landmarks, that is, to particularly salient buildings, squares, or crossroads, and are zero-dimensional; "paths", which are one-dimensional, for streets or rivers; "orientation frames", which are sets of places along with a system of coordinates that allow us to define distances and directions between pairs of places; and finally "regions", sets of places to which a global description applies – such as the definition of an outline, or the fact that the places are interconnected by a grid of paths. One important and difficult question is how detailed views of local environments are meshed with these schematized mental maps.

It is likely that a network of landmarks and paths, together with some global descriptions of regions (their outline, surface characteristics, etc.) also underlies our mental maps of large environments other than cities (territories with mountains, plains, rivers, roads, villages, etc.). In such maps, the zero-dimensional landmarks may be cities themselves.

So the grain structure extends beyond scenes perceivable at one glance: objects of greatly varying sizes may in the context of different activities be considered as points, ranging from objects in the visual field up to cities, and beyond; and objects of varying widths, from narrow paths to wide rivers, may be considered lines.

8.3 Locational knowledge and language

Language reflects the representations just described, but seems also to have its own idiosyncratic ways of structuring space.

Some aspects of shape representation are echoed in language: The use of the main axis of an object as a geometric description (as in *She rewound the vine along an horizontal lath*) gives support to the representation of shape proposed by Marr (1982) and others. The fact that one uses *in* to describe the relation of a gap to an object (*the crack in the vase*) suggests that the representation of such a vase is as an uncracked object with, so to speak, a negative part added.

The relational elements of perceptual representations play a role in making up the meaning of locative expressions, but sometimes indirectly: language makes "allowances", which obviously perceptual representations do not permit, and not all relations expressed occur in the perceptual representation – they must be extracted by abstracting metric information. But much of what language reveals are the schematizations comprised in the representations for action and spatial reasoning. As noted in the last section, to reach a distant object (or group of nearby objects), one need not pay attention to its internal details (or to the place distinctions between the objects in the group); one can think of the object (or the group) as one point. Linguistically, this is reflected, for instance, in some uses of *at*, as in *Jimmy is at the store*, where the store and Jimmy fuse to one point. As another example, consider a moving object: it seems very sensible to think of distinct positions of the object on its trajectory as points. In language, this is reflected in *The bus is at the 3rd Street stop*, where a place in the trajectory and the moving object are idealized to coincident points.

But there are circumstances in which a punctual conceptualization appears useful and a plausible part of a spatial representation, but is not reflected in language. So, though a city, for mental maps of the appropriate scale, would be conceptualized as a point, **John is at Paris* is not acceptable, even if uttered by somebody in San Francisco. And a room and its contents can profitably be seen as a point when one thinks of the distribution of rooms in a large building (one could represent the topology of the building by a graph, with the rooms as points and direct connections between rooms as arcs), yet one cannot say **the desk at the room*.

Conversely, there are conceptualizations that appear to be strictly for the benefit of language. It is doubtful that perceptual representations of object shape involve seeing a surface as some lamina (as in *the crack in the surface*), and it is not clear what purpose such a conceptualization serves in terms of spatial reasoning. Even with those conceptualizations that are useful to reasoning and occur in language, it is difficult to characterize the conditions under which a particular one is appropriate.

Having considered the relation of linguistic expressions to the knowledge in perceptual representations, and to the schematizations used in action and reasoning, we must ask what particular mixture of metric and relational information results from comprehension. A locative expression gives us only a constraint on location: if a spider is said to be *on a wall*, it could be anywhere on the wall. We cannot derive a full visual representation, unless we choose to assign a precisely defined default location to the spider. This is the solution adopted by Waltz and Boggess (1979) – but, as they note, this solution involves making unwarranted assumptions. These often have no harmful consequences, but sometimes we will need to remember that our positioning was hypothetical. If, for instance, we choose to assume the spider is to the right of a chair, we might need to remember later that we cannot rely on that assumption for further reasoning. Waltz and Boggess assign precise default locations because it allows them to reason efficiently (instead of testing the truth of some proposition by using inference rules and searching through the space of valid inferences, they can use procedures to test directly their spatial representation, which includes coordinates in some frame of reference), but they offer no solution for the problem of possible unwarranted conclusions. Still, I believe that we do place objects at more or less specific default positions when we construct a mental image that represents our understanding of a locative expression, and that we somehow keep track of the original constraint so we can retract unwarranted conclusions. How exactly this can be worked out is yet another open question.

In any case, because of the discrepancies between the spatial representations of scenes and the conceptualizations in language, and because we probably construct spatial representations in which we assign default locations to the objects talked about, part of comprehension must involve a step where, given the propositions yielded by the interpretation of a locative expression, we create appropriate spatial representations. Conversely, in production, the one or several propositions that will be translated into a locative expression may not come directly from the underlying representations, and this requires a complex extraction process. In the following sections, I will not discuss this element of decoding, and will only allude to its analogue in encoding.

8.4 Decoding

In a first sketch of decoding, I distinguished two tasks involved when normal conditions can be assumed: construct the normal situation type(s) associated with the spatial expression, and given such situation type(s), exploit the particular context to further specify the normal interpretation.

After discussing these, I will consider the problem of producing out-of-the-ordinary interpretations.

8.4.1 Generating the normal interpretation(s) of the expression

Given a spatial expression, the use types of the preposition in the expression, the pragmatic near principles, and general world knowledge, how can one construct the normal situation type(s) associated with the expression?

The main part of the normal situation type is a partial specification of the geometric meaning of the expression. Depending on whether the spatial relation has two or three arguments, there are two general schemata for the geometric meaning:

$$[A(S_I)](G_I(O_I), G_2(O_2))$$

and

$$[A(S_I)](G_I(O_I), G_2(O_2), G_3(O_3))$$

where S_I represents a predicate derived from the ideal meaning by a sense shift, A the tolerance shift, and G_i (with $i = 1, 2, 3$) the geometric description functions. The geometric meaning is not fully determined in the normal situation type – that is, by the expression together with world knowledge and an assumption of normality – since: (a) the actual identity of the objects O_I and O_2 is generally undefined outside a particular context (except for the referents of some proper names, or objects like *the sun*), and that of O_3 is undefined whenever it is an indexical; (b) the particular context may be needed to fully determine A and the G_i functions (and in fact, to reduce the number of matching use types to one only).

The difficulties of decoding become fully apparent when one notes that an expression, by itself, much under-determines the geometric meaning; general world knowledge and particular context must be consulted to determine the values of the parameters involved. Prepositions are ambiguous (each has typically several use types) and in any case the use types do not fully specify tolerance and geometric descriptions.

The problem is to find a use type, geometric descriptions, and a tolerance consistent with what is known about the normal behavior of the objects talked about (possibly several use types can be found). Initially, every use type of the preposition in the expression is a candidate for providing a blueprint to interpret the expression. We could pick a use type, hypothesize plausible geometric descriptions and tolerance, and then check whether the resulting geometric meaning and other instantiated use type constraints may be true, given our knowledge of objects. If there is a fit, a normal interpretation can be constructed from that use type; if not, the use type is rejected.

Table 8.1. *Examples from the catalogue of use types of* at, on, *and* in.

in:

N(spatial entity) in N(container)	spatial entity in container
N(gap/object:A) in N(object:B)	gap/object (A) "embedded" in physical object (B)
N(person) in N(clothing)	person in clothing
N(accident/object:A) in N(object:B)	accident/object (A) part of physical object (B)
N(spatial entity) in N(area)	spatial entity in area
...	...

on:

N(spatial entity:A) on N(object:B)	spatial entity (A) supported by physical object (B)
N(physical object) on N(area)	physical object on edge of geographical area
N(physical object) on N(vehicle)	physical object transported by large vehicle
N(object:A) on N(object:B)	accident/object(A) part of physical object (B)
...	...

at:

N(spatial entity) at N(place)	spatial entity at location
N(person) at N(artifact)	person using artifact
N(physical object) at N(path)	physical object on line and indexically defined crosspath
N(spatial entity) at sea	spatial entity 'at sea'
...	...

The catalogue of use types is a set of pattern-interpretation pairs, as illustrated by the examples offered in Table 8.1. (The interpretation has been replaced by a very succinct description, in italics; $N(x)$ denotes a noun-phrase referring to an object of category x; the use of the letters A and B should be self-explanatory.)

The interpretation consists of a set of constraints, which can be subcategorized into those constraints that apply directly to the scene and those that apply to the context (see Table 7.1).

Pattern and selection restrictions constitute the first instruments for filtering out matching use types: we can immediately eliminate all use types whose pattern and selection restrictions exclude the noun-phrases in the expression. For instance, with *The pear is in the bowl*, this step will leave as active candidates the following use types: "spatial entity in container", "gap/object 'embedded' in physical object", and "accident/object part of physical object".

Let us now see how, given a use type, we can specify the geometric meaning as much as is warranted, and use the resulting specification to check whether the use type fits the expression. Note that a given use type fully determines S_I, so the definition of S_I in the geometric meaning follows from the use type tested; the difficulty is with the geometric descriptions and tolerance.

There are three sources of constraints on the geometric description functions: use types, pragmatic principles, and object knowledge. Use types constraints may take the form of a full specification of the global function involved: for instance, with "spatial object in container", the function applying to the reference object must be *Interior*. Or the constraint may simply define the ranges of the functions – thus, in the use type "spatial entity in area", the range of the reference object function must be the set of areas. In "person using artifact", both located and reference object must be mapped onto points, so the ranges of the two corresponding functions must be the set of points.

In general, a point is obtained by simply using *PtApprox* (as usual, after *Place* has applied). But for *the waiting line at the counter*, for instance, these points are obtained by applying the product of several functions, the last of which is *PtApprox*.

$$[A(Coincide)](PtApprox(Head(Place(Line))),$$
$$PtApprox(Front(Place(Counter)))))$$

How do we know to introduce these additional functions? The answer should come from the other two sources of constraints. The pragmatic principles suggest plausible metonymies: transfers to a typically salient part of the object, to its base, to its projection on the ground, or to its projection on the plane at infinity. And three categories of object knowledge provide additional constraints on geometric descriptions:

(a) Which part of the object is salient under which circumstances. Object knowledge should include such facts as "this particular part is salient in such and such type of context" (e.g., the space in a theater where the audience sits when audience activities are the topic, the top of a table, the seat of a chair).

(b) Which idealizations and conceptualizations of the object are commonly used. For example, knowledge about roads will specify that a road is frequently conceptualized as a line; knowledge about surfaces that a common conceptualization for a surface is as a very thin lamina; and it can be specified with lawns and football fields that they lend themselves to conceptualizations as surfaces, but not as two dimensional enclosures (one says *on the lawn/football field* but not *in the lawn/football field*).

(c) The typical shape and use of the object. In *the line at the counter* for instance, *Front* is suggested by general world knowledge about the use of counters.

Tolerance is also constrained by the use types, pragmatic principles, and object knowledge. For instance, the use type "spatial entity in container" and the use type "spatial entity supported by physical object" in effect define tolerance conditions (these specify when an object in a container need not be in its interior, and when the object on a surface can be separated from it). Object knowledge tells us that a person waiting at a door is typically within a few feet of it, thus defining the tolerance in *Jane is at the door.* As for the pragmatic principles, at this point, we have so far formulated only two near principles (shifting contrast and background grid), and the rather difficult corresponding examples will not be considered.

In any case, lexical, pragmatic, and object knowledge should allow us in principle to determine plausible geometric descriptions and tolerance – and then help us filter out matching use types and determine the normal interpretation. Let us consider some examples. For *The pear is in the bowl*, the use types' constraints on geometric descriptions suffice to define the normal interpretation. For each of the use types whose selection restrictions the sentence satisfies, the required geometric description function applying for the located object is simply the *Place* of the object; it is also *Place* for the reference object in "accident/object part of physical object", but *Interior* and *NormalRegion* must respectively follow the application of *Place* for "spatial entity in container" and "gap/object 'embedded' in physical object". The spatial relation between objects specified in each use type, together with general object knowledge, then allows us to eliminate all but one use type, the containment one; pears are not usually embedded in or part of bowls, while for pears to be spatially included in the interior of a bowl conforms to ordinary circumstances. All the other constraints of that use type can be asserted of the relevant objects; none leads to inconsistencies. These constraints are in fact few and simple: no indexicals, no highlighting, no particular conditions on context are involved. The use type specifies an acceptable tolerance: the pear may be part of a heap of objects contained in the bowl, but be itself outside the interior. A constraint on purpose tells us that the expression must be used to provide information on the location of the pear.

When more complex combinations of geometric description functions are involved, the process of disambiguation and instantiation is more difficult. For instance, if an object has a typically salient part, one would try both the part and the whole object as geometric descriptions, and select the one that fits best the requirements of the use type and of world knowledge. With *the waiting line at the counter*, the use type eventually selected, "person using artifact", requires that the objects be mapped onto points. Knowledge about waiting lines indicates that the head is functionally salient; and the head of a line lends itself better to being approximated to a point than the whole line itself, leading to the combination of functions in the geometric meaning of *the waiting line at the counter*. The use type specifies that close proximity is allowed instead of coincidence (though it says nothing about how close) – this in fact makes the use type acceptable as actual coincidence would have forced us to reject it. A more precise definition of the distance can be obtained from object knowledge about the normal use of counters. With *the line along the sidewalk*, on the other hand, *along* requires line segments as arguments, and since line segments are good approximations for a line and a sidewalk, there is no reason to pick out a part of the line. Selecting geometric descriptions involves looking for a "best" match, given a set of constraints originating in use types, pragmatic principles, and world knowledge.

Some approximations are suggested by the use type, but must be confirmed by general spatial reasoning about the objects rather than information explicitly attached to their representations. For instance, with

> *The top of the cloud cover is at 3000 feet.*
> *The box is three feet from the wall.*

one would not expect to find included in knowledge about tops of cloud covers the fact that they can be approximated by a horizontal plane, or in knowledge of boxes that they can be approximated to points. In the first example, the relevant use type of *at* requires a point, line, or plane as the first argument of its relation; spatial reasoning should lead us to choose a plane as the best approximation for the top of a cloud cover. With the box example, the relevant use type of *from* requires a point as the first argument of its relation; the typical box is conveniently approximated to a point, though another way to obtain a point is to pick out the point of the box closest to the wall. This yields two interpretations for the expression.

According to the pragmatic principles, the geometric description functions may map an object on its base, or its projection on the ground. One must consider here consistency with object knowledge, but also sometimes the characteristics of the objects' normal environments, since whether only horizontal coordinates matter to the hearer may be a contextual matter. So for *the block in the circle* (Figure 6.1), the overall volume of the block cannot be included in the area, requiring the selection of the base. But for *The house is above the apartment building* (Figure 5.1), one should know that, when speaking of the location of buildings, only the base matters.

In similar fashion, one could deduce that a geometric description is the projection at infinity – that appearances are what matter. For instance, if we are relating a star and an object on earth, reasoning from object knowledge should lead us to conclude that we must be talking about appearances. But with *The tower is to the right of the peak*, we may be talking about appearances or fact; there are two interpretations of that expression.

If we are trying to fit to the expression a use type that involves an indexical, the normal interpretation inherits the constraints on the indexical value from the use type. No further definition of this value is possible at the level of the normal interpretation. So, for instance, if we are trying to match the use type "physical object on line and indexically defined crosspath" on *The gas-station is at the freeway*, we can infer that in the normal interpretation of that sentence, there is in the context a crosspath such that either speaker and hearer are on it, or the speaker takes the point of view of someone on it, and the gas-station is where that path intersects the freeway. When we have a particular context available, we should use that information to identify that crosspath.

In the last step of generating the normal situation type, we will use knowledge of the normal properties of and interaction with the objects to draw pragmatic inferences which further determine the normal situation type, but do not stem from the matching use type. We saw the need for such inferences with *the teapot on the table*. As another example, consider *the nail in the board*. Having selected "gap/object 'embedded' in physical object" as the relevant use type, we can be more specific than simply asserting that the nail is embedded in the board; we know that the nail will typically be as in Figure 8.1(a) and not as in 8.1(b). What we know about the use of nails, about the properties of wood, and how a nail is inserted into it, make situation (b) very unlikely. And since a normal situation type is restricted to normal interactions of the objects related, it is restricted to the interpretation corresponding to Figure 8.1(a).

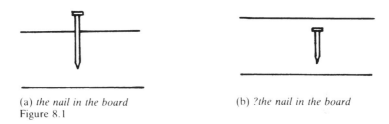

(a) *the nail in the board*
Figure 8.1

(b) *?the nail in the board*

Suppose we started from an unacceptable locative expression. Then, somewhere in the course of the process described, something would have gone awry; no use type would quite fit, inconsistencies would show up at some point for every hypothesized use type, set of geometric description functions, and tolerance. Thus the detection of anomalous sentences is one outcome of checking consistency for every use type tried.

This description of decoding calls upon some basic reasoning abilities which one must assume underlie language processing: checking consistency, selecting a best match, and drawing inferences. The modeling of these abilities corresponds to some fundamental research problems of artificial intelligence, but existing programs work only in the most primitive fashion and in simplified domains. The examples offered above underline the difficulties of extending these to more realistic domains.

8.4.2 Obtaining a context-specific interpretation

Given the particular context in which the spatial expression is uttered, it is usually possible to select one normal interpretation when the expression has several, and also to make the selected interpretation more specific. There are five main aspects to this narrowing down of possibilities: one will usually (a) identify the referents of the subject and object, (b) choose between possible geometric descriptions, (c) specify the tolerance, (d) assign a value to any indexical, and (e) draw additional pragmatic inferences. None of these tasks requires capabilities unique to locative expressions; they should be accomplished through general language processing abilities. These include the processes already mentioned in relation to decoding – i.e, ensuring consistency, selecting a best match, and drawing pragmatic inferences – but also selecting a maximally relevant expression and determining reference. I will give examples that illustrate each task except the referring of noun-phrases, since nothing in the problem of referring expressions is special to spatial expressions.

Consistency may be the key to disambiguating *the nails in the desk* (which amounts to choosing between two geometric descriptions for the reference object: the interior and the normal volume). If we know from the context that the nails are in a box, it would be inconsistent to assume that they nail the desk together; we must assume the containment use type. "Ambiguity" of geometric descriptions shows up also in *The box is three feet from the wall*, where the point corresponding to the located object could be the point closest to the wall, or an approximation of the whole box. Knowing the dimensions of the particular box involved might help select one interpretation: if the box is very small relative to three feet, the approximation solution is to be preferred; if it is quite large, picking the closest point is better; there is of course a relative size range for which both solutions are equivalent.

Often, it is not possible to specify the tolerance at the level of the normal situation type. Thus, if we say *Paul's house is to the right of the church*, without knowing something about the environment of Paul's house and the concerns of the speaker, we cannot tell whether the tolerance should be defined by a network of streets, by contrast with another house further from the relevant right axis of the church, or with the precision needed by a land surveyor (of course, another unknown is the point of view defining *the right*). To understand how a particular context might key us to one of the possibilities, one would need to understand relevance – how a system of knowledge representation might be devised that manifests relevance, and allows one to select the interpretation most relevant to the context of utterance. Relevance is one fundamental problem facing natural language processing research, but there has been so far little formal or computational work on it (I will return to the question of relevance below).

As another example relating to tolerance but also to indexicals, consider *The Queen is to the right of the Rook*. If we know that the speaker is considering game moves, we should assume that the game board defines tolerance; this interpretation has the highest relevance to the context. A similar appeal to relevance would lead us to select as point of view that of the player in focus.

Pragmatic inferences fall into three categories: Gricean inferences, inferences based on text cohesion, and those drawn from knowledge about objects and the physical world.

A Gricean inference occurs, for example, with *June is near her desk*, which is generally assumed to imply that June is not at her desk. This can be explained as an implicature arising from Grice's Cooperative Principle (Grice 1974). One of the Gricean maxims, the "maxim of quantity", states: "Make your contribution as informative as is required (for the current purposes of the exchange)". Naturally, the prickly point here is precisely defining the speaker's current purposes and the corresponding information requirements. *At* is more specific than *near*, but it is not true that speakers should always be as specific as their knowledge allows. To evaluate the information required by the current purposes of the exchange one must consider not only the facts involved and the speaker's goals, but also conventions about the appropriate level of specificity; in general, there is a default level of specificity of description. With objects, this is Rosch's "basic level" (1977);[2] there seems to be the equivalent of a basic level for spatial relations in scenes, but since scenes and situations are much more difficult to circumscribe than objects, their categorization properties have not been studied. For people sitting at desks, the default is *at*. Thus, if June was at her desk, one should expect the speaker not to say that she was *near her desk*, since that would be giving less information than the situation typically requires. So assuming that *June is near her desk* has been uttered by a cooperative speaker typically entitles the hearer to infer that June was not at her desk. This inference cannot, however, be made part of the normal interpretation of *June is near her desk*, since it cannot be assumed true in every context, even restricting ourselves only to normal contexts; in Section 8.5, I will give examples where the speaker would use *near* to describe someone sitting at a desk.

As an example of inferences involving both text cohesion and world knowledge, consider *There is a Picasso in my bedroom; next to it hangs a Miro*. One would normally infer from this that the Picasso was also hanging on a wall, and on the same wall as the Miro. Without going into detail on how these inferences might proceed, it is clear that neither the first, nor certainly the second, is part of the normal interpretation of *There is a Picasso in my bedroom*; they will arise from considering both the expression and its context.

I noted that decoding should involve checking that an expression is appropriate to the particular context, as perceived by the addressee. How can one evaluate the relevance of expressions to a context? Sperber and Wilson (1982) propose a way to define the relevance of a "proposition" relative to a context. Given a context – i.e., a set of propositions – a proposition P is more relevant to this context than a proposition Q, if more consequences can be drawn from the conjunction of the context with P than with Q. In other words, something "matters" in a given context if it has relatively many consequences in that context. This account has been criticized by Gazdar and Good (1982), who show that the number of implications has often little to do with relevance. Indeed, although there is some intuitive feeling that relevance has to do with being "of consequence", the number of non-trivial implications probably does not appropriately represent relevance; one would like to say that the "importance" of the consequences is what matters. Unfortunately, this leads us into circularity. Also, if we are to count pragmatic inferences from world knowledge in addition to "semantic" inferences (and Sperber and Wilson's definition is of very limited use otherwise), then the number of such inferences is infinite. One could decide to draw inferences from only a few selected (relevant) facts of world knowledge, but this brings in circularity again.

Another (and I would surmise better) way to look at relevance is to see it as relative to some communicative goals: an inappropriate expression may be true, but it does not satisfy the speaker's communicative goals, as the addressee understands them. Relevance becomes then entangled with the question of planning in language generation, a problem examined in the section on encoding. In comprehension, the hearer attempts to infer the speaker's plans (for instance, Allen and Perrault (1980) show how this allows an addressee to determine the implicit request underlying *The train to Windsor?* and answer cooperatively, given that the speaker is in a train station and the addressee behind the ticket window). "Irrelevance" would show up when some inconsistency appears in the realization of the hypothesized plan.

In any case, it is unlikely that relevance to a context is ensured by computing a "relevance factor"; more probably, the structure of memory and attention is such that only relevant propositions are focused upon.

8.4.3 *"Extra-ordinary" interpretations of locative expressions*

How are we to interpret locative expressions in contexts where "abnormal" conditions obtain? Conditions can be abnormal in several ways: the speaker may imagine aberrant worlds where physical laws do not hold; the objects may be, or be imagined to be, in outer space; they may be of abnormal shape, size, or material; or they may be positioned, interact with other objects, be used or dealt with in non-standard ways.

Generating the normal interpretation involves instantiating a matching use type, then drawing pragmatic inferences sanctioned by an assumption of normality. If, however, the particular context specifies that the objects' shape, orientation, size, etc. is out of the ordinary, one should forgo drawing some of these inferences. This will lead to an appropriate, though not normal interpretation for the expression. For instance, if we know that a table is lying sideways and are told *The teapot is on the table*, we would still find the use type "spatial entity supported by physical object" suitable, but the surface offering support must be that of a leg, as in Figure 8.2.

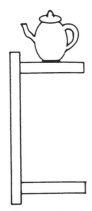

The teapot is on the table.
Figure 8.2

But in some cases, we cannot match any use type. What seems to happen then is that an acceptable interpretation is one that "closely" matches the normal situation type. Searle (1979) gives interesting examples of how a sentence can be used appropriately to describe outlandish situations. Considering *The cat is on the mat*, Searle notes that it would normally be interpreted according to Figure 8.3, with the mat supporting the cat.

He then describes a number of odd situations, asking whether or not *The cat is on the mat* is true in each one, and uses the resulting evidence to show

The cat is on the mat.
Figure 8.3

the importance of background assumptions in defining the truth conditions of the sentence. My own interest is in trying to understand when and why *The cat is on the mat* is judged true and appropriate in such situations:

(1) "...suppose that the cat and the mat are in exactly the relations depicted only they are both floating freely in outer space, ...In such a situation the scene would be just as well depicted if we turned the paper on edge or upside down since there is no gravitational field relative to which one is above the other."

(2) "...as we are strapped in the seats of our space ship in outer space we see a series of cat-mat pairs floating past our window. Oddly, they come in only two attitudes. From our point of view they are either as depicted in Figure 3 [analogous to Figure 8.3 above] or as would be depicted if Figure 3 were upside down."

(3) "Suppose the cat and the mat are in the spatial relations depicted in Figure 3, at the surface of the earth, but that each, cat and mat, are suspended on an intricate series of invisible wires so that the cat, though slightly in contact with the mat, exerts no pressure on it."

(4) "Suppose the cat and the mat are part of a stage set. The wires are there to facilitate rapid movement of the props, as the cat has to be moved from chair to mat to table."

Searle proposes still other scenarios, but these will suffice. Searle says that in cases (1) and (3), the question "Is the cat on the mat?" does not have a clear answer, and that "the meaning of the sentence *The cat is on the mat* does not have a clear application in the context as so far specified". But the sentence is literally true in case (2) when the cat "appears" above the mat to the passengers in the space ship, and in case (4). Such statements can be reformulated in terms of speakers' judgments, rather than sentence properties. Thus speakers would be generally hesitant about the appropriateness of *The cat is on the mat* in cases (1) and (3) (lacking further specification of context), but they will find that sentence appropriate and true in one of the two cat-mat interactions of case (2), and in (4).

What is going on here? First, the normal interpretation of *The cat is on the mat* is in accordance with Figure 8.3 above, except that something thin could be between the mat and the cat, say a rag or some straw: a mat in its normal function lies flat on the ground, and supports the cat on top of it. So in the prototypical case, three relations are implied: *Contact*, *Support*, and *Above* (the cat is above the mat).

Now in weird situations, one or two of these may not hold (may be false, or irrelevant), and yet speakers will feel confident that they can use *on*, trusting the addressee to use contextual evidence in such a way as to guess exactly how they are using *on*. As we have seen, implicit assumptions as to what matters or does not matter are tacitly communicated from speaker to addressee in uses that are more commonplace than these (for instance, hearers are able to judge that *in* has been used to mean strict, or only partial, or even no inclusion at all; or that appearance in the field of view is what matters in interpreting *The church is to the left of the tower*). It is interesting to try to discern the kind of subtle evidence people then rely upon. In (2), cat-and-mat pairs come in two types of configuration, one in which the cat appears to observers as above the mat, one in which it appears under. On the one hand, it is normal for the hearer to assume that the speaker is concerned with contrasting these two types; and on the other, one type resembles the normal situation type of *The cat is on the mat* more than the other. The speaker can thus be reasonably sure to be understood if he or she chooses to describe one situation by *The cat is on the mat* and the other by *The cat is not on the mat*. Note that if cat-and-mat pairs came in two kinds of configuration, both with the cat appearing below, but one with the cat some small distance from the mat and the other with the cat touching it, then we could say *The cat is on the mat* in the former case, and *The cat is not on the mat* in the latter.

In case (4), the context again suggests strongly that the participants in the exchange are concerned with contrasting distinct locations, and not with the support/no support distinction: although strictly speaking the cat is not on the mat when there is slight contact, the appearance is then identical to the normal situation type, and the use of *on* will go through. If, for instance, various cats were hanging from strings and touching the trays of various scales, though not supported by them, and if we were periodically interested in weighing the cats by lowering the strings until the cat rested all its weight on the scale, then presumably one could say *The cat is not yet on the scale* while urging the operator to lower the string. Here support has become the important contrast.

Thus, within certain limits, some distinctions can gain or lose import-ance, become relevant or irrelevant. The context can help the addressee figure out when this happens, and what precisely the speaker intends. Resemblance, and clues as to what the speaker wishes to contrast, can be used by the addressee to figure out deviant uses of the prepositions. Speakers can allow themselves these uses precisely because they can generally trust the hearer to make use of such clues and to evaluate resemblance precisely as they do.

8.5 Encoding

The appropriate way to look at language generation is as a process of planning to achieve certain goals (e.g., informing the addressee of some fact, getting the addressee to perform some action), given some linguistic tools – a lexicon and a grammar – and pragmatic and world knowledge (Cohen 1978; Appelt 1985). Even if one is concerned only with encoding, one still must resort to a planning analysis, since the form of the output is best understood by reference to goals and plans.

While the planning perspective nicely fits intuitions about language use and the related work is one very impressive achievement of artificial intelligence, no program written handles lexical selection itself as a planning problem. In Cohen, the planning process is limited to defining the needed speech acts with their propositional content; Appelt extends the planning process to the realization of linguistic expressions. Given propositions of which the speaker wishes to inform the addressee, his system (KAMP) is able to decide on different ways to distribute these propositions within one or several sentences. For instance, assume the speaker wants to request the addressee to remove a pump from a platform; KAMP first figures out that, to (a) perform the action, the addressee must (b) be informed of the tool to use, and (c) of the location of that tool. But there is no need to generate three sentences: "action subsumption" allows KAMP to satisfy all these goals with one sentence: *Remove the pump with the wrench in the tool box.* An action A_1 subsumes an action A_2, if "both A_1 and A_2 are part of the same plan, and action A_1 (in addition to producing the effects for which it was planned) also produces the effects for which A_2 was intended". The request can be made to subsume the actions of informing the addressee of the needed tool and its location, by filling first the instrument case of *remove* with a reference to the tool needed (*the wrench*), and then modifying that phrase by the appropriate locative phrase. Reference to the platform can be omitted because the addressee knows that the pump is attached to the platform only; mentioning the platform becomes a "phantom action".

Action subsumption allows the system flexibility in organizing the generated text, but for lexical choice, Appelt assumes essentially a straightforward correspondence between the underlying logical predicates and lexical items (e.g., the underlying representation contains a proposition asserting that a containment predicate is true of the wrench and the tool-box, and this predicate simply gets translated into lexical *in*). Appelt recognizes the inadequacy of this solution, noting that the judicious choice of lexical items allows a speaker to satisfy several goals simultaneously; in effect, action subsumption could profitably be applied to this problem.

In other words, Appelt assumes unanalyzed lexical items. Other work on language generation assumes lexical items decomposed into primitives. For instance, Goldman (1975) designed a generator with "conceptual dependency" (Schank 1975) as an underlying representation; he used a discrimination net[3] to zero in on a particular lexical item by making successive tests on the semantic representation. This allows him to choose, for instance, between *give* and *return*; if the recipient formerly owned the object, then it is *return*; if not, *give*. But this method assumes that one is always as specific as one can be (as one has the knowledge to be), while in fact, what gets expressed is picked out from what one knows on the basis of high level goals – yet Goldman uses no planning.

Ideally, one wants to bring together planning with a lexicon of analyzed items – with the kind of meaning analysis provided in the preceding chapters. This poses a difficult problem; not only must one devise a planning process to choose what to express, but testing a preposition for applicability in a given situation is an elaborate process, requiring more than verifying the presence of some primitive predicates in the underlying representation: use types are complex structures and their applicability depends on many aspects of the context, with geometric descriptions and tolerance adding further elements of variability. And whatever the form of the representation of the scene from which encoding proceeds (it occupies some point in the spectrum between a fully explicit image and a complex of abstract relations), it is unlikely that it contains direct expressions of the conditions derived from the use types (of the geometric meaning, for instance).

Whatever the speaker's top-level goal, there must appear at some point in the planning process the goal of expressing the spatial relation between two objects, using one as a reference object. But even after the planning process has determined that one object should be located with respect to another, the preposition to use cannot be selected by consideration of the scene alone. First, the permitted prepositions may depend on how the objects will get categorized, that is, on the head nouns of the – not yet generated – subject and object noun-phrases; second, as we saw in the discussion of relevance, a scene and given noun-phrases may still allow several prepositions – but ordinarily, the several communicative goals that the speaker has (besides expressing the relation of one object by reference to another) further restrict the prepositional choice.

As we saw in examining decoding, one locative expression may communicate many elements of meaning. Reliance on the addressee's knowledge of the world and reasoning abilities allows the speaker to pick one aspect of a situation, leaving the addressee to fill in missing details by drawing inferences. Action subsumption would clearly be useful here: expressing proposition P subsumes the action of informing of Q, if the addressee can infer Q from P given world knowledge. When choosing a preposition, the planner must decide on what it wants to communicate explicitly at that point and what it will leave to be inferred.

Focusing only on the selection of the preposition, let us assume appropriate noun-phrases have been generated, and divide the task of selecting the preposition into two steps: (a) finding the set of applicable prepositions, considering only constraints derived from use types, and (b) picking out the one preposition that satisfies best the overall communication plan. This division is not meant to be psychologically realistic, but just as a way to get a handle on the conditions defining the lexical selection task.

8.5.1 Finding matching use types
We are looking for all prepositions that have one or several use types whose constraints can be satisfied in the situation. We know which noun-phrase is subject, and which is object. At this point, we can choose from all locative expressions that can be constructed by plugging these noun-phrases into the use type patterns of all prepositions. The problem is then analogous to the one in decoding: given a use type, we must find plausible geometric descriptions and tolerance, such that the resulting geometric meaning is true of the situation at hand (in decoding, the partially specified geometric meaning had to be consistent with general object knowledge). As before, we must use pragmatic principles, use type constraints, and object knowledge to hypothesize geometric descriptions and tolerance; the purposes and concerns of the speaker may play a role in selecting appropriate geometric descriptions and tolerance (as exemplified by *The Queen is to the right of the Rook*). We can then check for the truth of the geometric meaning in the scene. Other use type constraints must be similarly checked. For any use type that matches, the corresponding preposition is one candidate. Some sort of discrimination net might be useful here, but with rather complex tests at the nodes, particularly given the dependence of geometric descriptions and tolerance on the context.

8.5.2 Communicative plan and preposition selection
The encoding step just described may leave us with several use types of different prepositions, all matching the situation at hand. Yet only one may be appropriate to the speaker's communicative goals (if not, we would assume that several expressions are appropriate); all the examples offered in the discussion of relevance illustrated this fact.

I will give one extended example that illustrates how lexical choice depends on communicative goals, the problems involved in refining the planning process to include lexical selection, and the potential of action subsumption for solving some of the problems involved. Imagine a scene with a man sitting at a desk, and an observer, on the other side of the desk, facing the man. This scene satisfies the constraints of one of the use types of five prepositions, yielding the possible following expressions:

> *The man was at the desk.*
> *The man was near the desk.*
> *The man was next to the desk.*
> *The man was across the desk.*
> *The man was behind the desk.*

But one can fabricate contexts such that only some of these are appropriate to the speaker's communicative needs and discourse plan. If, for instance, we follow the chosen phrase with *although he was obviously not working*, only the first and last expression would be appropriate, the first being preferable: *across* sounds now irrelevant:

> ?*The man was across the desk, although he was obviously not working.*

From the use of *at* or *behind*, it can be inferred that the man is in position to use his desk; *although* indicates that the man's idleness contradicts one of the implications of the preceding expression, namely that the man was working. It is not possible to express that contradiction so concisely if the preposition chosen is *across*. Assume as high level goals of the sentence: informing the addressee of the position of the man, of the fact that his position is indicative of work, of his idleness, and of the contradiction between the two latter. In the course of searching for a preposition to express the location, the planner will find that by using *at* or *behind*, the location action can be made to subsume mentioning that the position typically indicates work.

The sentences with *near* and *next to*, in the most typical context, imply that the man was not at the desk, and thus cannot be used in the situation described. This is the result of an implicature from Grice's Cooperative Principle – *The man was near the desk* uttered by a cooperative speaker typically entitles the addressee to infer that the man was not at the desk. But there are contexts in which the pragmatic implicature can be blocked: cases where the main focus of the exchange is the man's proximity to the desk. Assume the speaker is telling a story involving a man in a room and a gun in a desk drawer, and is asked: *Why couldn't you stop the man from getting his gun? Was he near the desk?*, an appropriate answer would be: *Yes. He was near the desk. In fact, he was at the desk.* So in this case, both *near* and *at* are assumed applicable.

I know of no work on focus that deals with this kind of phenomenon. Focus plays a role in KAMP, but only as it applies to the generation of referring expressions (e.g., it conditions the choice between a pronoun and a definite description). Understanding how different levels of categorization interact with focus and with pragmatic implicatures is a problem yet to be explored.

Finally, consider a detective story starting with:

> *Across the enormous desk, the man in the pin-striped suit, his face white against the back of his chair, was trembling like a jellyfish.*

By choosing *across* over *at*, the writer has introduced in that one prepositional phrase the presence of someone facing the man. If the author then goes on with "Exasperated, Phyllis Marlowe lowered her gun", the reader would have little doubt about where Phyllis Marlowe was. In other words, one lexical item communicates several facts: the existence and location of someone facing the man, and, together with information from other parts of the sentence (the face against the back of the chair) the fact that the man was probably sitting at the desk, rather than anywhere in the room.

Note that *behind* would have a slightly different effect: it less strongly suggests the presence of a yet unnamed observer; then, that observer could be anywhere in the part of the room on the front side of the desk, not necessarily directly in front of the man and close to the desk; also, *across* highlights the depth of the desk, the distance separating Marlowe from the man – with *behind*, the "enormousness" of the desk seems to attach to all its dimensions. Clearly, we are very far from being able to construct semantic models that take such subtleties into account, and one may prefer a theory that ignores them – yet they are worth observing, particularly since it is not clear they are unimportant to understanding language use.

Trying to imagine a planning process leading to the generation of the above sentence presents a nice challenge, as even a sketch of what would be involved indicates. Once one has decided to describe the position of the man with respect to the desk, one must determine that *across* is an applicable preposition, that the desk can be seen as a strip matched onto its top, and the characters as two points on either side of it. *At* and *behind* are also applicable, but *across* is preferred because it offers the possibility of suggesting the presence of someone facing the man early on and of creating suspense; mentioning just what the man is across from is left as a phantom action for this purpose. The clues that suggest there is probably a person facing him, rather than some object, are subtle: knowledge of narrative conventions and of the use of point of view in narratives is instrumental here; awareness of the alternatives (there must be some significant reason for the speaker not to use *at* or *behind*, and such a reason is more likely to be provided by a person than by an object) may reinforce that hypothesis. In any case, the planner must show that these inferences can be drawn by a typical addressee, and also that once Phyllis Marlowe is named, she will be identified with that person (for this, something like Kay's "parsimony principle" (1981) should be called upon, reflecting the fact that, in interpreting narratives, one should not hypothesize unnecessary partici-pants).

Action subsumption would come in as follows: among the higher level goals of the sentence must be to introduce the name of the heroine, and her position and orientation in the room. Actions to achieve the latter get subsumed by the action of describing the location of the man with respect to the desk by means of *across*. Introducing Marlowe's name gets subsumed by describing the agent of *lowered the gun*.

8.6 Object knowledge

This section surveys the attributes and properties of objects that can be relevant to the decoding and encoding tasks.

At the highest level, we find general knowledge relating to all physical entities – knowledge about matter, gravity, balance, movement, and appearance. We need to know, for example, that two material entities cannot be in the same place at the same time; all entities with mass are subject to the pull of gravity; all immobile objects must be supported, unless they are lighter than air; the apparent size of objects varies in inverse proportion with the viewing distance.

One must also have an account of the general properties of solids, liquids, gases, etc. In discussing the canonical geometric description for different classes of objects, I described some of the needed spatial properties. Other examples of necessary knowledge items include: liquids will take the shape of their container and have a flat horizontal surface when at rest (this is needed for interpreting *the water in the bowl*); liquids can easily be penetrated (it will help select the appropriate use type for the interpretation of *the stone in the water*). Hayes' "Ontology for liquids" (1978) is a good example of the kind of analysis and representation needed here.

Let us now go over the knowledge concerning particular object kinds. The attributes and properties below are defined mostly only at the basic level; occasionally some constraints exist at the superordinate level (e.g., there are upper and lower limits to the size of "pieces of furniture"). Note that the first four properties are physical properties; all the others are interactional properties:

> shape
> size
> gravitational properties
> characteristic orientation
> geometric conceptualizations
> typical physical context
> function
> actions performed with the object
> normal interaction with another object
> interactionally salient parts
> perceptually salient parts

- shape

The normal shape of each kind of rigid object (a table, cup, lemon, etc.), and the normal constraints on shape deformations for flexible objects (a string, pocket, leaf), are defined, though relatively loosely, at the basic level. Definition is much more specific at the specialization level. The best method of description for the shape of the various kinds of objects is probably in terms of a prototype and of allowed deviations from it. Interpretation obviously depends on objects' shape.

- size

Interpretation of a locative expression patterned on "A is at X", with X being a place in the ordinary sense (*Jon is at the store* and *my cabin at the lake*), depends on the size of objects A and X. Indeed such a sentence is true and appropriate when A is some "small" distance from X; what counts as small depends, among other things, on the sizes of A and X (Section 9.1).

- gravitational properties

A teapot will not normally hold of itself to the side of a table. A speck of dust will. Therefore, the teapot in *the teapot on the table* must be on a free top surface; but the dust in *the dust on the table* may be on any surface.

- characteristic orientation

In its characteristic orientation, a pine tree has a vertical trunk. The characteristic orientation of a table is with legs under and top horizontal. Such characteristic orientations are necessary in specifying the normal interpretations of *the tree on the meadow* and *the cup on the table*.

- geometric conceptualizations

A road and a river can be conceptualized as lines (*the city on the road/river*). A country cannot be conceptualized as a point (**at England*).

- typical physical context

If a door is in its typical context, that is, part of a wall, then one can only use its own axis to interpret *behind the door*. The sentence:

John is behind the door

is not true in Figure 8.4.

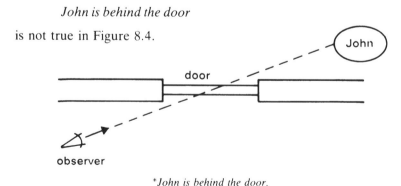

*John is behind the door.

Figure 8.4

Otherwise (in a hardware store for example) an observer's line of sight may override the door's cross-axis. (But there is also a loose usage where every object in the room past the door can be described as *behind the door*.)

• function

Function is important to the use of prepositions. For instance, because of the respective functions of a tray and a dish, though a dish and a tray may be essentially identical in shape, one says *the potato in the dish*, but not *the potato in the tray*.

In the case of the cage-like table in Figure 8.5:

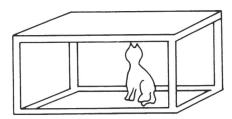

*The cat is in the table
Figure 8.5

one will not say *The cat is in the table*, but *The cat is under the table*. The preposition chosen reflects the salience of the function of the table, which is to support by means of the table top (the top is thus salient; *table* is then used as a metonymic substitute for its top), and not to contain by means of the underside "interior".

Function comes in explicitly in one use type associated with *at*: "person using artifact" (as with *John is at his desk*). And with *to the right of the chair*, "the right" can be defined by reference to a typical user of the chair.

• actions performed with the object

One moves caps onto bottles, not the opposite; this makes *the bottle in the cap* inappropriate.

• normal interaction with another object

This may contribute some conditions to the normal situation type; see for instance the example with nails and a board in Section 8.4.1.

• interactionally salient parts

The inside of a car, the top of a table, the head of a waiting line, are salient parts in functional interactions, which leads to metonymies in now familiar examples. The base of an object (of a building, any object on the ground, etc.) is salient in the ordinary interaction of moving about it or reaching it.

• perceptually salient parts

In *the chair under the tree*, "tree" is used as a metonymic substitute for "the branch part of the tree". The branch part is a perceptually salient part of the tree. This must be included in the knowledge about trees. Again because of metonymies, one should know, for each kind of object, which part is typically visible.

8.7 Conclusion

This sketch of decoding and encoding has assumed representations for facts like "this part of this kind of object is salient in such and such context", "appearances are what matter in this context", etc. Should we assume these representations consist of explicit propositions? Somehow propositions predicating that "what is of concern here is such and such" do not seem to satisfactorily account for the sense that some part of our knowledge is foregrounded. One would prefer to think of memory and attention structured in such a way that the selections necessary to encoding and decoding would be automatic. This suggests parallel connectionist models of memory and language use (Hinton and Anderson 1981; Dell 1985; McClelland 1985; Waltz and Pollack 1985).

Such models might also hold promise for other problematic aspects of the descriptions in this chapter. Use types were assumed to consist of well-defined constraints, so that checking whether a constraint is satisfied in a given situation, or consistent with a certain body of knowledge, is a more or less straightforward process. But what if a constraint is defined in fuzzy fashion (e.g., a "large" vehicle)? In such cases, it may not be possible to settle upon a fixed set of contextual parameters on which interpretations depend; it may, in effect, be impossible to characterize precisely the functions of context involved – and possible that for any such set of parameters, one can come up with a context such that a parameter outside the set matters (this is one way Searle (1979) argues for the existence of a background of assumptions and beliefs which cannot be made entirely explicit). Here, as in the processes by which some out of the ordinary interpretations are obtained, evaluation of similarity (e.g., between a prototypical "large" vehicle – say, a bus – and a particular one, or between the normal interpretation of *The cat is on the mat* and one of Searle's odd cat-and-mat situations) is crucial; such evaluation depends on considering simultaneously many aspects of the entities compared and of their context. In theory, distributed parallel architectures might offer a way to deal with such difficulties, since any contextual factor in an interconnected network might eventually bear on the assessment of similarity. But they still require analyzing objects and contexts into elements, and all possible ways to do so must be predicted in advance; if one believes in the notion of background, this would be impossible.

9   The three basic topological prepositions

At, on and *in* constitute in English a fundamental set of prepositions, with a large number of distinct types of uses derived from three ideal meanings which are cognitively basic, essentially topological, relations (the ideal meanings of *at* and *in*, respectively coincidence and surrounding, are topological relations, preserved under elastic deformations,[1] but the ideal meaning of *on* involves the physical relation of support in addition to the topological relation of contiguity in the three-dimensional case).

This chapter will present an informal description of the use types of each preposition. Each use type will be labelled by a brief summary phrase – e.g., "person using artifact" – simply intended as a pointer, a label for the purposes of this text. The categories mentioned in the label are only indicative; the use type description, which includes a pattern and an interpretation (a collection of constraints of the sort listed in Table 7.1), will specify precise selection restrictions.

Being principally concerned with locative expressions where the subject is a noun-phrase, I will not consider use types where the subject is restricted to being a clause, or where a locative occurs in the case frame of a verb, because in those situations there are often special conditions on prepositional choice that depend on the verb type. However, I will generally indicate if a particular use type allows events or states as located objects. The category "spatial entity" will denote the broadest category of locatable entities, that is, everything which is sufficiently spatially defined that it can be located: physical objects, geometrical objects (points, lines, etc.), accidents (holes, bends, breaks, etc.), some events (e.g., a meeting), activities (e.g., the referent of *we were sleeping*), and states (e.g., *it was hot*).

I have intentionally omitted some very idiomatic uses when they do not bring any new insight into use types and ideal meanings. The use types are not presented in order of increasing idiomaticity; instead, I have usually put next to each other use types whose similarities and dissimilarities I wanted to emphasize.

This classification has been built from a collection of examples gathered over several years. In addition, I have consulted the Oxford English Dictionary, the American Heritage Dictionary, and also Lindkvist's study of *at, on* and *in* (1950) – a classification based on 29,000 excerpts from English literature from 1500 to 1950 – excluding or adapting examples not current in contemporary American English.

9.1 The preposition "at"

The use types of *at* center around one ideal meaning:

at: for a point to coincide with another.

Because the first point corresponds to the Figure and the second to the Ground, the first is typically mapped onto an object, and the second onto a fixed earth location. Most commonly, an expression with *at* asserts that those two points, each specified by a different description, overlap in space, and the various use types, listed below, can be seen as variations on this theme:

> Spatial entity at location
> Spatial entity "at sea"
> Spatial entity at generic place
> Person at institution
> Person using artifact
> Spatial entity at landmark in highlighted medium
> Physical object on line and indexically defined crosspath
> Physical object at a distance from point, line, or plane

* "Spatial entity at location"
  Here is a representative set of examples in the use type:

> *The book is at the place where you left it.*
> *Julie is at the post-office.*
> *Paul is at Yosemite.*
> *There are lounging chairs at the beach.*
> *There is a Christmas party at the office.*

The normal interpretation of each of these expressions involves some object put – or some event occurring – on, in, or very close to another object which defines a location. The two objects are conceptualized as coincident points.

Note that one will not say *Joe is at the bush* if Joe is lying next to the bush: close proximity is not a sufficient condition for the appropriate use of *at*. Such a sentence can only be made acceptable by assuming a context in which Joe is running, and at that precise instant has reached the bush; that is, the reference object must be seen as a point on a trajectory. When the located object is in motion and the reference object is a landmark on its trajectory, one may use *at* with almost any reference object; otherwise, *at* is acceptable only with a restricted class of reference objects. Such special conditions seem conventional, and justify distinguishing two use types: "spatial entity at location" and "spatial entity at landmark in highlighted medium" (of which the trajectory requirement is a special case). Another use type closely related to "spatial entity at location" is "person using artifact"; it differs in its implication that the person is using the artifact, rather than simply being close to it. So, as I describe the selection restrictions for "spatial entity at a location", it should be kept in mind that when *at* occurs with objects outside the categories specified, one must either assume that the located object is at a landmark in a highlighted medium, or that the located object is using the reference object – the former must then be a person and the latter an artifact.

The only selection restriction on the subject of the locative expression in this use type is simply a consequence of the ideal meaning: it must refer to an entity that can be viewed as a point. This translates into the condition that the objects be bounded in all directions; or more exactly that they be primarily conceived of as bounded. Indeed, real objects are always so bounded; outside of geometry, unboundedness can only be a conceptualization. For instance, a road is in effect bounded, but since one usually experiences only a limited length of it at any one time, it is viewed as an unbounded strip or line. As such an "infinite" object cannot be viewed as a point, it cannot be the located object in this use of *at*. One will not say

?The freeway is at the lake.

except marginally perhaps, intending *the freeway* to stand for a salient, bounded part of it, probably an entrance.

The subject may also denote an event (*The meeting was at Mary's, Let us have a picnic at Lake Anza*). In defining a place for various kinds of spatial entities, I did not include events; an appropriate definition of the place might be the closure of the union of the regions occupied by participants in the event. While it is not precisely clear how the notion of conceptualization carries over to such spatial entities, it does seem that any activity can take place *at* a location, the only restrictions stemming from physical possibility (it would be hard to drive a truck *at a bar*).

The ideal meaning imposes the same restriction on the reference object: it must be bounded. So pathways and, generally, objects viewed as lines are excluded. *The gas station is at the freeway* is acceptable, but it does not simply mean that the gas station is located anywhere on or next to the freeway; it requires the selection of a bounded part of the freeway, and the example falls into another use type. At the same time, not every bounded object can be a reference object, so "location" in the label is a makeshift name for a category that includes:

(1) Entities denoted by the words *place, spot, location*, etc.

(2) Any dwelling (buildings, etc.).

(3) Some subunits of buildings, for instance apartments and stores. The discriminating characteristic here is whether the subunit is typically considered in the context of the whole unit, conceptualized as one cell of a cellular structure (as with rooms and corridors), or as a point in a larger environment, mainly in the context of movement between the subunit and locations outside the unit, as with stores and apartments:

> *Jonas is at the store/apartment.*
> **Jonas is at the bedroom/corridor.*

(4) Various geographical locations. A piece of land such that a set of adjoining similar pieces covers a portion of the earth cannot be the reference object in this use of *at*. So, as countries, states, counties, regions, neighborhoods, etc., divide the map, one does not say

> **at England/California/the county/the neighborhood/...*

To understand the intuitive basis of this restriction, imagine moving away from a surface until a given area shrinks to a point. Clearly, two adjacent areas of similar size will blend into one point. To get distinct points, we must start with areas that are disjoint, not contiguous.

Interestingly, this explanation allows one to predict that certain expressions with *at*, though *a priori* odd, will be possible, provided we make up contexts in which the reference object is naturally conceptualized as one of a set of disjoint geographical locations. For instance, yards and gardens are at first sight restricted to following *in*, that is, they are conceptualized as two- or three-dimensional enclosure (three-dimensional fits my own intuitions best, but I cannot fully exclude two-dimensional). But in fact it is possible to imagine a context where *at* is acceptable: of somebody working in a junkyard, one could say

> *He is at the yard.*

reflecting a view of the yard as one of a set of separate locations where the person could be. Similarly one will not say

> **Mary is at the garden.*

if the garden adjoins a house. But when thinking of a garden as one of a set of places in a city, one may use *at*:

> *Paul is at the community garden.*

So most geographical entities can be reference objects in this use type – albeit sometimes by forcing an unusual conceptualization – but very large entities tend to be excluded (which is natural, since a punctual conceptualization would tend to be inappropriate). Here is a partial list of geographical locations that may follow *at*: village, town, square, fair, estate, ranch, airport, lake, pool, beach, meadow, clearing, park, play-ground. Most proper names denoting an object in any of the above categories may also follow *at*, with the exception of towns or islands which must be small (*at Portola Valley*, but **at New York*; *at Ellis Island*, but **at Crete*). Excluded from being the object of *at* in this use type are forest, plain, prairie, desert, etc.

Note that the expressions with *at* are appropriate under special contextual conditions that will be specified below; the permissible contexts are often not the ones that first come to mind and the corresponding expressions may initially sound odd. Thus

> *?The restaurant is at the village.*

is, on the face of it, odd. But

> *There is a good restaurant at a village 6 miles from here.*

is fine.

(5) Geometrical points. Finally, the reference object may be an Euclidean point:

> *One focus of the ellipse is at the intersection of the two lines.*

Let us now turn to the spatial relation between the two objects. In the case of geometrical points, the use of *at* implies exact coincidence of the two points involved. *At* implies the closest relation within the range of significantly distinguished locations (Section 4.2); in geometry, this means coincidence – there is no tolerance for deviation from the ideal meaning. But with physical objects, the located object may be in, on, just on the edge of, or even just above – in other words, closely associated with – the reference object. With specific phrases, one will often infer that only one of these relations holds: for instance, the boy in *the boy at the beach* will be inferred to be on the beach, the man in *the man at the store* assumed to be in the store, the house in *the house at the lake* assumed to be on the edge of the lake. We can draw these inferences from general knowledge about the kind of things the subject and object denote, and from characteristics of the particular context at hand.

What is the maximum distance that may separate two physical objects, A and X, so that one can still say "A is at X"? First, the answer depends on the kind of objects that A and X are – distances clearly differ with *Jonas is at the store* and *my cabin at the lake*. But it is not simply size that matters; we judge that the objects are sufficiently close in subtle ways. Thus if the cabin in *the cabin at the lake* is in a town, the actual distance will depend on the size of that town, since any cabin there will tend to be *at the lake*.

Again, at first sight, if a boat is sailing on a lake, or if Jimmy is swimming in the pool, one would not say

> *My boat is at the lake.*
> *Jimmy is at the pool.*

But in fact, if I were in San Francisco and had left my boat moored at some lake hundreds of miles away in the Sierras, I would say just that first sentence, even if I knew a friend was just then racing the boat on the lake. Similarly, if I were far from the pool, there would be nothing wrong with uttering the second sentence, even if I knew Jimmy was then swimming, not sitting by the pool. This brings up some contextual constraints involved in this use type. There is a viewpoint contrast between this use of *at* and the use of, say, *in* and *on*: with either of the latter, we take a close-up view and our knowledge of the position is rather precise; but in using *at*, we take a remote view, our knowledge is often indirect, inferred (for instance, Jimmy told us he was going to the pool), and imprecise – we usually do not know whether the located object is in, or on, or on the edge of, the reference object (though we might). So it is generally inappropriate to say *My boat is at the lake*, or *Jimmy is at the pool*, if one is close to the lake or the pool, and one sees the boat sailing, or Jimmy swimming.[2]

This remote/close-up viewpoint distinction contrasts *at* not only with *on* and *in*, but also with *next to, besides*, or *by* (in the sense of *near*). Compare the sentences in each of the following pairs:

> *Jonas is at/in the store.*
> *June is at/in the supermarket.*
> *Lou is at/on the beach.*
> *Jimmy is at/next to the pool.*
> *Sue is at/by the lake.*

To clarify the implications of this contrast, let us compare *June is at the supermarket* and *June is in the supermarket*. Assume the speaker believes June to be in the supermarket. The following list illustrates some ways in which one chooses between the two expressions; it does not provide a set of complete conditions. I assume throughout that the speaker takes the point of view defined by his or her own position; otherwise the conditions do not apply.

(1) *At* will be required if speaker and addressee are close to each other and far from the supermarket. What counts as "far" is difficult to make precise. The ordinary Euclidean metric does not apply. For instance, space in a city is organized by salient boundaries: of buildings, yards, streets, etc. The applicable metric has more to do with how many of these boundaries are crossed than with straight Euclidean distance. Thus, if I am across the street from the supermarket, I am more likely to use *at* than if I am in the parking lot, although the actual distance may be the same.

(2) *In* will be required if speaker and addressee are close to each other in the supermarket.

(3) *At* will be preferred if the speaker's knowledge of June's position is not based on direct perception; conversely, *in* will be preferred if the speaker can see June, or more generally has direct perceptual evidence of her presence in the supermarket.

(4) *In* will be required if the speaker needs to contrast the interior with the exterior, for instance when the addressee expects June to be just outside the supermarket.

(5) There is a tolerance for sentences with *at* not to be rigorously true at the time of speaking. Thus I could well say *June is at the supermarket*, not knowing, and not caring, whether she had already arrived there. No such laxity is allowed with *June is in the supermarket*.

All the conditions just stated follow from associating *at* with a remote point of view, and *in* with a close-up one, though "follow" must clearly be interpreted loosely. In the same loose fashion, the remote viewpoint restriction derives from the ideal meaning of *at*: if the reference object is to be viewed as a point, and if it is rather large, quite obviously one must view it as if from a great distance. Again here, although we sense some intuitive validity in this derivation, it is hard to see how one could find a rigorous inferential path.

These connections between the ideal meaning, a remote viewpoint, and the five conditions above open a very interesting window onto some language processes that the notion of inference, whether logical or pragmatic, cannot explain. It is as if there were echoes in the conceptual system, associations by analogy rather than logical necessity or even typical co-occurrence – phenomena which would seem difficult to formalize. Seeing an object as a point does not logically imply that one is far from it, though it is suggestive of seeing from far away by analogy with the fact that an object appears to grow smaller as one moves away from it. Yet a speaker who says *June is at the supermarket* is not literally seeing June as a distant point. Similarly, direct perception does not imply that one is close to the object, nor imprecise knowledge that one is far from it; it only suggests these. This kind of loose logic (it relies on suggestion rather than implication), and the neither-yes-nor-no character of many intuitions about use (manifested in preference, as opposed to necessity) are very prevalent in language, and add difficulties to decoding and encoding.

● "Spatial entity 'at sea'"

This use type covers expressions like:

> *The Titanic will never be at sea again.*
> *We had a ball at sea.*
> *The marijuana containers are already at sea.*

These expressions imply that an object or person is travelling on a sea, or that an event is taking place during such travel. The subject is trivially restricted to objects that can be carried on a vessel, to the vessel itself, or to events that can occur on a vessel. The reference object is always *sea*, understood generically (not a particular sea).

One cannot say that this use of *at* is arbitrary: none of *along*, *under*, or *against* could be used. The place of the located object overlaps with the place of some indeterminate sea, a relation very close to the ideal meaning of *at*. The divergence is that the "generic sea" has no dimension and cannot be viewed as a point; but going from the concept of a particular sea to that of sea as an object kind is not unlike seeing an entity as a point, in that the particular is abstracted out. One thus finds the ideal meaning of *at* expressed here.

- "Spatial entity at generic place"
The reference object is also conceived generically in:

> *He likes to spend his vacations at the seaside.*
> *She owns a cabin at the mountains.*
> *Have fun at the ocean!*

Although we use the definite article, it is clearly absurd to look for a referent of *the seaside*. Such expressions seem to be restricted to mountains, seaside, etc., and to be used in the context of leisure activities. Thus

> **?She owns a factory at the mountains.*

is strange. The relation to the ideal meaning is analogous to that in the last use type.

- "Person at institution"
The sentences:

> *Several hundred workers at the cannery are on strike.*
> *My son is at the University.*
> *Professor Jones is at Berkeley.*

need not be strictly speaking locative, but they may indicate a person's place of employment, or more generally formal affiliation with an institution: the workers are not necessarily at the cannery during any particular period while the strike lasts, and Professor Jones may be on sabbatical, but an institution is usually associated with a given location, and such affiliations mean that people are frequently at that location. So the expressions are related to those in the use type "spatial entity at location". One can in fact construct parallel expressions synonymous with the ones above falling clearly into the use type "spatial entity at location", where the verb denotes the activity performed at the institution, for instance, *My son studies at the University.* The ideal meaning of *at* is thus expressed here, as it is in that use type.

- "Person using artifact"
  Consider:

> *Maggie is at her desk.*
> *There is nobody at the counter.*
> *The man at the stove is making crepes.*
> *Jessie is at his typewriter.*
> *There is a student at the blackboard.*

These expressions imply that a person is engaged in the normal use of the reference object – an artifact. The normal position of use of the artifact must be with the user next to it, neither in nor on it:

> **Jill is at her bed.*
> **Lew is at the stool.*

The artifact may not be one that one holds or carries around in typical use:

> **Jill is at the teapot.*

with the exception of some very idiomatic expressions:

> *Jill is always at her books.*
> *Lew is always at his pots.*

Neither can the artifact be a vehicle or something one moves:

> **The woman was at her grocery cart.*
> **They climbed mountains at their bicycles.*

again with some idiomatic exceptions:

> *the farmer at his plough*

Objects which do not have a clear use are not appropriate reference objects:

> **The art dealer was at the painting.*

The subject may refer to a group of persons, as in *There is a waiting line at the counter.*

Using *Maggie is at her desk* as an example, I have argued that the normal use condition could not be inferred pragmatically, that convention was involved; in other words, the above examples are not simply special cases of "spatial entity at location". Though the sentence always leads us to assume a normal interaction (so Maggie is not *at her desk* if, for instance, she is on her knees cleaning the floor just next to the desk), this is not sufficient to assert that convention rather than a pragmatic inference is involved. Since the most natural conclusion to draw from the fact that Maggie is very close to her desk is that she is using it, one could claim that *Maggie is at her desk* is not false when she is cleaning the floor, but it is uncooperative; the speaker should know that the addressee will infer that Maggie is using the desk. But such a pragmatic inference should be "cancellable" (Grice 1974): if the sentence by itself risks misleading, but its conventional meaning admits the possibility that Maggie is not using the desk, the speaker need only warn the addressee, by means of an added *but* clause for instance:

*?*Maggie is at her desk, but she is cleaning the floor.*

But this sentence seems contradictory. A second strong argument for conventionality and the need for a separate use type is that the inference does not go through when we express close proximity in some other fashion, as with *Maggie is by/(next to) her desk.*

It is possible to use *at* to describe the place of some objects as close to an artifact:

The swivel chair is at Joan's desk.

But here too, the function of the desk is involved. It is assumed that the swivel chair is placed so a person sitting on it would be *at Joan's desk* (it would not be appropriate if the chair were on the other side of the desk). And the sentence:

*The refrigerator is at the desk.

is unacceptable, because a refrigerator has no functional interaction with a desk.

Functional interaction seems less strongly associated with the use of *at* in examples with doors, gates, entrances, windows:

There is a man at the door.
She saw a woman at the window.

One tends to think of a man at the door as intending to enter (would a working house painter be *at the door?*), but I did find the second example in a book where it was only implied that the woman was near the window, not using it (i.e., looking out through it).

The ideal meaning of *at* is expressed here in the most straightforward fashion: the two objects are closely associated with each other and their dimensions are irrelevant.

• "Spatial entity at landmark in highlighted medium"

A medium[3] for an object is a region of space which contains it and is conceptualized as being of greater dimensionality than the object. In this use type, the reference object is a landmark (a salient object) within a medium, and the located object is close to or coincident with it. So in

> *The bus is at the 3rd Street stop.*

the medium is the bus run on which the stops are landmarks; located object and landmark are seen as points. But the landmark reference object can be a line or a surface: the implied medium is then a surface or a piece of three dimensional space, and the located object coincides with the reference object, or is part of it – the ideal meaning is generalized to higher dimensions:

> *Are the days at the equator always 12 hours long?*
> *There are bubbles at the surface of the water.*

In the first example, the implied medium is the surface of the earth; in the second, the body of water.

The use of *at* somehow brings to the fore the existence of a medium, in a way that *next to, by, in,* or *on* do not, that is, *at* works as a device for emphasizing the medium. But to use such a device, there must be a medium that it is useful to highlight. When objects are typically only part of a "trivial" medium – that is, when typically all one can say about them is that they are in three-dimensional space, or on the ground or some supporting surface – then there is no medium worth emphasizing. Most separate, movable objects (teapots, boxes, books, etc.) are in this category. This is why sentences like **The newspaper is at the teapot* are strange. On the other hand, when objects are intrinsically or typically part of a non-trivial medium, sentences with *at* sound perfectly natural. In particular, sentences where the reference object is an object part are at once recognized as accceptable, the medium being then the whole of which the reference object is a part:

> *There is a star at the top of the tree.*
> *There are two atoms at each node of this crystal.*
> *There are always kids standing at the corner.*
> *The semipalmated plover has a narrow white band at the neck.*
> *He was standing at the edge of the cliff.*
> *The camp is at a bend in the river.*

Note that in many of these sentences, the whole object is referred to; it is then in the foreground anyway. But the use of *at* emphasizes its role as a medium: our mind travels over the whole object, and picks a point or a line in it – which it does not do if we substitute *on, around, by,* etc., for *at*.

A context in which movement within a medium is alluded to, or implied, offers naturally the possibility of highlighting. Thus, verbs like *meet, gather,* etc. which imply movement to a meeting point may be followed by an *at* prepositional phrase with almost any reference object (they are not followed by *to*, because they refer to the termination of the movement rather than the movement itself):

> *They met at the big oak tree.*
> *The cattle gathered at the river.*[4]

Phrases with *at* are also natural complements of superlatives, since superlatives imply that one is considering a range of values and selecting a subset; if the values vary with position in space, we have a highlighted medium, namely the space over which these values are compared:

> *The grass is highest at the fence.*

A medium can also be a set of alternate points. Thus, assume we are playing a game in which players take fixed positions, each close to an object (a tree, a bush, a bench, etc.). One could say

> *This time, Jill will be at the tree, Paul at the bush, and Lew at the bench.*

Or a medium can be a series of objects:

> *He opened the book at page 65.*
> *The elevator is at the third floor.*

I do not see any way to infer pragmatically (say from the use type "spatial entity at location" together with aspects of the context) the characteristics of this set of uses of *at*, specifically the requirement that highlighting occur – thus a separate use type is justified.

• "Physical object on a line and indexically defined crosspath"
  In:

> *The gas station is at the freeway.*
> *There is a campsite at the river.*

the gas station is at the intersection of the freeway with some indexically defined crosspath, and the campsite is where a similar crosspath intersects the river. The reference object must be a linear object (or conceptualized as such). In the simplest case, speaker and addressee are on the crosspath, some distance from the reference object, and concerned with a specific direction of travel. In more complex cases, the speaker imagines the point of view of some possibly hypothetical traveller on the crossroad, a point of view distinct from either speaker's or addressee's.

This use type resembles the preceding one: there is a background medium, the crossroad, with a landmark on it; but that landmark is not the freeway as a whole, only the part that intersects the road. But, most importantly, the phrase would be false if the gas station were six miles from the intersection suggested by the context, while *He was standing at the edge of the cliff* would be true for any location along the cliff's edge. Although the medium may be an indexical of a sort in the last use type, that is, it is usually implicit in the context, its existence is only a precondition for the appropriate use of *at*; it is not indispensable to recovering the location intended by the speaker, as it is in this use type.

A hearer might be able to make sense of *The gas station is at the freeway*, given the preceding use type and necessary world knowledge, relying on the salience of the crossroad to infer pragmatically the location of the gas station, but no speaker could predict that such a use is allowed. The notion of an "idiom of encoding" (Makkai 1972; Fillmore 1979) might be useful here. An idiom of encoding is one that a language user might understand, given knowledge of the grammar and vocabulary, but without knowing that it is a conventional way of saying what it says. In our framework, the freeway sentence could be considered an idiom of encoding, if we take the preceding use type as the meaning of the preposition in our vocabulary: a language user could not predict the usability of the freeway sentence, on the basis of that use type, though he or she might be able to interpret it.

The ideal meaning is expressed here as the coincidence of two points – one is mapped onto the intersection of the linear reference object with the crosspath, the other onto the located object.

- "Physical object at a distance from point, line, or plane"
  In

> *The first rest stop is at a distance of three miles.*
> *The mine is at a depth of 300 feet.*
> *The airplane is at 10,000 feet.*

the object of the preposition does not refer to the position of the located object, but rather to a distance which separates that object from a contextually determined reference point, line, or plane. In the first example, there is a reference point most probably associated with the place of the speaker and/or addressee; in the last two examples, there is a reference plane coincident with the surface of the earth. The ideal meaning of *at* is embedded. For instance, in the first example, assuming the reference point is with the speaker, we have:

> *Coincide(PtApprox(RestStop),X)*

where X is a point such that:

> *Distance(PtApprox(Speaker),X)=3 miles*

The relation between X and the point approximating the rest stop is exactly the ideal meaning of *at*. One could think of the sentence as derived by deletion from *The rest stop is at a place three miles from here.*

9.2 The preposition "on"

I have adopted as the ideal meaning of *on*:

> *on*: for a geometrical construct X to be contiguous with a line or surface Y; if Y is the surface of an object O_Y, and X is the space occupied by another object O_X, for O_Y to support O_X.

The use types are:

> Spatial entity supported by physical object
> Accident/object as part of physical object
> Physical object attached to another
> Physical object transported by a large vehicle
> Physical object contiguous with another
> Physical object contiguous with a wall
> Physical object on part of itself
> Physical object over another
> Spatial entity located on geographical location
> Physical or geometrical object contiguous with a line
> Physical object contiguous with edge of geographical area

• "Spatial entity supported by physical object"

An object is supported by another if its weight presses or pulls upon it; the supporting object then resists the push or pull (these naive ideas about the physics of support are the only ones relevant to semantic structure). Talmy (1985) describes the important role played by the notions of exertion of force and resistance to force in structuring both grammar and some lexical domains. Among prepositions, he cites *against* as clearly expressing this dynamic, but so does *on* in a large class of uses, the force being weight.

There are many different ways two objects can cohere so one supports the other. In the prototypical case, the located object rests on a free, horizontal, upward facing surface of the reference object; this need not be a top surface, though it almost always is an outer surface (otherwise *in* is preferred):

> *the suitcase on the stairway*
> *the man on the chair*
> *the music score on the piano*

The surface may not be horizontal, and may support only part of the weight of the located object:

> *the ladder on the wall*
> *the painting on the easel*

But the located object may also hang:

> *the coat on the hanger*
> *the laundry on the line*

adhere:

> *the label on the box*
> *the steam on the window*
> *the paint on the walls*
> *the stain on the cloth*
> *the fly on the ceiling*

be joined by nails, screws, or other mechanical devices:

> *the lamp on the ceiling*
> *the knob on the door*

have its movement restricted because of its geometry and that of the reference object:

> *the ring on his finger*
> *The key is on the door.*
> *the shoes on her feet*

The joining may be so intimate that the relation shades into a "part of" relation – objecthood itself is not a clear-cut attribute. In

> *the characters on the page*

one may be speaking of small material bodies of ink adhering to the paper, or the characters may be viewed as part of a page (this example should then be fitted in the use type "accident/object part of physical object").

The located object in this use type can be any physical object, event or activity (support and contiguity then usually hold of the agent), and the reference object can be an object part or a physical surface in addition to an ordinary object:

> *He slept on the tile floor.*
> *the sweat on his forehead*
> *There is a film of oil on the surface of this tool.*

It cannot be a point or a line. In the following examples:[5]

> *A gnat lighted on the tip of the pencil.*
> *The balance beam rests on a knife edge.*

the tip of the pencil and the knife edge are not conceived respectively as a geometric point and a line, but as offering a very small or thin surface for support.

We know that support may be indirect – that is the two objects may be separated by other objects, thus not contiguous. Acceptability of such expressions does not depend only on the thinness of the intermediary object(s): thus, in Figure 9.1(a), "Ulysses" is *on the table*, but the lid is not on the table in 9.1(b), even if it is closer to the table than "Ulysses". And in 9.1(c), although the brick is as high as the jar, the lid is *on the table* again.

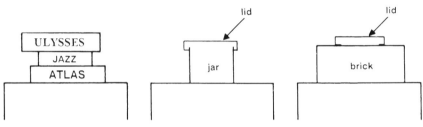

(a) *"Ulysses" is on the table.*   (b) **The lid is on the table.*   (c) *The lid is on the table.*
Figure 9.1

Salience helps explain these apparent contradictions. The relation between the lid and its jar is salient, it typically matters (we can infer from it that the jar is closed, that its contents are protected, etc.); to ignore it would be misleading. The relations between "Ulysses" and the book under, or between the lid and the brick, are not salient in the same manner.

Boggess (1979) notes that one would not say in 9.1(a) above: *"Ulysses" is on the atlas.* In her account, this relates to object hierarchies that play a role in search strategies. Someone who wishes to direct an addressee to some object in a complex environment, say a room with many objects, makes use of an imposed hierarchy. The arcs in this hierarchy represent relations of direct support and immediate inclusion; some nodes are landmarks, being particularly salient, usually because of their size relative to the objects just below them in the hierarchy. An efficient way to direct someone is then to point to the landmarks along a path from the root to the desired object. So one might say something like *The keys are on the brick on the desk in the living room* (Boggess' example).[6]

This hierarchy gives clues to the use of *on* with indirect support. One can say *A is on B* when an object C separates A from B, only if B is a landmark. The atlas in 9.1(a) cannot constitute such a landmark, but the table clearly does, thus the difference in acceptability between *"Ulysses" is on the table* and ?[*]*"Ulysses" is on the atlas.* Note that if the atlas were very much larger than the books above it, or salient in other ways (for instance, if it was always stored in the same place, and if the speaker knew the addressee was aware of that fact), *"Ulysses" is on the atlas* could be appropriate.

One must consider not only the salience of objects but also the salience of relations to explain the use of *on* in the case of indirect support. The inappropriateness of *The lid is on the table* in 9.1(b) is not explained by the salience of the jar as an object, since in 9.1(c), with a brick that has the same claim to salience as the jar, that sentence would be acceptable.

If there is contiguity and support, but also containment, then *in* generally takes precedence over *on*; so *on* generally implies contiguity with an outer surface of the reference object. But sometimes *on* can be used although there is surrounding: in one type of case, contiguity is highly relevant (Section 6.2); in the other, surrounding is limited, and containment becomes a minor function in relation to support:

> *the potato on/in the dish*
> *the man on/in the chair*

Note that one could not say:

> **the man on the armchair*
> **the man in the stool*
> **the pear on the bowl*

which shows that the degree of surrounding constrains the choice between *on* and *in*. Only *on* is acceptable with trays: the function of a tray is exclusively conceived as one of support:

> **The potato is in the tray.*

Finally, in *Jo is on the bus*, there is containment, but this example will be covered by another use type ("physical object transported by a large vehicle").

• "Accident/object part of physical object"
The located object is part of the reference object in:

> *the carving on the stone*
> *the crack on the wall*
> *the windows on the front of the building*
> *the handle on the basket*
> *the lines on his forehead*
> *the mark on the scale*
> *a bump on his head*
> *the freckles on his face*

A variety of spatial entities besides three-dimensional physical parts can be so located: surface accidents, gaps, etc. The located object must constitute a separate relief, something that appears as if it were "stuck" on the rest of the object and the rest of the object offered a surface for support, thus the unacceptability of:

> *the surface on the table*
> *the rim on the vase*

- "Physical object attached to another"

On can be used to express a relation of attachment; there may or may not be support, suggesting that attachment is the more important relation:

> *a dog on a leash*
> *a medal on a chain*
> *the pears on the branch*

- "Physical object transported by a large vehicle"
  In:

> *the children on the bus*
> *the crew on the boat*
> *the police officers on the subway*
> *The luggage is still on the plane.*

on is used, although containment is salient. The vehicle must have a relatively large surface or floor that supports the travellers. If the vehicle is small, surrounding becomes more salient, and *on* becomes less acceptable:

> *the customer on the taxi*
> *the fisherman on the canoe*

are not acceptable. The vehicle must be in the course of travel, even if it is not moving at the particular moment at which the sentence applies.
- "Physical object contiguous with another"
  In

> *the lock on his forehead*
> *The collar felt stiff on the nape of his neck.*
> *with his head bowed on his breast*
> *Do not put your dirty fingers on my clean suit!*

the located object is not supported by the reference object. These examples all involve body parts; except for these and similar exceptions, support is required when *on* is used to relate two physical objects. When there is contiguity without support, one must use *against*. Thus of two boxes side by side, or of a chair against a door, one will not say:

> *The blue box is on the red one.*
> *The chair is on the door.*

(Another exception is *On the left wall, there is a chest of drawers*, but that example and others with *wall* are very idiomatic, and justify a particular use type.)

We find here that a term implies different relations, depending on which distinctions are significant (a similar phenomenon explained why *at* implies exact coincidence with geometric points). If the related objects are such that it is typically "important" to distinguish situations where one supports the other from situations where the two simply touch, then *on* is restricted to the situations with support and contrasts with *against*, which must be used in the absence of support. If, on the other hand, the distinction is irrelevant, as it normally is for body parts, then the contrast between *on* and *against* disappears (or at least no longer occurs along the dimension of support). If I put my hand on your shoulder, it typically matters little whether I let its weight rest on you or not; *on* cannot then imply that a relation of support holds as opposed to simple contact.

In

> *the shadow on the wall*
> *the image on the movie screen*
> *a point on a plane*

support is irrelevant since shadows, screen images, and points are immaterial. Contiguity is only an appearance with shadows and images: shadows appear like planar objects (although they actually correspond to the intersection of a conical shaded region with a surface), touching the plane on which they appear; a similar description applies to screen images.

So support is irrelevant in this use type, either because the objects are immaterial or because its presence or absence is typically of no consequence: there is only contiguity, real or apparent.

Note that although contiguity itself is symmetric, all examples in this use type are asymmetric:

> **the wall on the shadow*
> **his forehead on the lock*
> **a plane on a point*

No doubt, this reflects the normal Figure/Ground relationship. Yet one also feels that the situation described should resemble one of support: since the supporting object is typically larger and more stable than the supported object, such a resemblance would demand that the larger and more stable of the two objects be the reference object.

- "Physical object contiguous with a wall"

In

> *On the left wall, there is a chest of drawers.*

the wall does not support the chest. Such examples appear quite idiomatic. Thus, a restricting qualifier like *left, back* or *further* must be present, or one must use *against*:

> *?* The chest of drawers is on the wall.*
> *The chest of drawers is against the wall*

The sentence with *on* suggests that the chest is supported by the wall. The only words that can be substituted for *wall* with the same effect are very close synonyms (e.g., *partition*).

• "Physical object on part of itself"

When an object is resting on a supporting surface, one may use *on* to indicate its relation to a part of it contiguous with the supporting surface:

> *the man on his back*
> *a table on three legs*
> *Can you stand on your feet?*

The ideal meaning clearly underlies the interpretation of those phrases: the situation described resembles one of support; it is as if the lowest part of the located object provided support for the rest. The sentence:

> *He stood, supported by two strong legs.*

provides evidence for this way of conceptualizing the relation between object and part.

Another possibility is for located and reference objects to be distinct parts of the same object:

> *the head on his broad shoulders*

Again, the head appears as if supported by the shoulders.

• "Physical object over another"

There are some examples where there is neither support nor contiguity; the located object is, or appears to be, over (in the sense that a mask is *over* a face) the reference object:

> *the dark clouds on the island*
> *His eye fixed, through the telescopic sight, upon the crosshair on the*
> *soldier's chest.*

These cannot be misunderstood, because of what we know about clouds and gun-sights. Although those are the only such examples I found, I suppose one could make up still others where the same conditions hold: the range of possible relations between located and reference object in these examples excludes contiguity or support, or contiguity and support do not correspond to significant distinctions for these objects, so the use of *on* can simply indicate superposition without contact.

• "Spatial entity located on geographical location"
There are a number of geographical locations with which one may or must use *on* to indicate that an object or an event is located in them. In these situations, the ideas of support and contiguity, though not very remote, are not central; simple location in the area is implied:

> *the players on the football field*
> *There is a demonstration on the plaza.*
> *The biology lab is on the campus.*
> *They exploded an A-bomb on a small island.*
> *The highest mountain on the continent is Mont Blanc.*
> *The ceiling lights on the third floor are not working.*
> *There is a parking space on the next block.*

Support and contiguity are implied with the football field and with the plaza (for the participants in the demonstration), but it is clear that focus is not on these. They are irrelevant in the other examples (except perhaps in the campus example, where if the geometric description is taken to be the ground area, the biology lab is at least indirectly supported by it).

With the third floor and the football field, one cannot substitute *in* for *on* to express general location, for no discernible reason other than convention, since one says

> *the furniture in the basement*
> *the grape pickers in the field*

In the other examples, one can use *in* instead of *on* to express general location in an almost synonymous manner, although use of *in* seems rarer.

Here is a partial list of areas that can be used as reference objects in this use type – first those with which one can also use *in* to mean general location: island, peninsula, land, continent, plain, prairie, pasture, estate; second, those with which only *on* is acceptable: shore, beach, coast, promontory, cape, earth, ranch, farm, campus, mountain (in the singular only; one says *in the mountains*), any landing or playing field, floor, and block.

• "Physical or geometrical object contiguous with a line"
Examples of locative expressions in this use type are:

> *a point on the bisector line*
> *Is Lima on the equator?*
> *The lake is on a straight line leading from here to the peak.*
> *a village on the border*
> *The sun was on the horizon.*
> *He stood on the edge of the cliff.*
> *a city on the road to Versailles*

The reference object may be an imaginary line (equator, border, etc.), an edge, or a pathway, which is then viewed as a line by approximation.

- "Physical object contiguous with edge of geographical area"

The areas allowed in this use type fall into three categories: open spaces, bodies of water, and all manner of pathways:

> *a shop on the main square*
> *a garden on the lake*
> *a city on the ocean*
> *the store on Polk Street*
> *a room on the patio*
> *a house on the park*
> *the gas station on the freeway*

Cities, states, etc., cannot be used here:

> **a city on Kansas*
> **a suburb on New York*

The located object must be contiguous with the edge of the area, but it must also be outside that area. This is not true if one says *on the edge of X* as opposed to *on X*. Thus, in:

> *a playground on the edge of the park*

the playground could be inside the park.

The located object must be attached and relatively large. One cannot say:

> **The truck is on the park.*
> **the stone on the lake*

to mean that the truck is on the edge of the park, and the stone next to the lake. The located object itself may be an area; yet such examples are not reversible:

> **the lake on the park*
> **the street on the nearby playground*

This accords with the normal Figure/Ground relationship. Typically, parks are conceptually movable with respect to lakes – being less conspicuous and less clearly bounded than lakes. And, typically, the location of playgrounds is not as well known as that of streets, which makes playgrounds conceptually movable with respect to streets.

9.3 The preposition "in"

The ideal meaning is:

in: inclusion of a geometric construct in a one-, two-, or three-dimensional geometric construct

The descriptions in this section are very succinct, since much has been covered in Section 4.1. Here are the use types of *in* considered:

Spatial entity in container
Gap/object "embedded" in physical object
Physical object "in the air"
Physical object in outline of another, or of a group of objects
Spatial entity in part of space or environment
Accident/object part of physical or geometric object
Person in clothing
Spatial entity in area
Physical object in a roadway
Person in institution
Participant in institution

• "Spatial entity in container"
The three-dimensional reference object has an interior, in which the located object, also three-dimensional, is fully or partially contained. The interior may be fully surrounded by the object:

the preserves in the sealed jar

it may be defined by a cup-like concavity:

the milk in the glass
The baby is sleeping in the cradle.
hands in the pocket

by two planes, lines, or quasi-cylindrical objects meeting at an angle:

the chair in the corner
the man in the blue chair
the garbage in the gutter
Point C is in angle r.
The cat was sitting in the fork of the two branches.

it may consist of several spaces bounded by two planes at an angle:

the dried flowers in the book

or be the hole of a torus shaped object:

the foot in the stirrup
the finger in the ring

or the reference object may itself be a hole:

the man in the doorway
the mouse in the hole in the wall

Complete closure is relatively rare, so some boundaries of the interior will usually be imaginary, but quite well-defined. For instance, one side of the interior of a container is a plane through its rim, two sides of the interior of a tunnel are planes through its ends. One may have to imagine the boundaries in more than one or two places:

the bird in a cage
a bird in the hand

Occasionally, boundaries are vague:

The child hid in the folds of her dress.

Possible reference objects for this use type include: bowls, boxes, bottles, envelopes, pockets, closets, cabinets, stomachs, mouths, cars, graves, rooms, buildings, rings, pipes, funnels, seats with a backrest (not stools), arms, windows (as openings), doorways, trenches, gorges, grooves, crevices, etc.

To summarize the detailed description of Section 4.1: when the reference object is a container with an upward facing opening, the located object may be entirely outside its interior if it is one of a group of objects supported by the container; only complete containment may be meant, depending on what the speaker deems to matter; and with reference objects like *corner*, context plays a role in determining how far the corner extends.

Not every concavity qualifies as an interior, and permits the use of *in*; the interior must be functionally significant for artifacts. When the concavity is facing downward, the choice between *in* and *under* is a matter of relevance (see Figure 1.4). With an arch for instance, containment is irrelevant, having no functional significance, so *under* is preferred:

the crowd (*in/under) the arch

• "Gap/object 'embedded' in physical object"
In:

the fish in the water
the nail in the board

the located object is included in the normalized region defined by the reference object, that is, in the part of space its shape would occupy prior to penetration. This goes also for a surface conceptualized as a very thin lamina:

the crack in the surface

The appropriate geometric description differs from the one used in the preceding use type, and the importance of the distinction is reflected in the fact that conjunctions like:

> *There are nails and a hammer in the box.*

cannot be interpreted with the nails "nailed" into, that is embedded in, the box.

This use type includes cases where the located object is a hole or a gap, because the same geometric description function then applies to the reference object:

> *the hole in the wall*
> *the crack in the bowl*
> *a gap in the border*

Note also the acceptability of conjunctions such as:

> *There are holes and nails in this board.*

This use type also includes examples where the located object is dissolved or blended into the reference object:

> *sugar and milk in the coffee*

The naive understanding here is one of particles of sugar and milk having penetrated gaps between particles of coffee. A similar understanding underlies:

> *the water in the washcloth*

Note the use of *inside* with various types of embedding. *Inside* cannot be used with immersion, or "embedding" into a liquid: **inside the water.* But one says *inside the clay*, which contrasts with *in the clay* by implying total containment. *Inside* seems to require the reference object to have an inner side (this excludes **inside the grass, *inside the tree* – except to mean "inside the trunk of the tree" – **inside the coffee*, and **inside the shade*, as it should). Thus it seems that one has no conception of the inner surface of a liquid in which an object is immersed, but one does if the surrounding substance is solid, like clay.

• "Physical object 'in the air'"

The physical object is assumed not only to be "embedded" in the air (this is true typically of most objects), but also to be either entirely surrounded by air, and/or raised high from its typical position:

> *the bird in the air*
> *He raised his glass in the air.*

- "Physical object in outline of another, or of a group of objects"
In

> *the bird in the tree*
> *the squirrel in the grass*
> *a cabin in a grove of aspens*
> *straw in his hair*
> *the worm in the strawberries*

the located object is located within the space defined by the outline of the reference entity – whether that entity consists of a single object or of a group of objects.

- "Spatial entity in part of space or environment"
Here, the located object is included in the overall volume defined by the part of space or environment. This volume will sometimes be unbounded or have vaguely defined boundaries:

> *There is a chair in the middle of the room.*
> *He disappeared in the depths of the mine.*
> *He lives in the vicinity.*
> *the best restaurant in the world*
> *There is no supermarket in the neighborhood.*

Light and shade also define an "environment", often vaguely bounded or unbounded:

> *They sat in the shadow of a tree.*

- "Accident/object part of physical or geometric object"
The located object may be an actual physical part of the reference object:

> *the muscles in his legs*
> *the man in the picture*
> *a page in a book*

or it may be a geometric accident, as in:

> *the crease in his pants*
> *the curve in the road*

The reference object may be one- or two-dimensional:

> *There are points in the line that correspond to integers.*
> *a sharp angle in the edge of the cliff*
> *a bump in the surface*

The part must appear as if surrounded by the rest of the object (**the leg in the table*).

The reference object may also be a group of solid objects, of which the located object is a member:

> *a man in the crowd*
> *Jimmy is in the line for buying tickets.*
> *bodies in the solar system*

- "Person in clothing"
  In

> *a man in a red hat*
> *a woman in high heeled shoes*
> *a Santa Claus in a red coat*

the normal Figure/Ground relationship is inverted. The relation implied is that the person is wearing the clothing, and surrounding is not required:

> *the general in golden epaulets*

But surrounding is clearly at the root of this use and actually occurs in the large majority of cases.

- "Spatial entity in area"
  One cannot use *in* with any piece of surface to mean "included in the area". A line drawn on the top of a table is not *in the top of the table*, but a line drawn on a page might be *in the margin*, though it would be *on the page*, not *in*. The reference object must be one of several areas arising from dividing a surface. One presumably would not be *in* a piece of land alone in outer space, even if there were several such colonies in space, as long as they were separate: one would say *on*. The context surface must have at least two subareas, so one can contrast inclusion in one with inclusion in the other.

I can think of three domains in which such a representation is adequate: geometry (*in the rectangle, in the circle*, etc.), the divisions of a page (*in the margin*), and geography (*in the field, in England*). I have defined geographical locations as three-dimensional entities including air above and earth below (Section 5.1), but one conceptualization is as an area corresponding to the ground they occupy. The ground – this seemingly infinite, seemingly immobile surface which does not belong to a perceivable three-dimensional object – is then viewed as a two-dimensional space, naturally structured into adjacent bounded regions. What is relevant to human life in that space is inclusion in one or the other of these regions.

This division into cells must be intrinsic; it cannot be induced by the use of terms like *side, right half*, etc.:

> **Draw a line in the right half of the blackboard!*

Middle is an exception to this rule: *in the middle* is used regardless of the properties of the object of which it is the middle; in fact *on the middle* is not appropriate (such an exception should be specified in the selection restrictions of the use type).

Some areas are excluded by convention, indicated by the geometric conceptualizations allowed (Section 8.6) for "lawn" and "football field," from being reference objects in this use type:

> *the lounging chair in the lawn*
> *the ball in the football field*

The use of *in* in such cases suggests that the located object is buried. Bodies of water are allowed:

> *There is an island in the lake.*
> *There is an aircraft carrier in the bay.*

with some exceptions:

> *The boat is in the lake.*

will be interpreted as meaning the boat has capsized. A floating boat is *on the lake*.

• "Physical object in a roadway"
  In:

> *There is a truck in the road.*

the truck is perceived as an obstacle. I do not see any way to infer this from the fact that the truck is in the area defined by the road, together with knowledge of roads and trucks. If such an inference were possible, it would follow also from *the truck on the road* and it does not; there is no obvious reason for the idea of an obstacle to arise in connection with *in* rather than *on*.

• "Person in institution"
  The person is in the institution in a typical function associated with it:

> *the man in jail*
> *The children are in school*
> *My son is in the hospital.*
> *the women in church*

The man must be a prisoner, the children are engaged in students' activities, "my son" is a patient, and the women are attending a service. Note the absence of the article in the prepositional object, except with *hospital* (but one says *in hospital* in Britain).

• "Participant in institution"
  The difference with the last use type is that the person need not be

physically in the building of the institution for the locative construction to be true. Thus:

> *The children are in school.*

is actually ambiguous between this use type and the former one, since it could mean that the children are in the school building at this very time, or that they are students. But:

> *My son is in college*

can only be interpreted as meaning the second.

9.4 Conclusion

One principal claim of this book is that a large number of special conventions occurs in the spatial uses of the prepositions, but the motivation for the choice of preposition is generally quite clear, and lies with a link to some geometric ideal – the essence of the preposition's meaning. Since the number of special conventions must of necessity be finite, this led to asserting that the set of uses of a preposition divides into use types derived from a geometric ideal. I believe this study of *at, on,* and *in* brings substance and clarity to this claim. The metaphor of a musical theme (the ideal meaning) with variations (use types) is instructive, in that, though there is no question that a resemblance is seen between the theme and a variation, there are no simple rules that transform one into the other. There are many different ways the ideal meaning can be manifested in a use type. So, though it is clear that it makes sense to use a given preposition in some situation, it would often also make sense to use another. Only convention justifies the correct choice.

As with all categorization in natural language, the distinctions between use types are sometimes, but not always, well-drawn. So, for instance, it is not clear whether one would want *the man at the door* to fit in "person using artifact" or in "spatial entity at location". I think such doubt reflects actual wavering of a language user's intuitions: in such cases, he or she is not quite sure in which category the expression falls. In interpreting the expression, a hearer will favor but not require that the man be using the door; that fact carries some weight in interpreting the expression, but it is not crucial. In general, use type constraints are not clear-cut. A formal representation of this categorical imprecision is difficult to imagine.

10   The projective prepositions

English includes a set of prepositions which are used to define directions about an object, and then specify the location of another object in relation to these directions. I have called these prepositions "projective", because all fundamentally involve the experience of viewing and the idea of a point of observation. Viewing, either in actual fact or through an act of imagination, allows human beings to specify a frame of reference. I will concentrate on the prepositions expressing basically relative position in an horizontal plane (only a few of these consist of one word, most are composite expressions):[1]

> *(at/on/to/by) the (left/right) of*
> *(at/on/in/to/by) the (left/right) {hand} side of*
> *(at/on/in/to/by) the (front/back/side) of*
> *in (front/back) of*
> *before/behind*
> *(right/back/left) of*

and consider those expressing vertical order only in passing:

> *above/below*
> *over/under*
> *(at/on/in/by) the (top/bottom) of*
> *on top of*

The frame of reference presupposed by these prepositions consists of six half-line axes[2] with origin at the reference object: the "front", "back", "right", "left", "up", and "down" axes. I will call these the **base axes**. One of the six base axes is associated with each projective preposition, except some composites with *side*, which may indicate right or left.

This chapter is not organized by preposition and use type, because description of the use-types is naturally factored between (a) the specification of the base axes, and (b) the specification of the parts of space on or near these axes where the located object must be. So Section 10.1 concerns the frame of reference: it examines how, given an appropriate use of a projective preposition, the addressee can infer the base axes by combining knowledge of the context and of the reference object. Since the answer depends only marginally on the particular preposition used, the discussion applies to all projective prepositions. Once a frame of reference is inferred, one of the base axes (or two axes, left and right, in combinations with *side* and no restricting qualifier) is selected according to which morpheme the preposition includes: *front, back, right, left, side, -fore,* or *-hind.* The remaining morphemes constituting the preposition (*at, on, in, be-,* etc.) signal different ways of constraining the location on or near the axis chosen, and some subtle but distinct contextual conditions of use. These are examined in Section 10.2, where the prepositions will be sorted into three overlapping groups. The question of the distinction between use types will be addressed in the course of these descriptions. In 10.3 ideal meanings are offered for a subset of the projective prepositions.

10.1 Frame of reference

A human being learns to construct a frame of reference starting from two basic experiences: the experience of his or her own body standing upright on horizontal ground, with eyes looking straight ahead (the "canonical position"), and the experience of encountering another human being face to face (the "canonical encounter") (Clark 1973). A frame of reference with a particular order of the base axes is associated with each experience. Indeed, the entire range of possible ways to specify a frame of reference is organized around these two experiences as prototypes, which I will call the **coincidence situation** and the **encounter situation** (for reasons that will soon become clear). After describing the two prototype situations and showing how they are manifested in a range of characteristic uses of the projective prepositions, I will give a detailed account of how a language user combines knowledge of the reference object and of the context to specify the frame of reference (properties of the located object bear only marginally on the specification of the frame of reference).

10.1.1 The two prototype situations

A human being in canonical position defines six half-line axes with origin at him/herself (Figure 10.1). The down axis follows the direction of the gravitational field and the up axis is opposed to it. The four other axes are in an horizontal plane: the direction in which the observer's eyes are facing defines the front axis, and the back axis is opposed to the front one; right and left axes are orthogonal to the front-back line.

With the picture plane taken as the ground plane, and the upward vertical orthogonal to that plane directed toward the reader (most figures from now on will follow that convention), we get horizontal axes arranged as in Figure 10.2.

The projective prepositions

For human beings, the direction of the perceptual apparatus is also the normal direction of movement, and an horizontal direction within the only plane of symmetry of the human body. The critical factor in determining "the front" is not the direction of movement itself, since crabs are said to walk "sideways" (Fillmore 1971). No similar example allows us to say whether symmetry or direction of vision is most important in defining a front, but it would seem the latter, since the experience of viewing shows through in every use of the projective prepositions.

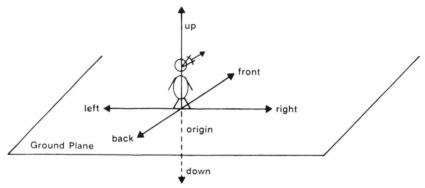

The canonical position
Figure 10.1

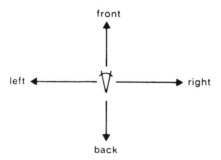

Horizontal axes of an observer in canonical position
Figure 10.2

Distinguishing right from left presents difficulties, because, "There are no simpler concepts in terms of which the notions 'left' and 'right' can be explicated" (Fillmore 1971). Even to define "clockwise order" one must finally resort to the notions right and left. As Fillmore puts it, "There is a basic sense of the terms 'left' and 'right' by which humans are taught to find left and right on their own bodies, and it is likely that this can be learned only by demonstration."

There is another way to define front, back, left and right axes, as exemplified by *The cat is to the right of Mary from where I stand*. Because of the phrase *from where I stand*, we know that the point of view adopted is not Mary's, but some observer's – in this instance, the speaker's. Here, the axes are as in Figure 10.3.

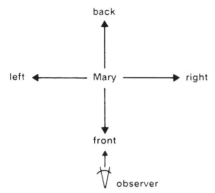

Horizontal axes defined by a canonical encounter
Figure 10.3

The situation depicted is the "canonical encounter": "What are the characteristics of the most usual interaction between two people, John and Mary? ...the most important property is that they will be facing each other a short distance apart. It is in this position that John and Mary are situated for the optimal perception of messages – both verbal and nonverbal – from the other person ...If John and Mary were side-by-side, or back-to-back, these conditions would no longer be optimal." (Clark 1973) In this situation, the speaker in effect "combines" the point of view of the person encountered with his or her own. Thus the axes are taken about Mary; the front and back axes are those of Mary, pointing in directions opposite to those of the onlooker; but right and left axes have the same direction as the observer's right and left, the opposite of Mary's right and left. Clark suggests this failure to reverse can be attributed to the symmetry of the left and right directions: indeed, this symmetry makes the left/right distinction hard to learn and even linguistically proficient adults often confuse the two. The difficulty would probably be overwhelming if, besides drawing the distinction correctly on themselves, speakers and hearers had to reverse right and left.

Thus, there are two possible orders of the axes: in the encounter situation, the base axes are in **mirror order** (clockwise is back-right-front-left), and in the coincidence situation (where observer and reference object in effect coincide), they are in **basic order** (clockwise is back-left-front-right).

10.1.2 Prepositional uses derived from the prototype situations
Of course a projective preposition may be used with an inanimate
reference object and without explicit reference to an observer. Yet, one
can always infer a point of observation (which I will call the **effective point
of observation**), and discern an encounter or a coincidence situation, if only
metaphorically. And once the mapping with one or the other prototype
situation is defined, the frame of reference (i.e., the base axes) is
completely determined.

By "point of observation " I mean an abstraction from the notion of
observer consisting of: a point or quasi-point in space (corresponding to
the observer's eye); the line of sight (a half axis oriented away from the
observer); and the observer's intrinsic up axis (not necessarily aligned with
the gravitational vertical). The other axes can be deduced from those
yielding a set similar to base axes in basic order, but the two play different
roles: base axes constitute a frame or reference about the reference object
for the purpose of locating objects; a point of observation encapsulates
where a real or imaginary observer stands and looks, allowing one to
ascribe base axes to the reference object.

A few characteristic examples should help clarify matters.

> *(1) The cat is in front of the tree.*

Here, we must assume an observer not explicitly mentioned, perhaps the
speaker. This is a metaphorical equivalent of an encounter situation, with
the tree playing the role of the person encountered. Observer and tree are
probably on the same horizontal ground, the observer in canonical
position. One can define base axes, in mirror order, with origin at the tree.
In front of the tree then points to a part of space between the tree and the
observer. The effective point of observation corresponds to the observer.

Note that a front can be induced on an inanimate object by facing it, but
a right orientation cannot be induced on an object situated on the speaker's
right, which points to the salience of the canonical encounter and of the
front direction (Kimball 1974).

> *(2) The red billiard ball was in front of the white one.*

This example could be interpreted like the preceding one, but if the
white ball is rolling, one may think of it as some "observer" with line of
sight in its direction of movement. This is a metaphorical equivalent of the
coincidence situation, with an effective point of observation coincident
with the reference object (i.e., the white ball). This point of observation is
virtual, since it does not correspond to an actual observer. One can define
base axes in basic order with origin at the center of the white ball. *In front
of* then points to a part of space adjacent to the white ball and with the
front axis as its axis of symmetry.

> *(3) The seats at the back of the theater were empty.*

The back of a theater (for someone inside it) is normally defined by imagining some observer placed inside the theater, at its center, and facing the stage. The axes of this virtual observer, in basic order, will serve to define internal parts of space corresponding to *on the right side of, at the back of,* etc.

> *(4) The bag is behind the chair.*

This may be interpreted using an imaginary observer sitting in normal position in the chair. Since, for the purpose of this expression, one may think of the observer and the chair as indistinguishable, one can define base axes in basic order with origin at the chair, identical to the observer's axes. A coincidence situation underlies this use: the effective (and virtual) point of observation coincides with the chair.

> *(5) A circle is drawn on the right side of the page.*

This example illustrates the possibility of base axes rotated with respect to the vertical. If the page is pinned to a wall obliquely, *the right side* may still be defined intrinsically to the sheet of paper, as follows: base axes are ascribed to the page by a canonical observer facing it, with the page vertical and oriented for normal reading, and those axes are then rotated along with the page. This is a case of encounter: the base axes are in mirror order. An effective virtual point of observation can be specified, some distance from the wall on an orthogonal to the page at its center, with its own up axis tilted so it is parallel to the intrinsic top-bottom direction of the page.

In some cases, only two of the eight axes can be defined. For example, *to the right of the rocket* cannot be interpreted intrinsically to the rocket in the absence of gravity (Fillmore 1971), though *in front of the rocket* can; the location and facing direction of a virtual point of observation coincident with the rocket can be specified, but there is no axis to play the role of the vertical, so right and left base axes remain undefined.

The five examples offered illustrate the main theses of this chapter: one of the two prototype situations underlies every appropriate use of the projective prepositions, and an effective point of observation, real or virtual, can be defined in every case. That point of observation can either be matched onto the reference object (examples (2), (3), and (4)) – the prototype situation is then coincidence, and the base axes are in basic order; or it may be some distance from the reference object – the prototype is then encounter, and the base axes are in mirror order (examples (1) and (5)). The effective point of observation is related to the base axes in two ways: in the coincidence case, its own front, left, back, and right define corresponding base axes (Figure 10.4(a)); in the encounter case, base axes and axes of the point of observation are symmetric, the plane of symmetry being the bisector of the segment joining the point of observation to the reference object (Figure 10.4(b)).

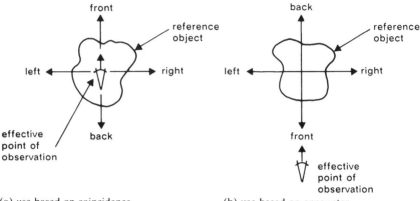

(a) use based on coincidence   (b) use based on encounter

Role of the coincidence and encounter situations in prepositional uses
Figure 10.4

In either case, the origin of the base axes is always with the reference object, being either that object itself when it is a point or viewed as a point, or some (usually central) point of it.[3]

The effective point of observation may correspond to an explicit or implicit observer in the context (speaker, hearer, or third person) (example (1)), to some typical user (examples (3) and (4)), or to some object which is seen as an observer by a metaphorical process (example (2)); or it may be obtained by rotation of the point of observation corresponding to a typical user (example (5)).

It is actually possible to define base axes in ways other than those illustrated by the above examples. Specification of the base axes involves several parameters (for instance, their origin, order, and the directions of the front and up axis provide a full specification), and there is great flexibility in the way elements from the situational and sentential context can be picked out to define each parameter: location and orientation characteristics from different sources may collaborate in defining the base axes.

Fillmore (1971) and Clark (1973), in two fundamental papers on the projective prepositions, miss some uses because they fail to see this last point. (Sondheimer (1974) clarifies many interesting details of these prepositions' uses, but fails to offer a complete picture for the same reason.) Clark introduces the two fundamental cases – one with base axes in basic order, and one where they are defined by the canonical encounter, in mirror order. He assumes that the axes are "intrinsic" in the first case, and "egocentric" in the second (that is, defined by an observer in the context). But in effect, these are independent dimensions: the intrinsic/egocentric possibilities can occur with either of the two order possibilities. So, at the very least, there are four categories: intrinsic and basic order (*in front of me*), intrinsic and mirror order (*in front of the closet*), egocentric and basic order (rare, but not impossible, as in *to the right of the stool* defined by the speaker while sitting on the stool), and finally egocentric and mirror order (*to the right of the vase*; if the vase is symmetric, one must resort to an observer in the context to define *the right*). (Note that I call "intrinsic" axes defined by a typical user of an object, which conforms to usual practice.) In fact, as we will see, there are even more categories, for two reasons: (a) the direction of the base axes may be intrinsic to objects other than the reference object, as in *The ashtray is on my desk, to the right of the phone book*, where the direction of the right axis is presumably defined intrinsically to the desk – parallel to its long axis – rather than the phone book (though the origin of that axis is at the phone book); (b) an observer and an object may contribute complementary constraints to the specification of the direction of the base axes, so that there are in effect "mixed" cases. As an example, consider *to the right of the road*: "the right" would be defined both by the geometry of the road – the front-back axis being normally coincident with its spine – and by an observer, real or imaginary, since there can be no right without an implied direction of travel.

Fillmore considers the different orders (basic and mirror) possible with axes intrinsic to the reference object (corresponding to the contrast between *in front of me* and *in front of the closet*), and "deictic" cases, where the base axes, in mirror order, are specified entirely by an observer in the context, but he also leaves out the other possibilities. I will use the term **deictic** to qualify base axes ascribed by recourse to an observer in the context, and **partly deictic** in examples like the one with the road.

10.1.3 Inferring base axes

To interpret an expression with a projective preposition, the addressee must figure out the frame of reference intended by the speaker. Conversely, a speaker building up such an expression must abide by certain rules, so the addressee can figure out the frame of reference intended.

What does figuring out a frame of reference imply? How is a frame of reference specified? One way to fully determine the six base axes is by (a) specifying the origin of the axes in relation to the reference object, (b) specifying the order of the horizontal axes as basic or mirror order, (c) selecting a given direction as that of the up axis, (d) selecting another direction, orthogonal to the up axis, as that of the front axis.

One difficulty with the above characterization is the expression "a given direction". A direction can be defined only in relation to some frame of reference taken – however provisorily – as absolute. In ordinary circumstances, the earth itself is conceived of as fixed; so at every point of its surface, one could define an absolute frame of reference using the vertical, together with, say, the north-south and east-west directions. But of these, only the vertical is so constantly obvious to human perception that it is always in the background as a privileged absolute reference direction. The other directions are specified in relation to objects in the environment.

The specification of the base axes entirely follows from that of the effective point of observation, real or virtual, chosen by the speaker. So any constraint on the set of base axes boomerangs as one on the effective point of observation, and vice-versa; I will speak in terms of one or the other, according to what is easier to grasp.

The following sections will examine how the various parameters defining the base axes – origin, order, and directions – can be related to located and reference objects, and to context, and how, as a context frequently holds many possibilities for frames of reference, an addressee can extract the one implied by the speaker.

10.1.4 Origin of the base axes

As noted, the origin of the base axes is always with the reference object. The located object may be outside, inside, or touching the reference object. When it is outside, the degree of precision appropriate to the specification of its location is often such that "with the reference object" is a sufficient definition of the origin. Thus, in *The house is to the right of the tree*, given the relative sizes of a normal house and tree and the inherent vagueness of the expression, there would be no sense in providing a precise location of the origin (moving it throughout the tree would bring only negligible shifts of the base axes, as far as the location of the house is concerned). In such cases, one may assume that the reference object is viewed as a point. If the reference object is very large, it may be necessary to pick out a point of it: depending on the context, this may simply be where an observer is looking (Section 10.2.4), or an intrinsically salient point – for instance, with *The squirrel is to the right of the tree*, the speaker may intend the axes to originate at the place where the trunk meets the ground.

In contrast, when the located object is inside, or touching, the reference object, it is always necessary to specify the origin more precisely than "with the reference object". It is often placed at the center of visual mass of the reference object (i.e., the center of gravity of an object of uniform density occupying the same space), or at some salient point. For instance, in *the seats in the (right hand side)/front of the classroom*, the axes delimiting front, sides, etc. may originate at the center of visual mass of the room, but if there were some salient line dividing the room (e.g., an aisle), the speaker could intend the origin to be on it.

10.1.5 Order of the horizontal base axes

As we have seen, the effective point of observation is chosen either as coincident with the reference object, in an analogy with a prototype situation of coincidence, or as away and facing it, in an analogy with a situation of encounter. In the first case, the base axes are in basic order, in the second in mirror order (Figure 10.4).

A speaker can choose axes in basic order in the following situations:

– the reference object is a person: the effective point of observation is chosen to correspond to that person (*She was seated to the right of the president*);

– the reference object is a moving object, or movable in one privileged direction (*in front of the arrow*): the effective point of observation is chosen so the direction of vision is that of the movement (movement only defines a front axis, but however the up axis is defined, right and left will be such that the order will be basic);

– the reference object is worn by or a part of a person (*in front of his nose, on the front/(right side) of your shirt*): the effective point of observation may then be defined by translating the point of observation associated with the person so its origin is with the reference object;

– the reference object is such that one sits or lies on it in typical use: the effective point of observation may be chosen as corresponding to the typical user (*to the right of the chair/bed*);

– the reference object is a room, building, etc.: the effective point of observation is chosen as that of a person at its center (Figure 10.5(a)); this is possible with spaces which are used facing a specific direction (theater, church, etc.) – the front is then ahead of the user, and the back behind.

In all these situations (this list, though not complete, probably covers most cases where axes in basic order are possible), the effective point of observation is clearly in very close association with the reference object, being in fact sometimes even coincident with it.

If it is possible to postulate an effective point of observation away from the reference object (corresponding for instance to an observer in the context, or to a typical user), one can construct a prepositional use based on an analogy with encounter. For instance, in a situation where the reference object is a room, garden, etc., it is possible to define the front by means of the main access (Figure 10.5(b)): it is as if the observer "encountered" the space of the room. Thus, *at the back of the room* may refer to an area furthest away from where an observer stands upon entering

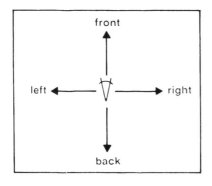
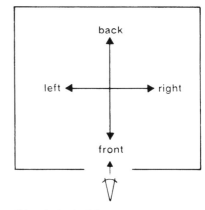

(a) *at the back of the classroom*   (b) *at the back of the room*
Figure 10.5

the room. There are of course many more commonplace examples of encounter (*in front of the closet, to the right of the tree*, etc.).

10.1.6 Direction of the base axes

"Direction" indicates here something more general than an oriented line: any parallel to such a line which points the same way has the same direction.[4] There are three possible sources of constraints on the directions of the up and front axes: first, gravity provides a directed line (oriented downward by convention) at every point in space, thus a **privileged direction**, a strong candidate for the direction of the down base axis; second, the reference object and/or other nearby objects may provide other privileged directions – candidates for the directions of the front and up axes; third, an observer – speaker, addressee, third person – can be used to specify these directions, either alone (purely deictic cases), or in conjunction with privileged directions (partly deictic cases).
• Privileged directions
  A privileged direction for the up axis is simply the gravitational vertical; but it can also be intrinsic to some object. A privileged direction for the front axis is always intrinsic to some object – sometimes the reference object (as with *in front of me*), but sometimes another (as with *The ashtray is on my desk, to the right of the phone book* when the base axes are parallel to the axes of the desk). In the latter case, the object providing privileged directions either supports or contains the reference object, or has the reference object as a part.
  Privileged directions intrinsic to objects arise because of a variety of factors: (1) the way they stand or sit in normal circumstances; (2) symmetry; (3) the way they are used; or (4) their resemblance to a human being.

(1) Many objects have a normal orientation with respect to the gravitational vertical – for instance, trees, tables, dishes, houses, animals, posters, etc. The direction of the base up axis may be specified as the upward direction intrinsic to that object; it will be aligned with the gravitational vertical when the object is in normal position, but at an angle otherwise. So in *All the branches in the tree above the first two are dead*, the direction of the up axis is defined intrinsically to the tree (note that is not the reference object), and the tree could have been felled so that direction would not coincide with the gravitational vertical. For objects that can be used indifferently with one orientation and "upside down" (a reversible place mat for instance), there are two privileged directions with respect to the object.

(2) Symmetry constrains the direction of the up and front axes: if an object has a plane of symmetry, up and front axes, when defined intrinsically to it, must be in that plane. So the front and up axes of a violin are in its plane of symmetry although its normal orientation (whether during performance, or when laid down) is not such that the up axis is vertical (and the front axis horizontal). The base axes may be parallel to the plane of symmetry of an object containing or supporting the reference object: for instance, if the two objects of *the radiator behind the wastebasket* are in a rectangular room, the speaker may choose to ascribe to the wastebasket a front axis horizontal and parallel to one of the room's planes of symmetry, overlooking him/herself as a point of observation.

(Note that for a violin, constraints other than those imposed by symmetry must be called upon to define the axes: the front must be the side with strings (for reasons explained further below); and the top must be where the tuning pegs are, presumably because of intuitions about balance, which make us favor the wide part of an object as its bottom.)

If an object offers several privileged directions, its environment may introduce an asymmetry that can be used to bring one in focus. For instance, a rectangular table offers four privileged front directions, but if it is against a wall, the only axis of symmetry for the wall/table configuration is normal to the wall. Since approach toward the wall side of the table is impossible (and since encounter is the only plausible underlying prototype), the front axis naturally faces away from the wall. There remains thus only one privileged front direction.

It may be that symmetry constrains the axes because of anthropomorphic metaphor: the human body has one main plane of symmetry, the vertical median plane, and in canonical position, the gravitational vertical and the line of sight are in that plane. But it seems also likely that one Gestalt principle of perceptual organization, the "symmetry principle" (Koffka 1935) is responsible for this. The principle states that symmetric patterns are "better" patterns (so that, for instance, a complex configuration will be preferentially segmented into symmetric patterns); this would also imply that we tend to divide objects along their axes of symmetry.

(3) Objects may provide privileged directions for the front axis also because of the way people normally use or interact with them, or because of anthropomorphic metaphor based on movement or feature-like characteristics. Examples of objects of the first kind are: chairs, closets, movie theaters, church naves, pieces of clothing, pictures, etc. With these, one can define a virtual effective point of observation corresponding to the normal user, and associated front and up privileged directions follow (as does the order of the axes). Normal use does not always indicate a unique set of privileged directions, since some objects have two types of normal users, each facing the other – theaters (actor and audience member), escutcheons (bearer and viewer), name tags (bearer and reader), etc. The speaker must then clarify which role he or she has in mind. Special users may settle upon conventions: the actor's viewpoint conventionally defines stage left and right, and the bearer's the left and right of an escutcheon (Fillmore 1971). Normally, the viewer would define the left and right of a name-tag, probably because reader (and writer) rather than bearer are most concerned with such distinctions. Even without such clearly distinct functions as audience/speaker, reader/bearer, etc., there may be more than one normal use of an object: so a road, door, corridor, etc., have two directions of use, a rectangular table has four.

For buildings, rooms, open spaces (gardens, squares, etc.) a salient use can be found in the way they are accessed (the underlying prototype is then encounter (Figure 10.5(b))). Naturally, there may be more than one way to gain access, but often one is salient: for instance, San Francisco's Golden Gate Park, a narrow rectangle, is most frequently entered from the city end as opposed to the ocean-side end, and that end is usually referred to as *the front of the park*; *the large meadow behind Stowe Lake* is interpreted with the front-back direction of the park ascribed to the lake.

(4) Anthropomorphic metaphor also gives rise to privileged directions. In a strict metaphor, the base axes would naturally be like those of a human being, that is, in basic order. But one can speak of anthropomorphic metaphor even when the underlying prototype is encounter and the axes in mirror order, since the object encountered is treated, somewhat loosely, as if it were another person.

An anthropomorphic metaphor may be motivated by movement: as with human beings when they walk normally, the direction of movement of a moving object defines a front axis direction, as already shown in several examples. Feature-like characteristics also suggest a privileged direction for the front axis: in an analogy with facial features, the side of an object with more striking features tends to be considered the front (Sondheimer 1974). This may explain why the strings of a violin indicate its front. As another example, consider a building with three blind walls and windows in the fourth; the front would probably be the side with windows, even if the only entrance is "in back". Right and left, however, would probably be defined in terms of an encounter with the windowed side. I do not know any case where right and left are defined as in Figure 10.6 (basic order) on the basis of feature-like characteristics alone. Generally, they will be reversed because the typical interaction suggested is that of contemplating those features, which leads to an encounter case.

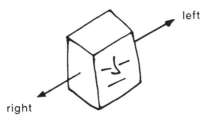

Figure 10.6

Privileged directions may be called "intrinsic", but with care, since they may be intrinsic to an object other than the reference object. Here are two examples besides the several already given: with *the Knight to the right of the Queen*, except in "Through the Looking-Glass", *the right of the Queen* would not normally refer to the Queen's right, but would be defined by an axis of the chessboard, given some player's point of view. And one could say *Paul is behind Tom* using the intrinsic reference frame of a theater, and not that of Tom: that is, Tom could be facing Paul, his back to the stage, with Paul further away from the stage than Tom (Sondheimer 1974).

• Purely deictic axes

Directions may be entirely defined by an observer – the speaker, addressee, third person, or some hypothetical observer other than an unmentioned standard user (excluded here since, by convention, that user defines intrinsic axes). With *The airport is to the left of the freeway, as you go south from San Francisco*, "you" refers to that hypothetical observer whose travel direction allows the addressee to choose between two opposed plausible front axes. In effect, in the purely deictic case, the observer defines not only directions, but the axes themselves, since the front axis must pass through the observer.

There are generally several candidates for the role of observer – most conspicuously the speaker and addressee. Strictly speaking, speaker and addressee cannot both occupy the same location, but, for the purpose of the locative expression at hand, one may consider that they do if they are next to each other and looking more or less in the same direction. But in some cases, such an approximation is not acceptable: so a speaker who faces the addressee must give a clue (linguistic, gestural, etc.) as to whom he or she intends as the observer.

An observer can be used to fully specify a front base axis in the following manner. If the observer is away from the reference object, then he or she must look toward the reference object, and the base axes follow in a standard case of encounter. If the apparent size of the reference object is "large", the base axes may depend on which point the observer picked to look at. If the reference object is small (a stool, fire-hydrant, etc.) and the observer is on it or touching it (sitting on the stool, with one foot on the fire-hydrant), then the front axis may be his or her own: so one might tell someone sitting on a stool *You dropped your handkerchief to the right of your stool.* If the observer is in the reference object, the base axes may be chosen as his or her own axes, but only if that object does not have any privileged directions. So one could say *the street to the right of the park* and mean a right defined by the way one is looking, given a park of indeterminate shape. If the reference object has privileged directions, they generally cannot be ignored and overridden by observer-induced axes; an observer cannot define *(on the right side)/(at the back) of the rectangular room* by facing along a diagonal. And an observer in a round room or coliseum could conceivably talk about something being *on the right side of the coliseum,* using his or her own facing direction to divide the space, but he or she must face toward the center (every diameter defines a privileged direction by virtue of its being an axis of symmetry). If the observer is at the center of the round space, then he or she may face any direction, and base axes may be defined accordingly: it is marginally possible to use *to the right of, at the back of,* etc. in this way.

• Partly deictic axes

When an environment offers several privileged front directions, one can sometimes select one by recourse to an observer. The observer then only partially constrains the base axes, and privileged directions provide other complementary constraints, as in the following examples:

(1) John is behind the door

Consider again a door in a room (Figure 10.7).

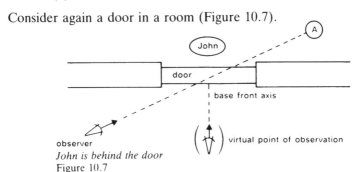

John is behind the door
Figure 10.7

Assume the speaker in the room intends himself or herself as the observer. As we saw, the base front ax's ascribed to the door must be orthogonal to it, since object A is not *behind the door* ; this leaves only two possible directions for that front axis. The presence of the observer in one of the spaces delimited by the door eliminates one of the directions: the base front axis must point toward that same space. The effective point of observation does not coincide with the observer: it is virtual, in the same room as the observer, on the cross-axis of the door, and some distance away from the door.

(2) *The airport is to the left of the freeway.*

Assume this is said by someone traveling on a road parallel to the freeway (Figure 10.8(a)): it can be interpreted by taking a virtual point of observation on the freeway facing the same direction as the traveler on the road.If that same sentence is spoken by the observer in Figure 10.8(b), the

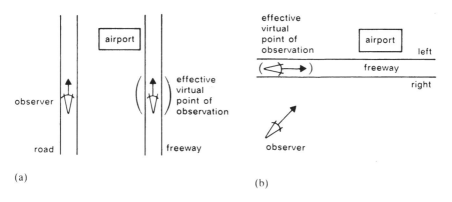

The airport is to the left of the freeway.
Figure 10.8

virtual point of observation is on the freeway, its front axis being the projection of the observer's front axis on the freeway.

(3) *the bicycle behind the tree*

A speaker at the top of a tower (Figure 10.9) may choose as effective point of observation his or her own projection on the ground. Any horizontal direction is privileged for the front axis; so one may override the observer's line of sight as the front axis (which would place the bicycle underground), replacing it with its projection on the ground.

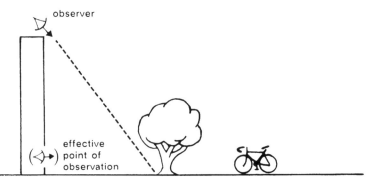

the bicycle behind the tree

Figure 10.9

In all these examples, an effective virtual point of observation is chosen which is the projection of the axes of an actual observer onto privileged directions offered by the reference or other object: this seems the principal way observer and privileged directions concur in defining base axes.

10.1.7 Choosing between conflicting frames of reference

Since several objects in a given context may be the source of privileged directions, and several observers could be used as sources of deictic axes, there are often many plausible frames of reference. Selecting the one intended by the speaker will be complex, involving consideration of many aspects of the context, linguistic and situational: cohesion, topic, speaker's and addressee's mutual beliefs (in particular about the contents of the addressee's awareness), purpose of the communication, perceptual salience, visibility, precision of the perceptual evaluation of alignment, of right angles, etc. The decisive factor generally comes down to relevance, as when relating chess pieces in a chess game, where only the board axes will matter and geometric and perceptual considerations are irrelevant.

So there are few specific hard and fast rules for selecting a reference frame. One can formulate some heuristics involving the geometry and size of the objects, the position of a potential observer, and the consequent perceptual salience. For instance, with the located object inside the reference object, symmetry axes of the reference object are very compelling: the direction of the up or front base axis tends to be parallel to them, and observers whose axes do not conform to this or objects other than the reference object can be ignored. This is true whether the candidate observer is also inside the reference object, as might be the case with *the table in the back of the room*, or must be outside it, as with *the picture on the right side of the page*.

With the located object outside the reference object:
– If the potential observer is in the reference object the latter's symmetry

axes are also compelling; so if I told someone in the backyard to look at *the redwood tree to the right of our backyard*, I could not mean a front axis defined by looking toward a corner of the yard. That is, inherent directions of the reference object are salient if the speaker is in it (whether in reality or imagination).

– The intrinsic axes of small objects can generally be ignored. *To the right of the pencil* is not likely to be defined by the pencil's own axes; in other words, small objects tend not to shape the space around them. In such cases, purely deictic axes or the privileged directions of objects supporting or containing the reference object should be used. One may also ignore the intrinsic axes of relatively large objects seen from a great distance. So looking from the a hilltop a mile away, *to the right of the house* is likely to be defined by the axes of the observer rather than those of the house: the characteristics of the house other than its location become less salient.

– If the reference object is linear and apparently unbounded (a road, a river, etc.), its own axis must be heeded (whether we say *in front of, in back of, to the right*, or *to the left of the river*, we must mean the river to act as a divider). And if the observer stands close to some clearly bounded linear or planar object, that object will appear, locally, unbounded, and the only axes allowed will be its own: it is impossible to use *behind the wall/fence* using axes other than those of the wall or fence when standing relatively close.

These heuristics reflect a few of the facts concerning perceptual salience that result from the structure of the perceptual system and the way we interact with our environment. It is extremely unlikely that human beings have anything like propositional expressions of such heuristics in mind, and a model of comprehension constructed with such explicit heuristics would thus be quite artificial and very probably miss many special occurrences. There are certainly many other cases like the one with the door in the wall (Figure 10.7); the reason purely deictic axes are not acceptable then is probably that occlusion by the wall forbids the judgment of alignment necessary to evaluate "behind". We cannot foresee all such special occurrences. Trying to formulate more general principles from which such specific heuristics would follow may not be the direction to go: it is arguable whether the proper level of description for these phenomena is with such artificial propositional abstractions.

10.2 Distinctions between the projective prepositions

The prepositions are classified below according to whether they can be used to express contact, inclusion in a part of space internal to, or external to, the reference object:

external only:

> *by the ((left/right) ⊗ side)/front/back of*
> *to the ((left/right) ⊗ side) of*
> *right/left/back of*
> *before/behind*
> *in front/back of*

mostly external, though some informants argue it can be internal in some contexts:

> *at the ((left/right) ⊗ side) of*

contact only:

> *on the front/back of*

internal only:

> *in the side/front/back of*
> *in the left/right {hand} side of*

either internal or external:

> *at the front/back of*
> *on the left/right of*

either internal, or external, or contact:

> *on the {(left/right) {hand}} side of*

There are potentially two main ways to account for the meaning of these expressions. An expression like *the child in the front of the car* could simply be interpreted by instantiating a use type attached to *in* (probably "spatial entity in container"), with subject *the child* and object *the front of the car*. If all locative constructions with *in the front of* can be interpreted by using such a compositional process, there need not be any special lexical entry for *in the front of*; but if, in some contexts, the result of decoding the expression starting from use types of *in* differs from its actual conditions of use, then we must put *in the front of* in the lexicon. To resolve this question, we need first a good understanding of the meanings of *side*, *front*, and *back*.

If a composite preposition needs a lexical entry of its own, we must still decide how many use types should be distinguished. It turns out that the distinctions between contact, location inside, and location outside the reference object (Sections 10.2.2-4), mark the division, either between use types, or between an idiomatic and a compositional preposition.

10.2.1 Object parts

Some expressions imply a division of an object into parts. These include:

the front/back/side/top/bottom of
the {left/right} side of

More exactly, the division into parts concerns a geometric construct, which is the geometric description of the entity referred to by the complement of the expression. The applicable geometric description is most often the place of the object (as in *the top of a block*), but it may occasionally be a non-trivial geometric description (e.g., the outline of the object, as in *The back of the tree is full of birds*). From here on, I will simply say "object" for "the relevant geometric construct corresponding to the entity referred to by the complement of the expression *the front/back/{left/right} side of* ".

Front, back, and *side* may refer to pieces of dimensionality *n*, or to pieces of dimensionality $(n-1)$ of an n-dimensional geometrical construct (Table 10.1), i.e., to a **chunk**, or a **face** of it. *Side, front,* and *back,* as faces, do not always coincide with the "natural" faces of an object, that is, with pieces of the object's surface delimited by a discontinuity; they may be determined instead by a point of view (a point of observation), and will then be called **projective faces** – my main concern here. One can then define base axes attached to the object (whether or not *front, side,* etc. occur as part of a composite preposition).

Table 10.1. *Dimensionality of chunks and faces.*

geometric construct	chunk	face
volume	volume	surface (exterior boundary)
area	area	line (edge)
line segment	line segment	point (end point)

Starting with the prototype case of a rectangular object seen from a point on one of its axes of symmetry, I will now describe the methods by which faces and chunks are delimited.

• Rectangular object with axes of symmetry as base axes

For a parallelepipedic or rectangular object viewed so the base axes are its symmetry axes, *front, back, left side* and *right side* (and in the three-dimensional case, *top* and *bottom*), as projective faces coincide with the natural faces encountered by the corresponding axes (Figure 10.10). Chunks are bounded by the corresponding face – the front chunk by the front face, etc. (the following descriptions will be restricted to a two-dimensional object, extension to a parallelepiped being straightforward); their sides are segments of the two edges adjacent to that face (Figure 10.11); the location of the fourth, inward boundary, depends on context which must contain some particularly relevant division line – for instance, a

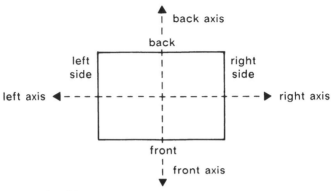

Faces of a rectangular object
Figure 10.10

salient division (e.g. a corridor in an apartment) parallel to the front-back axis may be used to divide right from left side (Figure 10.11(a)); and a division parallel to the left/right axis may divide front from back (Figure 10.11(b)). The dividing line need not cut the objects in two equal parts. For buildings, a salient division may be the inner surface of the exterior wall – informants often interpret *in the right side of the building* as being in the right wall. If there are two or more parallel salient divisions, then usually only the smallest (the least inclusive) of the chunks bounding on the outer boundary qualifies as *front, back,* or *side*.

If there is no salient physical division, then the terms may be understood as members of various contrast sets, dividing the object into equal parts. There is a two-way contrast between *left side* and *right side* which may be the one intended even without explicit reference to *right* or *left* (*One side of the table is red; the other...*). *Front* and *back* would usually be involved in a three-way contrast (front/middle/back; Figure 10.11(c)), although a two-way contrast (front/back) can be used. In *A is on the side of X*, one must assume a three-way contrast (side/middle/side; Figure 10.11(d)), otherwise the statement is vacuous. But *left* and *right side* cannot be involved in such a three-way contrast (left side/middle/right side) – that is, in the absence of

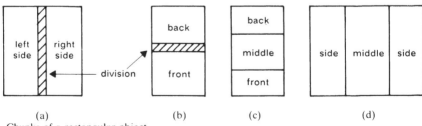

(a)   (b)   (c)   (d)
Chunks of a rectangular object
Figure 10.11

physically salient divisions: by *the right/left side of*, one seems to always mean half of the object.

The speaker may also have in mind a boundary relating to some particular purpose, although such a boundary is not physically marked (e.g., the maximum distance of good visibility will be used to pick out the seats *at the front of the theater*).

• Non-rectangular object

How are the projective faces of a non-rectangular object (or of a rectangular object viewed obliquely) delimited? In such situations, people call upon their ingenuity to divide the object boundary, using heuristics that occasionally lead to conflicting solutions. The resulting divisions will often be vague and ambiguous, and the careful speaker uses the terms with caution. Figure 10.12 shows plausible divisions of various plane figures. The limits of the faces are vague when not marked by slope discontinuities. Side and front (or side and back) may overlap.

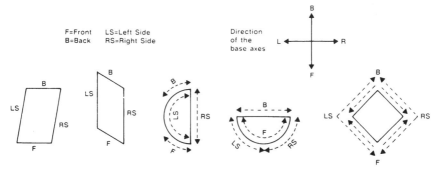

Faces for various object shapes
Figure 10.12

Some division heuristics are:

– try to approximate the object to a rectangle centered on its center of visual mass and with sides parallel to the base axes and place the projective faces' limits accordingly;

– the limits of natural faces (slope discontinuities) are important features: four of these can function as the limits of the projective faces, provided the resulting quadrilateral "sufficiently" resembles a rectangle with sides parallel to the base axes;

– what is visible from the point of observation is the front, what is invisible is the back, what is parallel to the line of sight is a side;

– what is furthest from the point of observation is the back, what is closest the front, the rest makes up the sides.[5]

Clearly, the last two heuristics yield different divisions for all but rectangular objects with base axes along axes of symmetry.

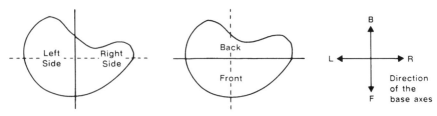

Chunks for a complex-shaped object
Figure 10.13

What about chunks? Again speakers must use their wits, and heuristics based on salient natural divisions, slope discontinuities, etc. Given a two-way contrast, one division procedure is to draw base axes with origin at the center of visual mass – right and left side are then delimited by the front-back axis, and front and back by the left-right axis (Figure 10.13).

Note that if an object is linear and unbounded, some faces or chunks cannot be defined: thus a road viewed by someone travelling on it has neither front nor back face.

10.2.2 Contiguity with the reference object

Prepositions that can be used to assert contiguity include:

on the front/back/({left/right} side) of

These are easily dealt with: the expressions are compositionally interpretable from a use type of *on* (generally "spatial entity supported by physical object"). Thus *A is on the front of X* simply means that A is in contact with and supported by the surface referred to by *the front of X* – either a face of a three-dimensional object (*the mural on the front of the building*), or a chunk of an area (*the table on the front of the stage*). The inward boundary of that chunk is context dependent, but determined by the same general procedures that determine the front, independently of the fact that *the front of* occurs after *on*: all conditions defining the use type "spatial entity supported by physical object" are then valid – for instance, there might be indirect support, e.g., a carpet between the table and the stage. The use type may also be "physical object contiguous with another", as with *He felt the pillow on the back of his head*, where no support is implied.

10.2.3 Location inside the reference object

Composite expressions starting with *at*, *on*, and *in*, allow the located object to be in the reference object. Some of them are compositional, others require lexical entries of their own – though when they do, certain features of their use are reminiscent of the meanings of the component morphemes.

• *in the front/back/({left/right} side) of*

The use of these expressions can be explained in terms of use types attached to *in*, taking *front*, *back*, and *side* to refer to chunks. Indeed, all idiosyncrasies of the use of sentences patterned after "A *is in* X" are true of "A *is in the front of* X". For instance, both sentence patterns have the same selection restrictions: one cannot say, meaning inclusion in the area, **in the front of the lawn/blackboard*, as one does not say **in the lawn/ blackboard*, but *in the front of the yard* is fine, as is *in the yard*. A is *in the front of X* if it is included in a chunk of some geometric construct bound to X, using the same geometric description function that would be required for *A is in X*: for instance, the bird *in the front of the tree* is in the front of the space delimited by the outline of the tree's branches, and the crack in *the crack in the front of the bowl* is in the volume enclosed by the normal surface of the bowl.

- *at the front/back of*

There are two possible compositional interpretations of these express-ions, depending on whether *the front* is taken to refer to a chunk or to a face. In the first case, the appropriate use type of *at* is "spatial entity at location", with the location being the chunk, in the second case it is "spatial entity at landmark in highlighted medium", the front boundary being the landmark in the whole object as medium. The conditions of use of *at the front of* sometimes point to one interpretation, and sometimes to the other, but never quite fit either. Moreover, speakers do not perceive *at the front of* as ambiguous in this way, so a special lexical entry for *at the front of* is necessary.

The conditions of use of *at the front of* are best described by contrasting it with *in the front of* – the two expressions compete when the located object is in the reference object. Although that contrast cannot be entirely traced to the distinction between *in* and *at*, there are clearly threads linking the two:

(a) In some sense, the closer something is to the front boundary of a hall, the more *at the front of the hall* it is. For example, if there were several people all in the front third, *the ones at the front* would be the ones closest to the front boundary. Also, if told that something is *at the front*, I would probably explore the space starting from that boundary, indicating thus my estimate of the probability curve for the location of the object. Neither of these observations is true of *in the front of*. The expressions *at the front/back of* denote graded concepts whose applicability decreases as the distance to the front (or from the back) increases. This points to the first compositional interpretation of *at the front of* (from "spatial entity at location"), with the located object close to the front boundary. But the maximum distance the located object can be from the front boundary is a function of the size of the whole object (it is roughly one third of its total length); this is a specification that could not arise from that compositional interpretation.

(b) *In the front/back of* is preferred to *at the front/back of* when the front chunk has a prominent physical inner boundary separating front from back. Thus *Jon is at the front of the car* is inappropriate if Jon is in the car, but either of *Jon is at/in the back of the theater*, with Jon inside the theater, is appropriate. This distinction is not predictable from either compositional interpretation of *at the front of*.

(c) *At the front/back of* is preferred if the located object is coincident with the front or back boundary (*There is a doorway at/*?in the back of the hall*). This points to the first compositional interpretation. The choice here is subtly sensitive to what is in the speaker's attention: if for example the speaker has in mind the location of somebody going to the door rather than the location of the door itself, then *in* sounds fine – as with *The exit is in the back of the hall*.

At the front of will have a lexical entry of its own, with a use type defined by the conditions just described. The preposition can also imply a located object outside the reference object, and that use is not compositional either (Section 10.2.4). Two use types should be distinguished here: there are significant distinctions between the conditions of use when the located object is inside and when it is outside, and those are not inferable from the inside/outside distinction; also, *at the front* cannot be vague between location inside and location outside – *Jon and Mary are at the front of the church* is inappropriate if Jon is inside, and Mary outside the church.

• *on the {left/right} side of*

The composites with *on*, in uses such as *The sheets are on the right side of the closet*, require their own lexical entries: they imply inclusion in a chunk of the reference object, and no use type of *on* allows this.

On the right side is vaguer than *in the right side*: with the former, the located object may be anywhere in the volume occupied by, or on the surface of the right side, while with the latter, the located object must be in the interior, the normal volume, etc., depending on which use type of *in* is involved: compare *I have a pain in/on the left side of my chest*.

These two prepositions can also be used with the located object outside the reference object, as in *The cemetery is on the left side of the church* (Section 10.2.4). Two use types should also be distinguished here: there are significant distinctions between the conditions of use in each case which are not inferable from the inside/outside contrast, and conjunctions such as *The organ and the cemetery are on the right side of the church* are unacceptable with the organ inside and the cemetery outside the church.

• *in the (left/right) hand side of*

These expressions require lexical entries of their own. There are two cases where *in the left side* and *in the left hand side* do not come out as synonymous. If the reference object is the observer or a part of the observer, then *in the left hand side* is not acceptable: e.g. *in the left hand side of my chest*. And, whereas *in the left side* could imply less than half the reference object, *in the left hand side* seems to always indicate half the reference object. Thus, an object *in the left side of the church* might be in the wall, or in a side chapel; but it would be in the left half of the church if it were *in the left hand side of the church.*

10.2.4 Location outside the reference object: basic subset of prepositions

Among prepositions which allow, or require, the located object to be outside the reference object, there is a basic subset consisting of:

> *to the right of*
> *to the left of*
> *in front of*
> *behind*

These have the most general conditions of application (*in back of*, although morphologically parallel to *in front of*, is not in this basic subgroup, as my informants tend to use *behind* instead). For simplicity, I assume a normal frame of reference throughout – that is, base up and down axes along the vertical, the other axes in an horizontal plane.

Each preposition in this set has one use type: no significant distinction allows one to differentiate two categories of uses.

What constraints on location with respect to the right axis are implied by sentences like *A is to the right of X?* The preposition *to the right* denotes a graded concept: although the located object may be some distance from the right axis, the right axis is a preferred location in several ways, which points to an ideal meaning implying location on that axis. I will first assume an idealized situation in which the reference and located objects are points, then describe the use of the prepositions where the reference object is spatially extended, and finally where the located object is spatially extended.

If the sentence *A is to the right of X* is used appropriately, where can we expect to find A? on the right axis (Figure 10.14(a))? within a 90 degree angle (the four prepositions would then each be assigned a quadrant) Figure 10.14(b))? or in the right hand half plane delimited by the front-back axis (Figure 10.14(c))?

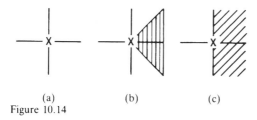

(a)   (b)   (c)
Figure 10.14

In fact, there is no position for A within the right hand half plane such that we could not, in some context, say *A is to the right of X*; position in the right hand half-plane may be the only constraint on the position of A. This is naturally the case if, in accordance with one of the salience pragmatic principles (see Section 6.1), one relates not the objects themselves, but their projections on the vertical plane at infinity normal to the line of sight. If depth (distances along parallels to the line of sight) is ignored, any position in the right hand half plane can be described as *to the right* of the reference object. But there are other cases, involving contrast, where any position in the right-hand half-plane also suffices. Consider the situation pictured in Figure 10.15. If there are no other objects present which fit the description *a glip*, then *The glip you are looking for is to the right of the blop* is a perfectly adequate specification. In other words, the loosest interpretation of the preposition is adequate, provided that obvious contrasts in the context allow the expression to fulfill its function of identifying the place of the located object.

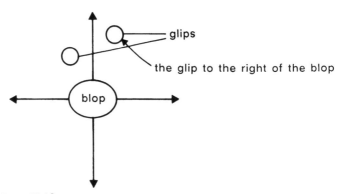

Figure 10.15

But in many cases, location in the right hand half plane is too imprecise a constraint. Greater precision is achieved in one of the following ways:

(a) One may use complex expressions: *to the right and behind*, *diagonally to the right*, *in front and to the right*, *directly to the right*, etc. These support associating a whole half plane with *to the right*: if the connective *and* in *A is to the right and behind X* operates according to its logical definition, then that sentence implies that A is to the right of X; and since the modifiers *diagonally*, *directly* (unlike *almost*, or *not quite*) restrict but do not negate the predicate to which they are attached, if *A is diagonally to the right of X*, then A is *to the right* of X.

(b) Context may suggest a preferred subspace in which the located object should typically be found. For example, one would normally assume that *the house to the right of ours* refers to the one directly to the right on the same street. A street constitutes a preferred subspace: description of a projective relation between two houses can often be assumed subject to the additional constraint that the houses are on the same street. Salient physical boundaries, specific knowledge about the normal use and environment of the objects, and cohesion, may all contribute cues to the selection of a preferred subspace; in effect, an ordinary pragmatic inference is involved here.

(c) The speaker, while assuming that the four prepositions point to overlapping half-planes (as in Figure 10.14(c)), may reason that he or she should select the "best" description among two conflicting possibilities: this would in effect restrict the angle in which the located object is to be found to 90 degrees (Figure 10.14(b)), since a competing description (*in front of* or *in back of*) would be selected for the complementary areas of the right hand half plane.

(d) If I said *Put this chair to the right of my desk!*, I would ordinarily consider my command fulfilled only if the chair were placed more or less on the right axis of the desk. One cannot claim here that interpreting *to the right* as "directly to the right" stems from the presence of a preferred subspace, nor is it a question of drawing an ordinary pragmatic inference, as with the assumptions that the chair is on the same horizontal ground as the desk, or next to the desk (an instance of the "nextness condition"). In contrast with these assumptions, location on the right base axis requires calling upon a special property of the concept *to the right*, namely that the right axis in effect exerts an attraction as a location: one must interpret *to the right* as "directly to the right", unless the context suggests otherwise.

(e) With several objects going by the same name in the right hand half plane, *the one to the right* is the one closest to the right axis (Figure 10.16). And typically, if told *A is to the right of B*, a hearer will identify A with the one most directly to the right. These conditions of use point to an ideal meaning implying location on the axis; they would then be predicted by the shifting contrast principle.

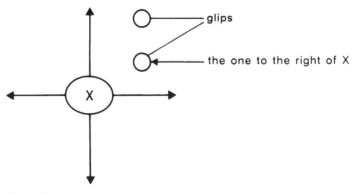

Figure 10.16

In any case, *to the right* is an instance of a graded concept with the right axis as its focal region, as shown by (d) and (e) and by the fact that, in the absence of any special cues, someone told *A is to the right of B* would probably explore first along the right base axis (probably from the reference object up to some "reasonable" distance).

What has been said of *to the right* applies *mutatis mutandis* to the other prepositions in the basic group. With *in front of*, location on the front axis is limited to the part between the reference object and the point of observation. However, the best explanation for this is probably pragmatic: if an object were located in front of the reference object, but behind the observer, it would be uncooperative (Grice 1974) not to use the observer as reference.

• Spatially extended reference object

Assume the located object punctual or small enough to be viewed as a point, and, for simplicity, in the same horizontal plane as a planar reference object. As the located object gets closer to the reference object, it becomes necessary to consider the dimensions and shape of the reference object and to specify the position of the located object in relation to its faces.

The reference object may be bounded in all directions, or it may be an apparently unbounded linear object (a road, fence, river, the Great Wall of China, etc.). If it is bounded, most of what has been said of *to the right*, when the reference object is punctual, remains true – in particular the tension between an ideal meaning placing the located object on the right base axis, and a loose interpretation placing it in the right-hand half-plane – provided one substitutes "a strip with axis the right base axis, and abutting on the reference object" for "the right base axis". A description of what this precisely implies for a variety of object shapes follows:

(a) Take a rectangular reference object with sides parallel to the base axes (Figure 10.17). Being in infinite strip 1 is like being on the right axis

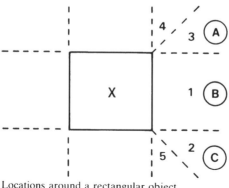

Locations around a rectangular object
Figure 10.17

for a point reference object; location in zones 1, 2, and 3 is like location in a quadrant delimited by obliques (as in Figure 10.14(b)), and location in the two quadrants on either side of the middle strip (zones 2, 3, 4, 5) is like location in a half-plane but not on the axis. So, for instance, A, B, and C could all in some context be described as *to the right of X*, but B is the most exactly to the right, and A is *to the right and behind X*.

(b) In Figure 10.18, *A is behind X* is appropriate. One must assume that

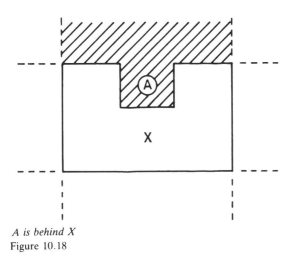

A is behind X
Figure 10.18

to be "ideally" (directly) behind X is fulfilled by any object in a strip abutting on the reference object's back face, as irregular as that face might be. So "the strip abutting on a face" should be defined in general as follows: Enclose the object between parallels to the base axes, so that each such parallel is tangent to the object. The right hand (respectively left hand, front, or back) strip extends toward the object up to the part of the boundary limited by the tangency points first encountered. This procedure requires the object to be bounded so it can be enclosed between those parallels, and thus does not apply to roads, rivers, etc.

(c) Unfortunately, with this algorithm, strips sometimes overlap. Thus in Figure 10.19, right and back strip overlap. An object in zone 1, 2, or 3, is *to the right of* X, ideally so if in 1. But is A *to the right of* X, or *behind* X? Both seem appropriate, as does the conjoined *to the right and behind*. Figure 10.20 shows the most likely choices of locative phrases for various figures; the ambiguity here reflects that encountered in attempts to specify the projective faces of the object – is the line "abc" in Figure 10.19 part of the right hand face or of the back face?

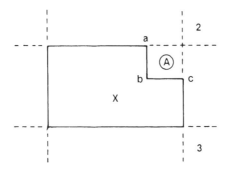

A is behind/(to the right of)/(behind and to the right of) X
Figure 10.19

In all these examples, some approximation by which the reference object is assimilated to a point is involved: the objects are embedded in a tolerance space. The examples in (b) and (c) above show that the "resolution" of this tolerance space is not homogeneous, not the same throughout the original space, otherwise reference and located objects would collapse to one point.

We have considered points, and figures that could be enclosed in a rectangle, but what of an unbounded linear object? A road may curve, but one of the base axis pairs must always be orthogonal to it: either the right and left, or the front and back axes. In the first case, the effective point of observation is on the road and looking along the road in one direction (Figure 10.21(a)) (*behind* and *in front of the road* are not interpretable then); in the second case, it is on one side of the road and looking toward it at a right angle (Figure 10.21(b)) (*to the right* and *to the left of the road* are not interpretable then). So in such cases, a small segment of the road is selected for the specification of the base axes, on which the observer (real or virtual) is located, or toward which he or she looks; that segment may then be enclosed between parallels to the base axes as we did with the rectangle in the example above (Figure 10.17), and either *in front of* and

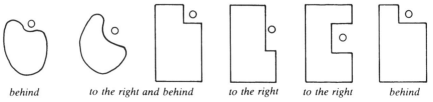

behind   to the right and behind   to the right   to the right   behind

Choice of expression for various reference object shapes and located object's position
Figure 10.20

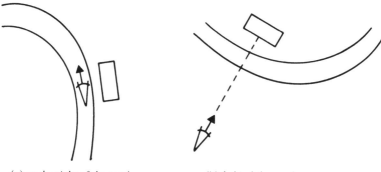

(a) *to the right of the road*   (b) *behind the road*

Figure 10.21

behind, or *to the right* and *to the left*, (but not both) can be similarly defined.

• Spatially extended located object

Assume a bounded reference object, enclosed between parallels to the base axes. A non-punctual located object may extend over one or more of the zones so delimited. Different judgments (*to the right, to the right and behind*, etc.) will emerge depending on which zone the located object intersects. Figure 10.22 gives reasonable choices for rectangular objects. Note that with conjoined expressions, the order of the conjuncts matters: if A extends partially over the right hand strip, one says *to the right and behind*; if over the back strip, then it is *behind and to the right*.

A is .... of X

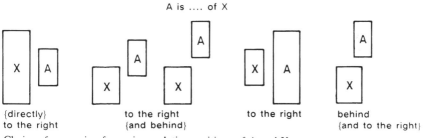

{directly}   to the right   to the right   behind
to the right   {and behind}   {and to the right}

Choice of expression for various relative positions of A and X

Figure 10.22

The garden in Figure 10.23(a) is *to the right and behind the house* – not that all of it is, but because some points of it are directly to the right, others directly behind, and still others to the right and behind. Another way to deal with an extended located object is to assume the locative expression true of only a salient part of it, in accordance with a salience pragmatic principle. That part must then be on the relevant base axis itself (or strip). Thus, one could say *The Thames is in front of me* in the situation depicted

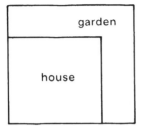

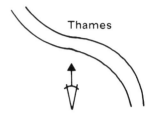

(a) *The garden is to the right and behind the house*   (b) *The Thames is in front of me*
Figure 10.23

in Figure 10.23(b), meaning that *in front of* is ideally true of a section of the Thames which stands out, by virtue of my looking at it. In *Behind this door lies a beautiful garden*, the salient part selected is the access.

If the reference object is linear unbounded, the located object may extend along a long portion of it. For instance, by *the land to the right of the road* (Figure 10.24(a)), one may intend to refer to the land along a considerable portion of the road: one then performs a sort of integration, with the point of observation moving along the road, and the land being in the space swept by the right axis. The linear object could even close on itself. Thus, in *the men behind the prison wall*, the men can be anywhere behind the wall, for all points of observation on a line around the wall (Figure 10.24(b)). The men are within the space covered by successive back axes as the point of observation moves along that line.

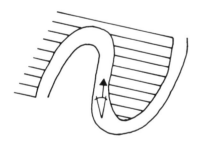

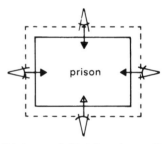

(a) *the land to the right of the road*   (b) *the men behind the prison wall*
Figure 10.24

10.2.5 Location outside: the other prepositions

This section will discuss only a few interesting points about five groups of prepositions.

● *on the (left/right) of*

These two prepositions clearly require a lexical entry of their own, with only one use type. The contrast between *on the right* and *to the right* is often construed as follows: *on the right* implies proximity between located and reference object, and *to the right* is neutral with respect to proximity (Leech 1969). But a closer look suggests that with *on the right*, the located object must not only be in proximity, it must also be next to the reference object: that is, given a salient set of objects satisfying a certain property (houses, the objects on my desk, etc.), the located object must be the closest to the reference object. So with *Jon's house is on the right of mine*, no other house must be between Jon's and mine, or else one should say *to the right of mine*.

If the located object is "far" from the reference object, even with no other object between them one must use *to the right*. What is the distance threshold (no doubt very vague) below which *on the right* is appropriate? In contrast with *near*, the definition of proximity in this case does not seem to depend on some implicit purpose, the speed of travel envisaged, etc., but appears rather perceptual, involving factors like the apparent size and distance of the two objects in the field of view (to be more specific would require systematic experimentation).

To the right evokes travel away from the reference and toward the located object: so *the red book to the left of "Ulysses"*, but not *on the left of "Ulysses"*, suggests a sweeping eye movement away from "Ulysses". Consistent with this are the qualifiers that can be combined with *to the right* but not with *on the right*, e.g. *further to the right, one inch to the right*, etc.

• *on the left/right side of*
These are clearly not compositional, since the located object may be away from the side considered; location outside defines a second use type for each preposition (the first is described in 10.2.3). As contrasted with *on the right*, *on the right side* draws attention to the external face of the reference object (thus *on the right side of the building* brings attention to the wall); both behave alike with respect to proximity.

• *at the left/right of*
These imply the closest proximity consistent with a reasonable world: *the bottle is at your left* suggests that the bottle is immediately accessible to hand, while it could be further away with *the bottle is on your left*.

• *at the front/back/{left/right} side of*
One plausible compositional interpretation for, say, *at the back of*, would make it mean "close to or coincident with the back boundary", but this would not work since in Figure 10.25, *A is at the back of X* is not true: the located object must be more or less in the cross-hatched area. Each preposition in this group should thus have a lexical entry of its own. So *at the front/back of* will have two use types, but *at the {left/right} side*, which cannot be used with the located object inside the reference object, only one.

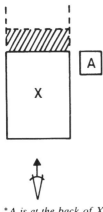

*A is at the back of X
Figure 10.25

● *to the front/back of*

These are mostly used in conjoined expressions like *on the right and to the front*, which means roughly the same as *on the right and in front*. The location so described cannot be more than 45 degrees away from the right axis, otherwise one must say *in front and to the right*. The order of the conjuncts matters: *?to the front and on the right* is odd.

10.3 Ideal meanings

I will define ideal meanings for the prepositions in the basic subgroup. Each has two ideal meanings, corresponding to the two prototype situations. Each ideal meaning involves a point of observation (P_{Obs}) and points as reference (P_{Ref}) and located (P_{Loc}) objects, all in the same horizontal plane. Base axes can be inferred from the point of observation and reference object: the two possible orders of these axes lead to the two ideal meanings (Figure 10.26(a) and 10.26(b)). So, for instance, *to the right* has two ideal meanings, say, *ToTheRight₂* and *ToTheRight₃*: *ToTheRight₂* is true of P_{Loc} and P_{Ref} iff P_{Obs} and P_{Ref} are coincident and P_{Loc} is on the right base axis so implied; *ToTheRight₃* is true of P_{Loc} and P_{Ref} iff P_{Obs} and P_{Ref} are apart and P_{Loc} is on the derived right base axis (the indices "2" and "3" indicate the fact that there are in effect two independent variables in the first case, and three in the second). Analogous definitions for the other prepositions are easy to formulate.

Throughout this chapter, every use of the projective prepositions has been described in terms of its relation to one or the other ideal meaning. To be sure, subject and object of the prepositions most commonly refer to physical objects, not geometrical points, yet the objects will often be viewed as points, or a part will be selected and viewed as a point; even

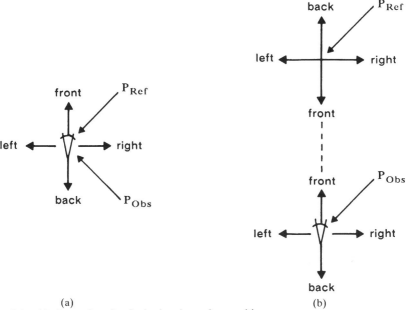

(a) (b)
Defining ideal meanings for the basic subset of prepositions
Figure 10.26

specifying the position of the located object in terms of its relation to the faces of the reference object can be discussed in terms of approximation to a point. The located object is not necessarily on one of the base axes, but position on the axis is privileged in several ways. The axes may be rotated with respect to the vertical, yet coincidence of the down axis with the gravitational vertical is also a privileged case. Coincidence of the point of observation with the reference object is often true only given a certain tolerance (as with *The bag is behind the chair* with the base axes defined by a sitter). The point of observation, usually an indexical, may correspond to an imaginary observer. All such processes only slightly obscure the derivation from the ideal meanings.

10.4 Conclusion

In attempting to collect data and describe the uses of these prepositions, one is struck by the vagueness and inconsistency of speakers' intuitions, as well as the degree of individual variation. Many of these expressions combine terms that are inherently vague, for instance *at* and *side*, and a wide range of contextual characteristics are apparently brought to bear on the interpretation of a given locative construction in ways that are complex and obscure. A variety of forces seem to pull one way or another: varying compositional interpretations, salience, contrast with other terms, influence of background elements, perspective on the objects, need to avoid ambiguity, etc. Giving an account of all of these in even a few cases would be very difficult, yet in some way a speaker subconsciously juggles them all in order to decide on the acceptability of a sentence. Presumably, there is no unique way to reach this decision, and distinct, even inconsistent, paths may be used on different occasions. As a result, it is difficult to come up with precise and satisfactory descriptions of these uses, and equally difficult to answer with certainty questions about whether some feature is conventional, whether a particular prepositional expression is compositional, etc. The lack of an appropriate theory of vagueness is most strongly felt in the case of these prepositions.

One may wonder why such vague and unreliable expressions have not fallen out of the language. One reason is that speakers rely extensively on their addressees to make assumptions similar to their own. A speaker relies as much on the other's rationality, similarity of perception and experience, as on conventional properties of linguistic forms. A second reason is that error is admissible. Language need not be perfect, it may keep "design defects": vagueness, ambiguities, etc. These expressions may have stayed in the language because increased precision would be too costly compared to the gain, and because in case of a breakdown, there is usually room for rectification. It would be surprising if the very structure of language did not at times reflect that possibility.

Conclusion

Attempts to give an account of lexical meaning remain the weakest link in artificial intelligence and logical semantics. Neither discipline has ever offered lexical representations that satisfactorily account for speakers' uses; both have discovered that lexical meanings simply cannot be regimented into neat bundles of necessary and sufficient conditions. This book has been an attempt to understand that unruliness. Is it a result of the way world knowledge, pragmatic knowledge, and context interact with the linguistic code? Is it that language is full of idiosyncrasies that simply have to be learned one by one? The answer to both questions is "yes", and this work has focused on one domain to describe these aspects of language.

To account for the flexibility and open-endedness of language, for the interplay of regularity and irregularity, I have posited rules – and then ways to bend or break them (e.g., ideal meanings and shifts, use types and interpretations that do not fall into any use type). But these deviations interact with context very freely and it is difficult to uncover systematicities. In several places, I called upon similarity to explain some of these phenomena, but offered only very informal descriptions of how it operates. The descriptive framework offered here provided "hooks" on which to hang various aspects of prepositional use, but left many loose ends where only discursive means were available. Understanding similarity – how it is perceived and how it operates in semantic structure – is the next task in trying to build a more satisfactory theory. Defining lexical categories by means of necessary and sufficient conditions is only an approximation; it can account for the operation of similarity in many, but not all cases. The perception of similarity depends on global features of the entities compared (features one would often not include in describing these entities) and on their context;[1] and similarity affects lexical choice in unexpected ways. Both phenomena – the sources of perceived similarity and its effects on lexical choice – should be carefully considered. To return to a much-used example (the pear in the bowl in Figure 4.2), with a situation similar to that of containment in an open container, *in* can be used, although containment is no longer true. Handling this peculiarity as a conventional detail to be specified in the lexicon (within a use type) is only a stopgap solution; one wants instead a precise account of what underlies the perception of similarity, and rigorous principles which explain how such a preposition is chosen when the spatial relation it expresses is untrue, how it is that the context of the relation has then become more important than the relation itself.

The other important questions addressed in these pages concern the form and nature of our underlying spatial knowledge, and how language reveals it. Some of the capriciousness of spatial expressions disappears if one assumes that they are not shaped, as one would initially expect, by the canonical description; instead, approximations of objects and environments useful for movement, action, and spatial reasoning, approximations of shape that presumably play a role in their perceptual representations, perceptual organization principles, perceptual salience, etc. are at work behind locative expressions.

Finally, one main intent of these very detailed descriptions of prepositional uses was to show the degree to which language is inexplicit, and how shared tacit knowledge and aspects of perceptual mechanisms inform what is being expressed by a given sentence. Attempts to solve this problem with an extended use of traditional indexicals assume that one can settle on a predefined and finite set of contextual parameters that will bear on the truth-conditions of sentences. Many examples showed that it is unlikely this would allow us to account for all the context-dependency encountered: salience and speaker's concerns, for instance, are not observables easily captured by a set of parameters.

One important contribution of artificial intelligence has been to place language back where it belongs, within the cognitive system. But the nature of linguistic rules, and the way they articulate the underlying knowledge, remain superficially understood; this work should be seen as a prelude to a re-examination of these questions.

Notes

Introduction

1. It is possible that all lexical meanings are prototypically structured, which would make the question of compositionality one of combining prototypical meanings, a problem I do not address. Being primarily interested in the meaning of the prepositions, I will leave aside questions about the meaning of definite descriptions, quantified expressions, and so forth; all the spatial expressions considered will have noun-phrases with specific referents which will occur as arguments in their semantic representation. Also, since I focus on the spatial relations expressed, the role of syntactic structure in forming these semantic representations is incidental.

2. Two years after I started using the term "situation type" to describe the meaning of locative expressions, Barwise and Perry published their first work on "situation semantics" (1981). Possibly, my notion could be fitted into their more recent theoretical framework (1983), but a precise comparison would require several chapters and take us away from the main purpose of this book. Here, I will just point out two apparent differences: situation types include conditions for appropriateness as well as truth, and the notion of normality is central in my own framework.

1. Meaning and use of locative expressions

1. These particular formulae are adapted from Cooper (1968).

2. The simple relations model underlies most work on locatives within the computational paradigm (Cooper 1968; Winograd 1972; Miller and Johnson-Laird 1976; Boggess 1979; Waltz 1980). Boggess takes into account an additional level of complexity, namely the role that a few perceptual features of the objects play in determining the interpretation of locative expressions, but, as we will see, this is insufficient. In linguistics, early work on locatives came mostly from structuralists (Leech 1969; Bennett 1975). Although they do not require meaning to express the sentence truth-conditions, only to account for intralinguistic relationships, their representations resemble those just described. Implicit in Gruber (1965), Fillmore (1971), Talmy (1975) and Jackendoff (1983) is a view of spatial prepositions as expressing simple relations between physical objects. Recent work, such as that of Brugman (1981), Lindner (1981) and Talmy (1983), is more in accord with the views expressed here, but it gives neither a precise account of the relation of locative expressions to the real world of physical objects, nor of the respective roles of motivation and convention.

3. An intensional description of a category consists in necessary and sufficient conditions characterizing a member; an extensional description would be an enumeration of its members. These terms are not fully appropriate here, since a situation type is typically a fuzzy category.

4. Although the collection of phenomena that follows is taxonomically a hodge-podge, it represents a first "naive" appraisal of the ways in which the examples given deviate from the application of the simple geometric predicates, which is satisfactory for this initial exposition.

5. The asterisk will indicate all kinds of ill-formedness: syntactic, semantic, and what traditional linguists would call pragmatic.

2. Normal situation types

1. See note 3, Chapter 1.

2. The speaker could negate the'pragmatic implication, but by stressing both *in* and *under* in *The bread is not in the bowl, it is under the bowl*; he or she would then imply that *in* was not the best choice of words.

3. In trying to sort truth-conditions from pragmatic conditions, linguists often stumble into circular arguments: they set as a goal for their semantic theory an account of the truth-conditions of sentences; as for the truth-conditions of a sentence, they are precisely those which the theory explains.

4. See Labov (1973), Rosch (1977), and Coleman and Kay (1981). For a brief explication of the notion of prototype, see Chapter 4.

5. This example is from Talmy (1978a).

6. "Connected" refers to the topological intuition of an object made of one piece (as with a disk, or plane with a disk removed); a plane from which a circular line has been removed, on the other hand, is not connected.

3. Purpose

1. It is unclear whether the descriptions of purpose that follow are present in the speaker's mind. As Winograd and Flores (1985) explain, an utterance may appear to be the result of applying certain linguistic strategies to fulfill some well-defined goal; but such an analysis may not describe the psychological reality of linguistic activity. A better model is one where a complex system is subjected to perturbations from the outside world. In such a model, what we see as a purpose will be the net observable result of a very large number of distributed mechanisms and operations; but until we are able to discern the details of such a model, it will be profitable to observe the regularities that link what "appears" as purpose with linguistic choices.

2. Schegloff (1971), Rumelhart (1974), and Shanon (1979) consider the problem of choice of reference entity, but only for the specification of geographical location.

3. The source of this "confusion" might be in the following developmental facts. An infant, at a very early stage, behaves according to the rule: "an object is any bounded volume of space that can move from place to place along trajectories" (Bower 1974). Later, as it discovers the relation "inside", and learns that two

objects, one inside the other, can move as one, its behavior conforms with: "two objects cannot be in the same place simultaneously unless one is *inside* the other".

4. One should not look for too close a relation between this use of the terms and their use in Gestalt psychology. Figure/Ground in the Gestalt sense is a perceptual relation, while in Talmy's sense, it is a conceptual relation. In

   the desk to the left of the chair

   the chair does not act as perceptual background for the desk, although, in Talmy's sense, the desk is the Figure and the chair the Ground.

5. This example is adapted from Talmy (1978a).

4. Ideal meanings

1. The base of a generalized cylinder can be any closed curve.
2. Geoffrey Nunberg suggested this example.
3. Both examples are from Roger N. Shepard.
4. Topology is the study of those properties of figures that are unaffected by "elastic deformations" (homeomorphisms) – that is deformations that exclude tearing or joining. The image of a rubber sheet may help explain this. Take any figure, and imagine it made of rubber. All figures obtained by stretching or shrinking this rubber object are topologically equivalent (thus a sphere is equivalent to a cube, but a torus is distinct from a sphere, because one cannot obtain one by elastic deformations of the other), and all relations and properties that remain true under such stretching and shrinking are topological properties and relations.

   Piaget and Inhelder's "topological relations" do not conform to this mathematical definition (see Weinzweig 1978); proximity, for instance, is metric rather than topological. They do not define the other relations (order, enclosure, separation) in clear or consistent fashion, but in at least some instances, they mean the topological relations one would normally associate with them. So, for instance, in some of their experiments, they illustrate these relations as follows: A, B, and C are in that order on an oriented line (order), a figure is inside a closed surface topologically equivalent to a sphere (enclosure), two figures share no point (separation). All these relations remain true under elastic deformations. Interestingly, in some of Piaget and Inhelder's experiments, a topological relation is involved only if one considers geometric conceptualizations: for instance, strictly speaking, a bowl is topologically equivalent to a disk, and has no inside or outside; however if we project in imagination a closed figure on the bowl (closing the inner surface of the bowl with a plane at the top), then we can define surrounding in strict topological fashion.

5. Geometric descriptions

1. This example is from Nunberg (1977).
2. These constraints on elementary geometric description functions occasionally

result in somewhat counterintuitive semantic representations. Thus, with *the tree on the meadow*, one might prefer to say that the place of the visible part of the tree is *on the meadow* rather than that a part of the place of the tree, the part above ground, is *on the meadow*. One could try defining the functions so such intuitions are honored and there is no type mismatch in building up the semantic representations. But such ordering intuitions are often very fuzzy. Predicate calculus forces on us choices and distinctions without any intuitive basis (this, *a priori*, points to its inadequacy for the representation of natural language meaning). For instance, we have to decide whether we want to represent *The bird is in the bush* by:

$$Included(Part(Place(Bird)), Interior(Outline(VisiblePart(Place(Bush)))))$$

or, redefining the domain and range of *Part, Interior, Outline,* and *VisiblePart* so that they are always given arguments of the proper type, by:

$$Included(Place(Part(Bird)), Place(Interior(Outline(VisiblePart(Bush)))))$$

There is really no fact of naive epistemology that could motivate us to choose between the two representations. The solution adopted here has the practical advantage of being simple and of yielding semantic representations that could be used in reasoning about spatial knowledge without leading to inconsistencies.

6. Pragmatic factors

1. Patrick Hayes introduced me to the notion of a tolerance space.

7. Use types

1. This example was suggested by Ivan Sag.
2. Rosch (1976) formulates a similar principle to account for the "basic level" of categorization: "Basic level objects should be the most inclusive level of classification at which objects have numbers of attributes in common." But, as a psychologist, she means this to be an empirical, not a logical, criterion, the numbers of attributes being decided by experimental procedures (e.g., asking informants to list attributes).

8. Decoding and encoding

1. To be precise, I should say here "intensional objects". Out of context, a phrase like *the red clock* cannot be tied to any particular object in the world; yet we can in one sense think of it as a single object with certain properties (it is red, shows time, etc.). Such "objects" are called intensional objects.
2. The basic level of categorization is the level at which we tend to name an object in the absence of any specific contextual cues; thus, upon being shown the image of a chair and being asked "What is this?", we are more likely to say "a chair" than "a piece of furniture", or "a kitchen chair". "A piece of furniture" is a description at the superordinate level, "a kitchen chair" at the specialization level.

3. A discrimination net is a binary tree, with tests at the nodes; one branch is taken if the answer to the test is "true", the other if it is "false". If the net is used for lexical selection, at the end nodes will be lexical items selected by the succession of test results along the corresponding path from the root.

9. The three basic topological prepositions

1. For a definition of elastic deformations, see note 4 in Chapter 4.
2. Most typically, the speaker takes the point of view implied by his or her position, or the addressee's, but as Fillmore has shown with *come* and *go* (1971), a speaker may take yet other points of view – for instance that of the persons talked about, or even, less specifically, the speaker may position him/herself in imagination anywhere, according to some momentary interest, focus of attention, etc. The speaker could then use *at* when close to the reference object. For instance, one could look at Jimmy swimming and say *His mother does not know he is at the pool.*
3. The term is borrowed from Roger N. Shepard (in class). Using "background" has the unfortunate result of often having two "backgrounds" to consider in relation to the same sentence: the physical background (medium) for a given object and the background of attention, where relative "highlighting" places the first background. "Medium" seems thus a better choice.
4. This example is from Roger N. Shepard.
5. These examples are from Roger N. Shepard.
6. One also sometimes relates an object to one salient, but near it. If we also consider proximity, the relational graph is no longer a tree, but the general procedure for choosing reference objects remains the same.

10. The projective prepositions

1. These two lists include a fundamental set of such prepositions, but there are others, e.g., *on one side, on the far side, toward the back, at the extreme left.* Composites with *edge* are excluded, since they depend only on the geometry of the reference object, and not on a point of observation. For the same reason, *side* in these lists is always meant in the sense that an object has two sides (to be contrasted with front or back), and not four or six.

   The following notations are used throughout this chapter: if a, b, c, etc. are strings, the string "ab" means the concatenation of a and b, the string "a/b/../k" means any of a, or b, .., or k; "{a} " means that a is optional; "a $\otimes$ b" means one of: a, or b, or ab.
2. A half-line axis is a straight line starting at some point and extending to infinity in one direction only. A description of the frame of reference in terms of six half-line axes is more convenient than one in terms of three oriented axes extending to infinity in both directions, since the composite prepositions make direct reference to six directions, although opposite axes are not always symmetric: Clark (1973) shows using dimensional adjectives (*deep, high*, etc.) and common sense facts about perception that the directions "ahead" on the front-back line, and "upward" on the vertical, are in some sense "positive"; right and left however are completely symmetric.

3. Take *A is behind X*: if X is a point or viewed as a point, "behind" always extends up to X, which is thus naturally chosen as the point of coordinate zero. If the reference object is not punctual, the origin is at some point of it: with prepositions referring to positions inside the reference object (as with *the seats at the back of the theater*), such a point exactly separates front from back on the front-back line, and right from left on the right-left line; with prepositions referring to positions outside the reference object (e.g., *behind*), it will be convenient to keep the same origin for all the base axes, though the located object cannot then be on the whole of the relevant axis.

4. In other words, a direction is an equivalence class of directed lines defined by the following equivalence relation: two such lines are equivalent if they are parallel and point the same way.

5. Here is Alice's solution to the division problem for a circle. A caterpillar seated on a mushroom is telling Alice: "'...one side [of the mushroom] will make you grow taller, and the other side will make you grow shorter.'...Alice remained looking thoughtfully at the mushroom, trying to make out which were the two sides of it; and as it was perfectly round, she found this a very difficult question. However, at last she stretched her arms around it as far as they would go, and broke off a bit of the edge with each hand. 'And now which is which?' she said to herself, and nibbled a little of the right-hand bit to try the effect." This passage brings up several points. First, this is a case of encounter. Second, when an object has no natural discontinuities to mark faces or chunks, the use of *front*, *side*, and *back* is not very natural, yet the hearer will then get busy trying to use any cue – any mark on the object or contextual cue – to make sense of it – as does Alice. Third, Alice uses a two-way contrast system (left side/right side). Finally, in her interpretation, front and back would overlap with the left and right side.

Conclusion

1. Goldmeier (1972), who studied similarity for various geometric designs, showed that similarity cannot be described as partial identity, or as identity of proportions or relations, but depends on "agreement with respect to the *singular* whole qualities which determine the phenomenal appearance of a figure". Such "whole quality" is determined, for instance, by the presence or absence of corners, intersections, etc. I am suggesting a study of similarity, as careful as Goldmeier's, but dealing with conceptual structure.

References

Allen, J. F., and Perrault, C. R. 1980. Analyzing intention in utterances. *Artificial Intelligence* 15: 143-178.

Anderson, J. R. 1978 Arguments concerning representations for mental imagery. *Psychological Review* 85: 249-2 77.

Appelt, D. E. *Planning English sentences.* 1985. Cambridge, England: Cambridge University Press.

Barwise, J. 1981. Scenes and other situations. *Journal of Philosophy* 78: 369-97.

Barwise, J. and Perry, J. 1981. Semantic innocence and uncompromising situations. *Midwest Studies in Philosophy* 6: 387-404.

Barwise, J. and Perry, J. 1983. *Situations and attitudes.* Cambridge, Mass.: The MIT Press.

Bennett, D. C. 1975. *Spatial and temporal uses of English prepositions: an essay in stratificational semantics.* London: Longman.

Block, N. (ed.). 1981. *Imagery.* Cambridge, Mass.: The MIT Press.

Block, N. 1983. Mental pictures and cognitive science. *The Philosophical Review* 92, 4: 499-541.

Bobrow, D. G. and Winograd, T. 1977. An overview of KRL: a knowledge representation language. *Cognitive Science* 1: 3-46.

Boggess, L. C. 1979. *Computational interpretation of English spatial prepositions.* Ph.D. dissertation. Urbana, Ill.: University of Illinois.

Bower, T. G. 1974. *Development in infancy.* San Francisco: W.H. Freeman.

Brady, J. M. (ed.). 1982. *Computer vision.* Amsterdam: North-Holland.

Brady, J. M. et al. 1984. *Robotics and artificial intelligence.* New York; Springer Verlag.

Brugman, C. 1981. *The story of over.* Unpublished Master's thesis. Berkeley, California.: University of California.

Clark, H. H. 1973. Space, time, semantics, and the child. *Cognitive development and the acquisition of language,* ed. T.E. Moore, 65-110. New York: Academic Press.

Cohen, P. 1978. *On knowing what to say: planning speech acts.* Technical Report No. 118. Department of Computer Science, University of Toronto.

Coleman, L. and Kay, P. 1981. Prototype semantics. *Language,* 57: 26-44.

Cooper, G. S. 1968. *A semantic analysis of English locative prepositions.* Bolt Beranek and Newman report No. 1587. Springfield, Va.: Clearinghouse for Federal Scientific and Technical Information.

Dell, G. S. 1985. Positive feedback in hierarchical connectionist models: applications to language production. *Cognitive Science* 9, 2: 3-24.

201

Dennett, D. C. 1981. The nature of images and the introspective trap. *Imagery*, ed. N. Block, 51-62.

Denofsky, M. E. 1976. *How near is near: a near specialist.* MIT Artificial Intelligence Laboratory memo no. 344. Cambridge, Mass.

Dreyfus, H. L. 1979. *What computers can't do.* New York: Harper & Row.

Fillmore, C. J. 1971. *Santa Cruz lectures on deixis*, presented at the University of California, Santa Cruz. Bloomington, Ind.: University Linguistics Club. Mimeographed.

Fillmore, C. J. 1975. An alternative to checklist theories of meaning. *Proceedings of the First Annual Meeting of the Berkeley Linguistics Society*, 123-31. Berkeley, Calif.: University of California.

Fillmore, C. J. 1979. Innocence: a second idealization for linguistics. *Proceedings of the Fifth Annual Meeting of the Berkeley Linguistics Society*, 63-76. Berkeley, Calif.: University of California.

Fillmore, C. J., Kay, P. and O'Connor, M. C. 1985. *Regularity and idiomaticity in grammatical constructions: the case of* let *alone.* Unpublished manuscript. Berkeley, Calif.: Department of Linguistics, University of California.

Finke, R. A. 1980. Levels of equivalence in imagery and perception. *Psychological Review* 87: 113-39.

Forbus, K. D. 1983. Qualitative reasoning about space and motion. *Mental Models*, ed. D. Gentner and A. L. Stevens 53-73. Hillsdale, N.J.: Erlbaum Associates.

Gazdar, G. 1979. *Pragmatics: implicature, presupposition, and logical form.* New York: Academic Press.

Gazdar, G. and Good, D. 1982. On a notion of relevance: comments on Sperber and Wilson's paper. *Mutual knowledge*, ed. N. V. Smith, 88-100. London: Academic Press.

Goldman, N. 1975. Conceptual generation. *Conceptual information processing*, ed. R. Schank, 289-371. Amsterdam: North-Holland.

Goldmeier, E. 1972. *Similarity in visually perceived forms.* New York: International Universities Press.

Grice, H. P. 1974. Logic and conversation. *Syntax and semantics*, vol. 3, ed. P. Cole and J. L. Morgan, 41-58. New York: Academic Press.

Gruber, J. S. 1965. *Studies in lexical relations.* PhD dissertation, Cambridge, Mass.: MIT. Reprint, 1976, in *Lexical structures in syntax and semantics.* Amsterdam: North-Holland.

Hayes, P. J. 1978. *Naive physics: ontology for liquids.* Geneva, Switzerland: Institute of Semantic and Cognitive Studies.

Hayes, P. J. 1979. *The naive physics manifesto.* Geneva, Switzerland: Institute of Semantic and Cognitive Studies.

Hinton, G. E. and Anderson, John A. 1981. *Parallel models of associative memory.* Hillsdale, N.J.: Erlbaum Associates.

Jackendoff, R. 1983. *Semantics and cognition.* Cambridge, Mass.: The MIT Press.

Johnson-Laird, P. N. 1977. Procedural semantics. *Cognition* 5: 189-214.

Kameyama, M. 1980. *Putting on in Japanese.* Unpublished manuscript. Stanford, Calif.: Department of Linguistics, Stanford University.

Kay, P. 1981. *Three properties of the ideal reader.* Unpublished manuscript. Berkeley, Calif.: Department of Linguistics, University of California.

Kimball, J. P. 1974. *The grammar of facing.* Bloomington, Ind.: Indiana University Linguistics Club. Mimeographed.

Koffka, K. 1935. *Principles of gestalt psychology.* New York: Harcourt, Brace & World.

Kosslyn, S. M. 1981. Research on mental imagery: some goals and directions. *Cognition* 10: 173-79.

Kuipers, B. 1978. Modeling spatial knowledge. *Cognitive Science* 2: 129-53.

Labov, W. 1973. The boundaries of words and their meanings. *New ways of analyzing variation in English*, ed. C.-J. N. Bailey and R. W. Shuy. 340-373. Washington D.C.: Georgetown University Press.

Lakoff, G. 1970. A note on vagueness and ambiguity. *Linguistic Inquiry* 1: 357-59.

Lakoff, G. and Johnson, M. 1980. *Metaphors we live by.* Chicago: University of Chicago Press.

Leech, G. N. 1969. *Towards a semantic description of English.* Bloomington: Indiana University Press.

Lindkvist, K-G. 1950. *Studies on the local sense of the prepositions 'in', 'at', 'on', and 'to' in Modern English.* Lund Studies in English, no. 22. Reprint, Nendeln, Liechtenstein: Klaus Reprint, 1968.

Lindner, S. 1981. *A lexico-semantic analysis of verb-particle constructions with "up" and "out."* PhD dissertation. San Diego, Calif.: University of California.

Lynch, K. 1960. *The image of the city.* Cambridge, Mass.: The MIT Press.

Makkai, A. 1972. *Idiom structure in English.* The Hague: Mouton.

Marr, D. 1981. Artificial intelligence: a personal view. *Mind design*, ed. J. Haugeland. Cambridge, Mass.: MIT Press.

Marr, D. 1982. *Vision.* New York: Freeman and Co.

Maturana, H. R. 1978. Biology of language: the epistemology of reality. *Psychology and biology of language and thought: essays in honor of Eric Lenneberg*, ed. G. A. Miller and E. Lenneberg, 27-63. New York: Academic Press.

McClelland, J. L. 1985. Putting knowledge in its place: a scheme for programming parallel processing structures on the fly. *Cognitive Science* 9, 2: 113-46.

McDermott, D. and Davis, E. 1984. Planning routes through uncertain territory. *Artificial Intelligence* 22: 107-56.

McKeon, R. (ed.). 1941. *The basic works of Aristotle.* New York: Random House.

Miller, G. A. and Johnson-Laird, P. N. 1976. *Language and perception.* Cambridge, Mass.: Harvard University Press.

Montague, R. 1974. Pragmatics. *Formal philosophy: selected papers*, ed. R. H. Thompson. New Haven: Yale University Press.

Nunberg, G. 1977. *The pragmatics of reference.* Ph.D. dissertation, The City University of New York.

Palmer, S. E. 1975. Visual perception and world knowledge. *Explorations in cognition*, ed. D. A. Norman et al. San Francisco: W. H. Freeman.

Paul, R. P. 1981. *Robot manipulators: mathematics, programming, and control.* Cambridge, Mass.: The MIT Press.

Piaget, J. and Inhelder, B. 1967. *La conception de l'espace chez l'enfant.* Translation, *The child's conception of space.* Translated by F. J. Langdon and J. L. Lunzer. New York: W. W. Norton and Company.

Roberts, F. S. 1973. Tolerance geometry. *Notre Dame Journal of Formal Logic* 14: 68-76.

Rosch, E. 1976. Classifications of real-world objects: origins and representations in cognition. *La mémoire sémantique*, special issue of the *Bulletin de Psychologie*, ed. S. Ehrlich and E. Tulving, 242-250.

Rosch, E. 1977. Human categorization. *Advances in cross-cultural psychology*, vol. 1, ed. N. Warren, 1-49. London: Academic Press.

Rosch, E. and Mervis, C. B. 1975. Family resemblances: Studies in the internal structure of categories. *Cognitive Psychology* 7: 573-605.

Rumelhart, D. E. 1974. *The room theory*. Unpublished manuscript. San Diego, Calif.: The University of California at San Diego.

Russell, B. 1905. On denoting. *Mind* 14, 479-49 3. Reprint. Feigler and Sellars, 1949, 103-115.

Schank, R. C. 1975. *Conceptual information processing*. Amsterdam: North-Holland.

Schegloff, E. A. 1971. Notes on a conversational practice: formulating place. *Studies in social interaction*, ed. D. Sudnow, 95-135. Glencoe, Ill.: Free Press.

Searle, J. R. 1979. Literal meaning. *Expression and meaning*. Cambridge, England: Cambridge University Press.

Shanon, B. 1979. Where questions. *Proceedings of the 17th Annual Meeting of the Association for Computational Linguistics*, 73-5. San Diego, Calif.: University of California at San Diego.

Shepard, R. N. 1978. The mental image. *American Psychologist* 33: 123-37.

Shepard, R. N. and Podgorny, P. 1978. Cognitive processes that resemble perceptual processes, *Handbook of learning and cognitive processes*, vol. 5, ed. W. K. Estes. Hillsdale, N.J.: Erlbaum Associates.

Siegel, A. W. and White, S. H. 1975. The development of spatial representation of large-scale environments. *Advances in child development and behavior*, vol. 10, ed. W. Reese. New York: Academic Press.

Sondheimer, N. K. 1974. *English as a basis for command languages for machines and some problems of spatial reference*. Computer Sciences Technical Report No. 205. Madison, Wisc.: University of Wisconsin.

Sondheimer, N. K. 1976. Spatial reference and natural-language machine control. *International Journal of Man-Machine Studies* 8: 329-36.

Sperber, D. and Wilson, D. 1982. Mutual knowledge and relevance in theories of comprehension. *Mutual knowledge*, ed. N. V. Smith, 61-85. London: Academic Press.

Strawson, P. F. 1950. On referring. *Mind* 59: 320-44. Reprint *Philosophy and ordinary language*, ed. Caton, 1963, Urbana, Ill.: University of Illinois Press.

Talmy, L. 1975. Semantics and syntax of motion. *Syntax and semantics*, vol. 4, ed. John P. Kimball, 181-238. New York: Academic Press.

Talmy, L. 1978a. Figure and ground in complex sentences. *Universals of Human Language*, vol. 4, ed. J. H. Greenberg et al., 625-49. Stanford, Calif.: Stanford University Press.

Talmy, L. 1978b. The relation of grammar to cognition—a synopsis. *Theoretical Issues in Natural Language Processing-2*. 14-24. Urbana, Ill.: Coordinated Science Laboratory, University of Illinois.

Talmy, L. 1985. Force dynamics in language and thought. Parasession on causatives and agenting. Chicago Linguistics Society, 21st Annual Meeting. University of Chicago.

Waltz, D. L. 1980. Generating and understanding scene descriptions. *Elements of discourse understanding*, ed. A. Joshi et al. Cambridge, England: Cambridge University Press.

Waltz, D. L. and Boggess, L. C. 1979. Visual analog representations for natural language understanding. Paper presented at IJCAI-79, Tokyo, Japan, August 1979.

Waltz, D. L. and Pollack, J. B. 1985. Massively parallel parsing: A strongly interactive model of natural language processing. *Cognitive Science* 9, 2: 51-74.

Weinzweig, A. I. 1978. Mathematical foundations for the development of spatial concepts in children. *Recent research concerning the development of spatial and geometric concepts*, 105-176. Columbus, Ohio: ERIC Center for Science, Mathematics and Environmental Education.

Wilson, D. M. 1975. *Presupposition and non-truth-conditional semantics*. London: Academic Press.

Winograd, T. 1972. *Understanding natural language*. New York: Academic Press.

Winograd, T. 1976. Towards a procedural understanding of semantics. *Revue Internationale de Philosophie* 3: 260-303.

Winograd, T. 1980. What does it mean to understand language? *Cognitive Science* 4: 209-41.

Winograd, T. and Flores, F. 1985. *Understanding computers and cognition*. Norwood, N.J.: Ablex.

Woods, W. A. 1978. *Procedural semantics as a theory of meaning*. Paper delivered at the Sloan Workshop on Computational Aspects of Linguistic Structure and Discourse Setting. Philadelphia, Pa.: University of Pennsylvania.

Zadeh, L. A. 1971. Quantitative fuzzy semantics. *Information Sciences* 3: 159-76.

Zadeh, L. A. 1974. *A fuzzy-algorithmic approach to the definition of complex or imprecise concepts*. Electronics Research Laboratory memo no. ERL-M474. Berkeley, Calif.: University of California.

Zeeman, E. C. 1962. The topology of the brain and visual perception. *The Topology of 3-Manifolds*, 240-256. Englewood Cliffs, N.J.: Prentice Hall.

Zwicky, A. M., and Saddock, J. M. 1975. Ambiguity tests and how to fail them. *Syntax and Semantics*, vol. 4, ed. J. P. Kimball. 1-36. New York: Academic Press.

Index

Printed in Great Britain
by Amazon